MW00995206

HAWK
RECON

For Bertie, with love, and Steven Winters, combat medic with the 173rd, K.I.A. 1968

Also by the author – Outlaw Artist

HAWK RECON

RECON

Head Hunters of the A Shau Valley

WILLIAM 'DOC' OSGOOD

Pen & Sword
MILITARY

AN IMPRINT OF PEN & SWORD BOOKS LTD.
YORKSHIRE - PHILADELPHIA

First published in Great Britain in 2023 by
PEN AND SWORD MILITARY
An imprint of
Pen & Sword Books Limited
Yorkshire – Philadelphia

Copyright © William 'Doc' Osgood, 2023

ISBN 978 1 52678 293 9

The right of William 'Doc' Osgood to be identified as Author of this work
has been asserted by him in accordance with the Copyright,
Designs and Patents Act 1988.

All rights reserved. No part of this book may be reproduced, stored in a retrieval
system or transmitted, in any form or by any means, without the written
permission of the author.

Typeset in Times New Roman 11.5/15.5 by
SJmagic DESIGN SERVICES, India.
Printed and bound in the UK by CPI Group (UK) Ltd.

Pen & Sword Books Limited incorporates the imprints of Atlas, Archaeology,
Aviation, Discovery, Family History, Fiction, History, Maritime, Military, Military
Classics, Politics, Select, Transport, True Crime, Air World, Frontline Publishing,
Leo Cooper, Remember When, Seaforth Publishing, The Praetorian Press,
Wharncliffe Local History, Wharncliffe Transport, Wharncliffe True Crime and
White Owl.

For a complete list of Pen & Sword titles please contact
PEN & SWORD BOOKS LIMITED
George House, Units 12 & 13, Beevor Street, Off Pontefract Road,
Barnsley, South Yorkshire, S71 1HN, England
E-mail: enquiries@pen-and-sword.co.uk
Website: www.pen-and-sword.co.uk

or
PEN AND SWORD BOOKS
1950 Lawrence Rd, Havertown, PA 19083, USA
E-mail: uspen-and-sword@casematepublishers.com
Website: www.penandswordbooks.com

Contents

Preface

This is a book about brutal, bloody, close in war and combat characterized often by the ambush.

Sir Charles was the name we gave the enemy in Vietnam out of great respect. It was used often. We had other names, of course, and I had to use them in the book because no other way existed. Sorry about that! Sir Charles was scary. He was a damn good soldier and could kill you before you could say, "Nuts". As for the Viet Cong, Col. Charlie Beckwith, my commanding officer, said,

"These V.C. are the finest infantry soldiers I have ever seen!"

The making of Hawk Recon went on for over 50 years with time off to work as an Alaskan bush pilot, smuggle 'electronics' into Mexico, go surfing and skiing. I never stopped collecting photos and stories. I put together a reunion in Las Vegas of the Hawk Recon members and attended get togethers of the Vietnam Helicopter Pilot Association and Vietnam Helicopter Crew-member Association. Over the years, I talked with most all of the characters, traded letters and made countless phone call interviews! Thanks to them I received detailed descriptions of the large battle scene (after sitting between two of the pilots and gunners during it) plus photo copies of their instruments and emergency flight controls and how to use them, not to mention triggers and sights for rockets, grenades and bullets. As a part time medic crew member, actually trained to fly a Huey, and later as a professional pilot, I could really feel the aerial adventures. Most helpful was receiving the tapes of radio chatter while we were all together in the air dodging AA fire!

I visited the museum at Fort Campbell, home of the 101st Airborne Division, and wrote many a letter to libraries and government record storage facilities. I purchased maps and large black and white photos taken by different combat photographers, some of whom tagged along with us. I viewed available film of the 2/327, 101st and Hawk Recon. Seemed like the Hawk Recon were the darlings of the *Screaming Eagle* newspaper and their fantastic picture sloshing up a creek in the A Shau Valley graces the opening of the 101st 68-69 yearbook!

Armed with this material I was able to produce a story you can match faces and names with landmarks, and landmarks with maps and photos all at once!

Marking our trek into the future Hamburger Hill battlefield and ambush site was made possible by following a trail of our dead soldiers remembered by us and recorded by the US Army.

Then in 2018 I ventured into the area between Hue, Phu Bia, Camp Eagle, Lang Co village and slept in the A Shau Valley. I took a refreshing look at the terrain and watched the same valley fog creep down the hills.

Acknowledgements

Acknowledgements go first and foremost to Gary Linderer a tireless editor, writer and Airborne Ranger! Likewise, authors Kenn Miller and John Del Vecchio of the 101st airborne. My publisher in New York at Pen and Sword books, Chris Evans, for being so understanding and easy. Of course, a big thank you to my fellow Hawks and Hawk medics: Dean Ramsey, Doc White, Doc Brown, Willie Smith, Doc Wallace, LURCH aka Dan Hickman and Company A 2/327th, 101 who make this story as well as the crews of Eagle Dustoff the biggest heroes ever! Also, the entire 101st aviation group. Lastly the members of Company D, 3/187th, 101 the Rakkasans who broke me in and were happy to see me leave…thank God! Plus the 1/506th 'Currahhee's for helping us up on Berchtesgaden.

A very special Aloha goes to the people of Molokai who are the most charming and and just plain 'coolest' people I know. A big thank you to the Kaunakakai library and the entire staff: Cindy Delanty, Wanda Thompson, Vikashni Hoffman, Jeanne Lindquist and especially Pa'a'aina Kee for trying to help me most of all – with great enthusiasm!

The *Molokai Dispatch* newspaper helped with art work and great cover. Thanks!

Thanks to Zack from the Kite Factory for the professional photoshop art! And a heartfelt thanks to the beautiful. and talented actress/musician, Canadian Valerie Descheneaux, for encouragement and computer skills when needed most!

Gracious thanks to all my art teachers: Mrs Rich of Scotts Valley Elementary, Private (Korean war vet) Charles Wolters of Soquel High, plus, a huge thank you to Green Beret Dr. Joe Kerr!

Lastly, the peoples of Vietnam for their love and for showing me around again and remembering everything that went on. But most of all, the A Shau Valley Pacoh mountain tribes, people who fought on both sides and were often left behind by us. Good hunting and pure water!

Foreword

The 1st Brigade of the 101st Airborne Division arrived by ship in South Vietnam on July 29, 1965. Prior to this, US involvement in the Vietnam conflict consisted of advisory and support roles. The summer of that year would see American forces arrive in-country and begin actual combat operations through South Vietnam. This would involve major Army, Marine and Air Force units on land, and additional Naval forces patrolling the coast and inland waterways.

It wasn't long before US units discovered that the Viet Cong forces arrayed against them were an illusive foe. Finding and fixing them proved a difficult task. Trained to fight a conventional war in the temperate zones of Europe, American troops stumbled through the thick jungles, muddy rice paddies, and heavily forested mountains pursuing insurgents who were not only difficult to find, but who left snipers and booby traps on their backtrails which frustrated the pursuers and caused heavy casualties.

General William Westmoreland, Commander of US Forces in theater, quickly realized the need for small, well-trained reconnaissance units that could slip into enemy held territory and locate them without alerting them to their presence. Soon after the arrival of the 1st Brigade, 101st Airborne Division, Westmoreland authorized the formation of a Brigade Long Range Reconnaissance Patrol, which would consist of a 45-man platoon. The unit would initiate deep penetration patrols throughout the Brigade's area of operations. These heavily camouflaged six-man teams would soon prove their worth. Within the next six months, all US independent brigade and division units formed similar reconnaissance companies.

Battalion commanders saw the initial success of these recon teams. They began to realize that they, too, could benefit from such resources under their direct command. Col. David Hackworth, commanding officer of the 1st Battalion, 327th Infantry, one of the 1st Brigade, 101st Airborne Division's three maneuver battalions, asked for volunteers to join "Tiger Force", the newly formed battalion reconnaissance platoon.

Quickly, the 2nd Battalion, 327th Infantry, and the 2nd Battalion, 502nd Infantry, the other two maneuver battalions in the Division, formed their own recon platoons, naming them "Hawk Recon", and "Recondos", respectively. All three platoon-size elements began running patrols in their battalion areas of operations independently of their sister infantry companies.

Over the next seven years, Tiger Force, Hawk Recon, and Recondos established enviable fame for inflicting heavy casualties on the enemy. Operating in smaller units than the larger infantry companies, they were able to penetrate enemy base areas, often catching the VC and NVA forces by surprise. Hitting them hard and fast with raids and ambushes, then pulling back to bring in air and artillery strikes on the enemy positions, proved an amazingly effective way to wage war in the thick jungles of Vietnam. These all-volunteer units earned an enviable reputation for "out-guerillaing the guerillas".

Although a few books have been written since the end of the war about battalion reconnaissance units, they haven't gotten anywhere near the attention they deserve. William "Doc" Osgood, a combat medic with Hawk Recon during the height of the Vietnam War, has spent years researching and gathering material about Hawk Recon operations during his time with the unit. He writes in the slangy dialect of a young American citizen soldier from California, experiencing war for the first time. At a point in our history when many young men were burning their draft cards or fleeing to Canada, Doc saw it as his duty to serve. He's not flowery with his writing style, and pulls no punches. He tells it like it was. I must admit that I enjoyed reading his story. It's as dirty, as innocent, as lonely, as exciting, as humorous and as boring as the war in Vietnam actually was. It's a testimonial on realism, and I thank him from the bottom of my heart for writing it. The best history is always recorded by those who lived it. Good work, Doc!

Gary Linderer, F Company 58th Inf, Long Range Patrol, 101st
Screaming Eagles

Prologue

This is the story of the young, mostly teenage 'Witch Doctors'; combat medics in bloody action. It's about four men forced out of Green Beret school early due to all the medics being killed after the Tet battles in Vietnam. Only two of them would make it back in one piece.

The medics had a heavy load to bear and not only in the aide bags they humped. They were taught to kill and then bring the dead back to life, almost in the same instant. Talk about conflict!

The author, out of the frying pan and into the fire, started out in Company D, 3/187th, 101st Airborne right on schedule for sure death on Hamburger Hill. Luckily, he was transferred into the 2/327th,101st then commanded by none other than Col. Charlie Beckwith, the original Delta Force Green Beret. Actually, Charlie was probably the man who got the medics kicked out of Special Forces to fill his infantry ranks.

As Beckwith's Hawk Recon platoon's head medic, the author found himself in a heavy recon outfit. Reconnaissance, yes, but often used as a killer-attack unit. The Hawks packed extra fire power and stayed out in the boonies probably longer than any unit in the war, even crossing into Laos. 40-day missions were not unheard of. Much longer than SOG and LRPs.

I'll tell you now, this author is against the Vietnam war, and most others. However, I'm very proud of my combat peers for being gutsy warriors and surviving it. Just walking point into ambush sites, something I never did, is plain courageous. I am proud of the air medal I got, very proud, but laugh at the national defense ribbon.

If we have any good from war it has to be the drawing together of the races, at least in the bush where I was. I was in the medical corps, you know, like that funny TV show M.A.S.H. I could say I didn't hurt anybody; I tried to save people. Bullshit!

I became a killer.

We did try and help the poor villagers and especially kids by offering medical service. I would have tried very hard to save ANY enemy soldier who was in deep trouble after first trying very hard to kill him, of course. We did build schools and roads and bridges that tourists enjoy today. Not to mention the airports and harbors.

I know of one 101st aviation crew captained by Byron Edgington that, against direct orders, flew into a typhoon, at night, to pick up a mother in difficult labor. Baby boy went back to the village the next day, after a slight adjustment to Mom's birth canal, in a wooden ammo box cradle that was marked: US Army 105 shells.

I'm just glad I got to see war, otherwise I wouldn't have learned firsthand what our government is willing to do.

Chapter 1

Induction Center Riot

October 22, 1967

The radio screamed so loud it almost hurt! Mick and Keith and the boys screeched about: marching, charging feet, street fighting and palace revolution. Sounded about right. Sounded like our future. The room danced in chaos, drunken chaos. The wood bed frames had long since splintered and given way, the mattresses resting on the old carpet. The hotel room was overrun with wild young men. Paper airplanes systematically launched from our 12th storey window overlooking downtown Oakland. Some of the airplanes, being on fire as they were, spun in to crash and burn far below. Beer bottles were on display everywhere and one soared across the room cracking the thick glass table top.

"Oh Shit, now you did it," a teenager with red hair moaned.

"Fuck you, douche bag," was the reply from another boy with bad skin.

"Yeah, what are they gonna do … send us to Vietnam?" someone else chimed in.

"Probably … probably will, sport, and in just a few hours too," the bottle thrower declared.

I figured that everything breakable in our room, was broke. What a mess. I looked out a window and down the light shaft and noticed some garbage smoking twelve floors down. Hotel fire came to mind. An arm thrust rudely past me and outside holding a beer bottle.

"Bombs away," the arm's owner said. A few seconds passed and we were treated to a healthy CRASHHHH! from the air shaft where some of our suicide planes were still smoldering. I smiled and held my beer out

1

our window (without a view) ... a whole full quart! I turned to our silent crew ... seeking approval. I thought I saw somebody nod and my bomb just disappeared! It dropped like a greased brick and must have hit an air conditioner at the bottom. A terrible tearing noise followed by an eruption of beer, and slivers of glass, not unlike a small atomic detonation, flew up in shock waves! After that we all felt guilty, I think, so quieted down expecting a loud knock on the door. Some even tried to sleep.

We waited for the dawn and our fate because in the morning we would become soldiers during wartime.

I wore Levis, Ray-Ban aviator glasses and shoulder-length hair and today was the day I was born for, I thought. Down in the lobby a short Humfwick (head motherfucker who thinks he's in charge) barked our instructions.

"All right men, when the bus arrives, I want all to board quickly and remain seated."

We walked out of the hotel and climbed on the bus. At least most of us climbed on the bus.

"Where are we going ... San Quentin?" an inductee joked as we took our seats. I sat by a window and peered out through steel wire mesh rigged around all the glass.

In a bright sunlight the bus motored off but in a moment the driver pulled into a deserted parking garage, parked, and left the engine running; he listened to a hand-held radio pressed against his sweaty skin. We were parked facing the street at an exit, in shadow.

"What's the holdup?" someone wondered.

Forty-five minutes later the driver gunned the motor and we shot out into the street. Although the morning was in full bloom, the streets were empty as we approached the heart of the city. Empty that was except for the debris that littered the ground and skidded along the street in the wind. Something was wrong. No one was walking around and no cars were moving.

I turned to look out the rear window and noticed they were following us. None of us had seen the military bus pull in behind. Both buses stopped in the middle of the road. Suddenly the police made their move and swarmed out from the green bus. They were riot police. Some of the guys with me stood up. Jeez, I wondered what the hell was going on. We were surrounded. All the cops carried three-foot clubs and wore gloves, boots and helmets with face shields.

Again our bus lurched forward. We moved along, straddling a double yellow line, the police two abreast, ringing us, walking. We began to notice barricades down the side streets and that's when we saw the body. It was burned almost beyond all recognition. As we drove slowly by you could make out that it was a cop car, on its top, all four tires removed.

The wind began to howl through the vacant streets.

WWOOoooWWHOoooooo – "Don't go", it seemed to cry. Don't gooooOOOo Wwhoooooo.

"Did you hear that?" the red-haired kid in the front of me asked turning around puzzled. Was it the wind? We continued in silence. Minutes passed. We heard the sound again, it was like the devil himself, low, sinister.

HhhhhhHHHHH Nnoooo, don't go. No don't go … was that it?

Suddenly louder, "Hell no we won't go!"

It was a chant from people up ahead, like a parade; we were a parade? It was like a sick kind of parade. We were like the official guest of honor, the grand marshal and the float all rolled into one. In other words the center of attraction was us. We turned the corner and saw a river of humanity oozing the street; choking the side streets as far as we could see were more people. They were on the curb, on each side of us and so close you could see into their eyes. "Hell no we won't go!," roared the mob again. The earth shook!

The entire UC Berkeley population must have geared up today.

POW! A chunk of cement cracked my window! It left a mark of light-colored powder stuck on the crack in the glass at nose level. Next a skinny hippy charged through the crowd swinging a big sign and I calmly looked down into his mad little eyes while he heaved his weapon over the riot police and into the side of the bus.

She was blond, beautiful, and smiling at me. Everyone else was flashing the peace sign so I jabbed up and down a lazy upside down

'V' sign in return to show opposition. Like a Roman thumbs down! The crowd saw that and went wild. The girl smiled again, probably thought I was an infiltrator, I sure looked like one.

BAM, BAM. BAM … smash! Rocks struck the roof!

"Yeah peace, right on, dig it you motherfuckers," one of our guys shouted.

"Are we gonna have to fight our own people to get into the service?" he continued.

"If some asshole gets in my way, I'm gonna kick him a new one."

The bus parked in front of the induction center and some of the first guys had to climb over piles of demonstrators to get in the door.

"Hell no … we won't go," screamed the throng as I got off. The guy that had sat in front of me nudged my arm and said,

"See that chick over there … that's Joan Baez … Wow!"

The only person I recognized was the old lady; she was always on hand, holding her poster with the photos of dead babies and clutching her shawl. Usually alone, she guarded her post rain or shine, day or night, but today she brought her army. The peace army. I was impressed.

Inside we spent the day getting inspected, detected and some of us … rejected, just like in the song. In the afternoon I got bored waiting around and being that we were all sworn in and everything, started snooping around. I found myself walking into a big room overlooking the street. Inside the smoke-filled office were a bunch of men with rolled-up shirt sleeves. They were chain-smoking cigarettes and aiming movie cameras, mounted on huge tripods, out between gaps in the closed venetian blinds. I asked one guy who looked like Dennis the Menace's father,

"What's happen in' man?"

"Taking pictures of the hippies," was his answer. He glanced in my direction with a funny look as if he wasn't sure who I was all of a sudden. I stood in the center of the room, out of place in this crowd … which was usual for me.

The *Oakland Tribune* interviewed me and the reporter asked,

"What do you think about all of this?"

"I think a lot of those people outside couldn't care less about anyone dying anywhere, except maybe themselves. I think a lot of them are just out having a great time running around and throwing stuff."

I should have said: "I don't really give a damn about any of it ... I just want to stay alive but I believe some outside would go but are just plain cowards!"

In a way I could identify with the peace freaks, I could see myself out in the street if not for the fact that I was busy joining the Army at the moment

My picture was in the paper, they misquoted me but got the general message right. They printed:

"The 'kids' are out for 'kicks'".

I never used the word 'kids' or 'kicks'; that was old-people talk.

Chapter 2

Boot Camp

Our bus plowed through the rain and darkness. From the airport at Tacoma we were going out to Fort Lewis for basic training. Now I was getting somewhere, I thought, as we unloaded into some old buildings in the middle of the storm and introduced ourselves to plates of green powdered eggs. So this is the Army, I mused.

I was planning on making the service a career and later becoming a CIA agent. In two days I knew I never would. Two hours after arriving and of being bullied and screamed at, they told us to get some shut-eye – big day tomorrow.

About forty-five minutes later a 60-watt lightbulb exploded in my face! We met Drill SSG Maybry and his wicked sidekick, Corporal Fang. They literally kicked us out of the sack.

Maybry was a stout little bundle of meanness while Fang appeared like some decrepit teenage vampire. Our chief DI looked like Smokey the Bear with his charming WWI campaign hat, crew cut and southern accent. Later in the day Maybry strutted through our barracks glaring at us 'girls' until he stopped in front of me and said, "Osgood, what's wrong with you? Don't you know only two things fall outta the sky?" He had seen my Green Beret recruitment brochure with the paratroopers on it, that I used for a book marker. "Well dumb shit, got any idea at all … I ain't got all day?!"

I froze, I didn't know what to say to this individual. I had no idea. The barracks were as quiet as a bank at 4:30 as he pushed his beefy red face close to mine and screamed:

"BIRDS AND BIRD SHIT!"

He stomped off. The whole place erupted in raucous laughter with many a jeer and hoots. It was so funny he had to turn and add, "Osgood here wants to jump outta a perfectly good airplane." This time only a few snickers, mainly from the Puerto Ricans who were joining the National Guard, floated among our assembly. These really nasty 'weekend warriors' figured it was okay to ridicule me, a real soldier, because their daddy drill sergeant did. I should have smart-assed Maybry and told him "yes … the brave and the paid!"

Not long afterwards we got another DI. Unlike Maybry, he was young, had a CIB, and a yellow and black horse-head combat patch that shown like a true badge of courage. He was from the 1st Cavalry Division and was just back from Vietnam. One night in the orderly room he showed a couple of us slides of dead VC laying on a road with their heads and limbs shot off. His name was SGT Brown.

During basic we stood around in the rain a lot and on one particularly miserable morning were gathered around SGT Brown and SSG Maybry with our little canteen cups of hot cocoa. The cooks had actually made cocoa and delivered it to us out on the parade field. Touching.

I started to ask SGT Brown something about Vietnam, choked instead, and spit a fine spray of hot chocolate onto his starched, new, fatigue shirt front. Maybry rolled his eyes skyward and sneered, "Osgood, what the hell is wrong with you?"

Brown bit a grin and turned his well tanned country boy head.

They were pushing us through basic. They needed bodies. They saw that not everyone was coming back from their little Asian war.

As we marched around the basic training area, often passing other training company formations, we'd sing:

> GI beans and GI gravy
> damn, I should of joined the Navy.
> Tip your hat and show your curls,
> We are passing by the girls … !
> That's the Fort Lewis boogie what a
> crazy song!

7

Or ... if we were running in formation and Maybry felt like really singing Gung Ho:

> I want to be an Airborne Ranger
> I want to live a life of danger
> I want to go to Vietnam
> I want to kill ole Charlie Cong!

The DIs would bellow out the lines and we'd scream back repeating them, very dramatic!

Six weeks through basic the old sergeant who ran the armory reported a bayonet missing and what's more – I was the culprit! A screaming match erupted on the steps of the barrack while I explained to the 50-year-old moron that his card system had malfunctioned and allowed 'him' to lose a weapon. The old fucker cocked back grasping an M-14 bayonet like a hammer. You could smell the hate on him as his lips pulled back in a snarl and he started towards me, checking himself just in time.

Maybry was furious and actually made me climb into an almost empty 18ft x 15ft x 6ft Dipzy Dumpster trash container with a toothbrush, to scrub the fucker inside and out! It was kind of funny really; I didn't take it too seriously and knew I would never try and clean the whole thing. After five minutes of half-assed brushing, Maybry stuck his nose over the side of the bin and said,

"Osgood, what is wrong with you, don't you have anything better to do?"

I jumped out of the metal box and started to double time up the gravel path; Maybry put his arm out,

"Osgood ... will you relax ... slow down, will ya?"

Maybry was okay, he got me out of KP once to go out and qualify on the M-14 instead. We all chipped in and actually bought the man a gift before we graduated. Some kind of hunting gear. But the most amazing thing he ever did, after we'd been in training only two days was – and this was in formation in front of the whole company (E-3-2) – to inform us that:

"I don't want to ever go to Vietnam and get my ass shot off. I'll stay here and shoot the ass off ducks!"

I was shocked, dumbfounded. The career soldiers didn't want to go to war? How could that be? Wait a minute … something was wrong. The whole purpose of an army is to fight, why else would anyone join it? I was young; I would learn.

Our company was typical, I guess; we had a Gomer Pyle and a crazy Californian hippy wannabe snake eater … me. One guy shit right down on the floor of the company orderly room! He was discharged and it wasn't honorable.

Another guy could tell really, really funny jokes … for hours. Honest to God, he had thousands on tap and we spent a whole Sunday afternoon laughing our guts out!

By then I'd earned the nickname 'airborne' … and it wasn't used politely. The term meant paratrooper. I believe I was the only one headed to jump school.

When our test results came in … I was found qualified to be an Army pilot but I knew I'd never pass the eye exam.

In fact I wasn't quite the hero of basic training I thought I was going to be. I was just average on the rifle range and one day Maybry put me in front of the entire company to demonstrate my skills at rifle drill. Stuff like several ways to salute an officer while carrying a weapon and left shoulder … right shoulder, parade rest and attention … forward march! I wasn't a drill team commando and could not throw the M-14 up in the air, catch it with my teeth, fix a bayonet or any of that fancy shit. I couldn't even do the basic stuff and almost dropped my 'gun'! I think I could handle inspection arms though! My performance was totally embarrassing! But you know, after a day or two, I really didn't give a shit.

The neatest thing about boot camp wasn't being fired at with live machine gun bullets as we crawled under barbed wire, or them blowing live charges near us at the same time. It wasn't being hit with CS gas while we struggled to get our masks on underneath even more wire. The neatest thing I can remember was when they tried to trick us with the gas.

We had spent the whole day getting to learn all about tear gas, nerve gas and CS. CS is about forty times worse than any tear gas. CS is chemical Mace. The shit will slow you down. It WILL stop you and fuck up your whole world. They'd had us in a room, singing songs, and breathing pure tear gas. Nothing to it; it's like some kind of foul hairspray. CS is a different animal.

At the end of the day we assembled in company formation to board the buses parked and running. The sun was down behind the trees and it was getting dark. We were all tired, dirty and red eyed from crawling around and playing at chemical warfare. All of a sudden a monster ran out of the woods with a hissing flamethrower. This humanoid had large saucer size eyes and a pig's snout! I finally recognized the eyes and flat nose to be a gas mask. Instead of liquid fire, smoke billowed from the nozzle and hose connected to big tanks on the creature's back. We couldn't run … we were in a military formation. The figure raced past us all …: while we stood still cemented in even ranks. The thing's evil wand sizzled violently with sparks popping and odd-colored smoke pouring up into the air. A cloud descended slowly into our formation. Someone finally remembered what we'd been taught and yelled,

"GAS!"

I yanked off my helmet and threw it on the ground.

"Oh shit!" I muttered fumbling with my mask and container. I was all thumbs. I was in slow motion. I was going to get gassed, but good. I saw that the CS cloud covered the far end of our column and was down to knee level. All I could see down that way was combat boots sticking out underneath the fog. Helmets started striking the ground.

The last day I lugged my baggage out the door and asked Corporal Fang,

"Hey corporal, what's a 91A10?"

Everyone had mysterious numbers and letters on their new orders. Nobody had numbers like mine.

"It's a truck driver", he said, "or a medic or sumpin."

I had orders to be a 91A10. I was going to be a truck driver, a medic, or sumpin. I was screwed! I didn't want to be a medic, which is what the orders said. I wanted to be a Green Beret and blow shit up and fire exotic weapons. Besides, medics got killed all the time. I didn't want to kill anybody either, just blow shit up.

I dragged my new duffel bag down the steps of the barracks and towards the bus stop. It was almost Christmas 1967. The days of holding an assault rifle in one hand and a fist full of cock in the other while singing:

> This is my rifle, this is my gun ...
> This is for fighting and this is for
> fun ...

were over.

Drill SSG Maybry opened the orderly room door and headed my way. He turned to go up the steps in front of the barracks, stopped, and said to me:

"Osgood ... I don't know what's wrong with you, but ... keep your head down ... okay."

Chapter 3

Shot Class was a Pain in the Ass

After basic I was off to medics' school at Fort Sam Houston, Texas. I'd spent Christmas with my family and had shown up at the house looking like a hotel bus boy with shiny shoes, necktie and goofy bus-driver hat. On this leave I developed the habit of taking as much leave as possible and as often as possible.

One morning, not long after arrival at Fort Sam, a young GI who was on guard duty walked into our WWII style barracks. He carried an M-16 and laid it on his bunk before walking off to the latrine. I walked over and picked the thing up. It looked like a space gun to me. It was coal black, lightweight and thin. That was the first time I had ever seen the already famous Colt; I was impressed. My buddies and I had just seen the new movie, *Bonnie and Clyde* and we wanted to go out and hose down something with the rifle. Something like someone's car. We were actually ready to go downtown and buy our own 'guns', but calmer heads prevailed. The killing machine the Army was giving us would do; it was a beauty and evil as hell. Its nickname, 'Black Magic', was perfect.

Late one morning someone roused me from a deep sleep and told me to report to the mess hall for KP. I couldn't believe it, not again! I had gone through the miserable cluster fuck of grease and slime and sweat a couple of times already. KP was a whole day of pain and very hard work! I hated that crap and no way was I going to do it if I had anything to say in the matter. Dragging my feet into the chow hall, I approached one of the head lifers,

"Hey sarge, I can't work. I'm sick."

"Oh golly gee and what seems to be the problem this fine morning?" the typically overweight skinhead asked in a tone that was actually funny.

"I'm sick ... I got something wrong ... " I lied. "Why just look at my—" my eyes nearly popped out of my head ... a red rash was splotched all over my arms, "—arms ... yeah arms, that's it ... look at this shit all over my arms."

The NCO ran my ass up to the hospital on the hill and it turned out I had a good case of German measles and didn't know it. Just in time too. Great, no fucking KP, no boring classes and maybe some good food. I wasn't too excited about this medic business anyway; I knew I wouldn't be real good at it.

The hospital at Fort Sam was crammed full of burn patients from Vietnam. We knew better than to go up anywhere near the burn ward – they told us not to go but we already knew. The staff put me in isolation and I was joined one at a time by other members of my company who came down with the disease. Go train at a hospital and get sick ... it figured. While I was isolated in hospital, I never saw any of the burn victims but I did have a run in with the 'night crawler'.

Late one night I found myself lost in the corridors with no one around; it was uncanny, every floor, every station was deserted. I ran upstairs and again changed floors in the elevator, then back to the stairs and finally into the elevator again. I pressed the button for my floor and waited for the door to open. When it finally did, he was standing right in front of me blocking the way ... the 'night crawler!' It was the captain who walked the halls, like a robot, and now he was in my way looking at something above the door. The man was back from Vietnam with a bad case of malaria. Bumping into him made me determined to never catch that disease. Babbling incoherently with an ashen, sweat-covered face and shoulders, he looked away as I squeezed past him. A big handsome man with a shaved head was reduced to a quivering pulp with legs.

Steve Winters, a tall friendly guy with glasses from Tulsa, became my best friend in medic school. He was planning on jump school and Special Forces also. Like me he had enlisted for three years, a Green Beret requirement.

The days dragged by to the beat of marching feet going to classes and sometimes to the sound of drums and pipes. Some student played the

13

bagpipes and when he did the sound was hypnotic. I knew I would march into the jaws of death, under its spell, if given the chance. The sound of those bagpipes, I knew, produced an electric feeling that would transform the average Jody Q. Milktoast into a walking-tall, looking-fine, mean, lean, snake-eating, airborne-ranger killing machine, a legend in his own mind.

The tune of war also played loudly over South Vietnam about this time. The battles of Tet raged; Green Beret camps were overrun by tanks and US prisoners taken. We didn't read the papers or notice what Tet was all about. We heard about heavy fighting and hoped it would not end, cheating us from our fate.

The funniest thing that happened in medic school happened in shot class. First of all I was scared shitless. Nothing like getting cold steel rammed deep into your flesh with insanely sharp ... needles. I hated the idea of giving shots, at first, but soon learned that using the damn things was a whole lot better than getting them. They actually wanted us to stick one another with real needles and inject liquid into our bodies. Right from the git-go the instructor asked for volunteers. The old saying 'never volunteer for anything', came to mind because if ever a time not to volunteer was ripe, this was it! The instructor explained the technique of injecting medicine and then requested one of the volunteers to demonstrate on the other. Holy shit! I saw that the 'volunteers' the instructor picked were as nervous as rats at a dog show. On stage center stood two country bumpkins, a skinny guy and a fat one, a real Laurel and Hardy team. Laurel picked up the hypodermic needle off a tray and Hardy, stared straight ahead with a silly look. Laurel stabbed away, I forced myself to watch. I don't know how in the hell it happened, but the next sight we were treated to was a syringe sticking into Hardy's ribcage! Like an arrow it was. Laurel had missed completely the arm he was aiming at and Hardy didn't even know it! The needle was buried in the subject's side, but the plunger hung down limply like a white leech. The human pin cushion ever so slowly turned his head and looked down at the disgusting spectacle, then turned back to stare at us, searching our faces begging for a reasonable explanation. None available. The only help we gave him were titters, giggles, uncontrollable laughter and sick looks.

Chapter 4

Jump School

After combat medic school Steve Winters, James Maurice, David MacIntosh and myself bused over to Fort Benning for paratrooper school. Finally, we were getting somewhere I thought. Our class, the 45th training company, included Marines and Navy Seals. The atmosphere was very gung-ho, VERY gung-ho. Patches and decals of elite Army, Air Force, Marine and Navy teams and units were displayed. Navy UDT frogmen trained here while Seal teams double timed through the company streets in blue stretch pants tucked into strange and exotic green and black jungle boots. When we broke formation Marines screamed, "Recondo" or 'Force Recon!"

I ate it all up with a large spoon.

45th company was right next to the 'animal farm' where the troublemakers and deserters and those who had failed the program lived. In my barracks I was by myself. All my friends were in other buildings. Worse, was a Mexican and his dime-store record player that moved in with me. Julio only had one record, some broken-hearted teenage bullshit, that irritated from under my bed as he played it all night long. Julio and I were bunkies!

The school consisted of three, one-week phases: ground week, tower week and jump week. During ground week we did a whole lot of running and singing. Our old favorite from basic was popular at Benning also:

I want to be an Airborne Ranger
I want to live a life of danger
I want to go to Vietnam
I want to kill ole Charlie Cong

Or my absolute favorite:

> C-130 going down the strip
> Airborne Daddy gonna take a little trip
> Stand up, hook up, shuffle to the door
> We're all gonna jump from this big tin whore

Our training area had all kinds of mock up aircraft doors, 40ft wooden towers to jump out of and slide down suspended from steel cables, and of course the 250ft monster towers that hauled four jumpers up at one time. When my turn came for the 250-footer I was hoisted above the Georgia pine trees beneath an already deployed practice chute stretched out and held by a 30-ft metal ring. After my chute cut loose, I prepared for my first real PLF. About 50ft above ground zero, one of the school cadre or 'black hats' pointed a bullhorn at me and bellowed,

"That's it, you're a pro ... looking good jumper, you're a pro!"

I hit the ground like a 150 lb sack of over-ripe peaches, but passed tower week and felt ... like a pro?

We still stood microscopic, early morning inspections with super shiny boots and polished brass with many, many pushups for less than perfect uniforms. We still ran everywhere in the summer heat and one time had the Navy run circles around us. The Seals, in powder blue stretch-pants and jungle boots, ran past our formation at triple time I guess and circled us as we double-timed, pounding the red clay.

One very warm morning found the 45th company on the ramp at the airport. With hands on top of helmets, like PoWs, swarms of 'black hats' slapped, tugged and double-checked our efforts at strapping on a parachute for the first time. Climbing on the C-119 'flying boxcars' was a bitch and trying to wedge onto the red nylon webbing bench seat was a bitch, but the sitting and waiting and sweating down inside our clothes was just the shits! It was scary. It was so fucked up it was almost fun.

The pilots eased the throttles forward, watching the gauges for early signs of engine failure and pulled the old Fairchild off the ground. Little did we know that if they'd lost one engine now, and the airspeed wasn't high enough, we'd all flip upside down and burn to death on the hot runway not far below! At this time the jump masters heaved the doors open. Up until they did that we were in almost total darkness. When the doors flew open the effect was of watching a movie screen in a cave. Suddenly, moving scenery rushed by outside and trees alongside the runway were zinging past-really-close. We were in the air, but still hurtling down the strip. The engines take-off roar dominated all other noise while the jump masters moved around or looked out the door. This was their show and the 'black hats' made the most of it, looking cool in black t-shirts and caps with silver wings on powder blue oval cloth backgrounds. Our two 'master blasters' wore Air Force slim pack chutes with rip cords. One of them took his hat off and looked outside. I was amazed at how the slip stream played and beat ripples and wrinkles that jerked and fluttered the skin around on his tanned face, squinting eyes and red neck. These salty ass-kickers were great, often older, crew cut, NCO types, that added color to our green cluster fuck. The lifers strutted about the rear of the aircraft in the sunlight, holding onto the overhead jump cable with one hand and leaning out the door or checking the deck area for fouled gear. Suddenly one of the NCOs yelled,

"STAND UP!"

While he raised his arms in a vigorous lifting motion, we all tried to get up at once. But before we sorted ourselves out they screamed,

"HOOK UP!"

I slammed the open hook at the end of my yellow nylon static line, down around the steel cable and closed the sliding hook mouth, then safe-tied it shut, sealing it on the steel rope cable. Each hook had a hole through it and a corresponding piece of aircraft safety wire tied on the line next to the device. When I stuffed the wire through the hole and bent it at both ends, the hook and static line were set to yank the 'silk' out of my back pack.

Everyone tried to check the guy in front of him, but the best you could hope for was a glance at his static line to make sure it wasn't wrapped through your own harness … pulling you out the door on top of him! We all sounded off, "OKAY!" in succession and slapped the next in line on the ass. After the equipment check the next command was the dreaded:

"STAND IN THE DOOR!"

The first jumper braced with one jump boot hanging over the edge, slicing the air flow, while both his hands gripped the doorway about chest level. The first two jumpers could now get a good view of the red and green jump lights and the patchwork of greens, browns and gold, 1,200ft below.

The jump masters really got with it, double checking the static lines, talking with the pilots, looking out the door and eyeing the burning red light. One of them knelt down and watched the huge DZ slide into sight. He estimated the the time to arrival to be sixty seconds and the wind to be twenty knots. Green smoke burned on the DZ and the jump was on! The pilot flipped the jump light switch to green and the senior jump master instantly took another quick glance out the door for stray 'boxcars'. Looking both under and above our C-119. The black hat stepped up behind the paratrooper in the door, slammed him on the ass and hollered like his life was at stake, "GO!"

An Airborne Ranger just back from Nam, at the head of our stick put his feet together, toes down, while thrusting himself out the door. Stationed at Benning, on a secret mission, the Rangers got the honor of jumping with the jump school to keep current. He slapped and held onto both sides of his reserve chute, tucked his chin in and spun towards the ground in a blast of turbulence.

Our formation of C-119s puked out bodies and parachutes. Bodies swapped sides – crisscrossing at the back of the tail, narrowly missing one another.

Back where I was we waddled half-way to the exit and then had to try and run to keep up with the rest of the stick already leaving us behind. I hesitated in the door as the soldier in front of me disappeared out and around the fuselage. The tail boom and vertical stabilizer hung down in front of the door and suddenly spooked me. That was the last thing I saw. I closed my eyes and jumped as hard as I could to avoid skidding down the side of the airplane on my face. Like a large wave smashing me on the bottom I rolled in darkness before being jerked upright. My feet and legs swung up and almost kicked me in the head. I'd forgotten all about counting to five, but did remember to open my eyes and try to check the canopy to see if I'd live. My risers and shroud lines were all twisted and cinched down tight over the back of my neck but I managed to strain around enough to see a beautiful 28ft OD bubble of nylon over me. My exit had been sloppy which caused the malfunction and me to have to 'bicycle' my legs in order to spin around and un-twist the parachute cords. I spun like a rubber rat on a string. When I stopped revolving I'd lost 800ft.

I tried to stay clear of the other jumpers and watched in fascination as one student landed on top of another chute! The jumper on top ran to the edge of the canopy and jumped off, swinging free.

For a moment a splendiferous vista and floating, or almost flying, ride were mine. The view was incredible. All too soon the ground became a serious factor and I knew I'd better do something about it and quick. This was it, a real parachute landing fall coming up fast. Putting my feet together and my hands grasping high up on the risers, I pulled the thick nylon down to my chest and stared out at the horizon. A black object rushed up and clobbered me into the ground; I'd run into my own shadow – and mother earth! I jumped up happy as a sissy at camp, but no sooner did it dawn on me that I probably hadn't broken a leg, somebody yanked me off my feet. Actually, I was about to be dragged off the DZ by the wind!

First, I caught myself and started a series of ostrich hops, running in giant steps jerked along by the full canopy! I knew this couldn't last and wasn't too surprised when I tripped and landed squarely in a belly flop … my full weight … on the reserve, snapped on the front of my gut. In full panic I'd thrust my hands out at the last second to cushion the fall and my fingers speared through the ripcord handle, exploding open and spilling the snow-white reserve out onto the ground in front of God and everybody. Nearly pulled out of my boots, I was dragged along like a water skier in Death Valley tangled up in a mess of lines and nylon.

A rooster tail of dust followed along at a surprisingly snappy clip. Now for once I knew just what to do so I rolled onto my back and squeezed off a quick release. That action released half the shroud lines and collapsed the main. I stopped.

At the assembly point the NCOs and officers pointed out my white reserve to any that had failed to notice it. Kind of obvious …

like a tarantula on a wedding dress. It was VERY funny! I didn't care; the ride back to the company, in the back of an open truck, was like a dream. We lay in tired heaps in a swoon of happiness and a macho love of life. Life was never better. It was hard to believe we had done it.

Indeed, life was good for us young paratroopers. After that first jump we celebrated at the snack bar – where else? – drinking many delicious cold beers from large frosted plastic pitchers kept in the freezer. God it was grand! And so handy too, they put that snack bar right down the block from our living quarters. It was a lovely watering hole for us under-age drinkers. At that time we didn't know or care about NCO clubs, Officer clubs, or off post restaurants. We loved our little plastic and cheap snack bar! I think that two trees stood outside to give the illusion of scenery and shade in the 100-degree heat.

Steven Winters and then the rest of us also celebrated by buying new Corcoran jump boots from the PX, like the snack bar, situated right in the 45th company area. We were jumping so we needed the boots. They were kind of showy, an option!

The next day we made two more jumps in the Georgia springtime. After the third jump, we watched a flight unload its sticks. All the chutes deployed and drifted to earth normally, all that is, except one. You could tell this one guy was a runt from a mile away, as his buddies floated under him leaving him to hover in the waves of heat. While his mates bit the dust he drifted into a thermal and started going back up! He almost didn't make the DZ.

On our fourth jump our stick landed in the trees short of the field. I was already on the ground as a body came sailing down and landed in a 30ft pine tree right next to me. The jumper dangled a couple of feet off the ground. Tarzan pulled the safety clip out of his release mechanism, turned the lock, and smacked the release to drop clear of the harness. At that very instant a really 'gargantic' dust devil whipped out of nowhere lashing bits of wood and pine needles in our faces and bent the tree almost over to the ground. The boiling air snatched the chute out of the tree and shot it straight for the sun!

It was fully inflated, perfectly deployed and like a kite, the harness and backpack added the proper weight and balance for a tail. The last we saw of it, it was headed for the Gulf of Mexico, still climbing.

Our fifth and last jump was an equipment blast. Once out of the plane the deal was to drop the cargo bag off your harness and let it hang from a 15ft umbilical cord or drop line – hitting the ground on its own. I did all that, but my body did a good imitation of a heavy drop tank, hitting hard, with most of its weight slamming onto my head and jamming my helmet down over my eyes. I think I actually cracked my skull. My bunk mate, Julio, wasn't so lucky. He broke his leg. Too bad, no more Trini Munoz singing teen angel songs. I was rattled, but ran off the DZ feeling tall, like a real paratrooper. I had survived five jumps and earned my wings!

We got our silver jump wings and Special Forces patches – the famous 'electric butter knife' design. These patches are a gold sword with three lightning bolts behind. A black and gold Airborne tab rides above a blue background for the sword. The whole thing is in the shape of an Indian arrowhead, which indicated we'd be working with tribes.

The green beret was still a way down the road, but we got to wear an aviator style 'cunt cap', with the red and white parachute and glider patch. This patch was an embroidered circle. It was WWII vintage and pretty elite. Some of the old timers used to sew a silver dollar under the patch for good luck and/or a surprise weapon.

The school cadre came around and in a touching display of concern and efficiency told us they had arranged a car pool up to Fort Bragg and the JFK Special Warfare Center. This is when they handed me and my three pals Green Beret patches. I think it was a trick. We were all on cloud nine and didn't care or know that somebody was probably getting four sets of travel pay and that somebody wasn't going to be us. I was as happy as a pig eating out a dead cow as we roared off post in a blast of rock and roll. Airborne all the way!

Rainy Night in Georgia and *Dust in the Wind* were top 40 that summer.

Chapter 5

The Dirty Dozen

The boys and I turned left into the JFK Special Warfare Center and had to slow down for a formation of Green Berets double timing down the street. I stuck my head out the window and asked a soldier rummaging through his car trunk in the parking lot, "Hey … where do you report in around here?"

He stood up, spun around and bent over again, his green beret and white cloth jump wings framed in our car window.

"Ah … some more cannon fodder I see. The training group orderly room is right over there and up aways," he pointed.

Finally, I was getting somewhere, I thought. These guys lived in modern air-conditioned barracks and had semi-private ROOMS! The berets were a different breed, that was for sure. Later, I actually saw, NCOs, 'sergeants' pulling KP right along with us lowlifes.

For the first couple of weeks, we made formations, dodged work details the best we could and went to sleep out under the pine trees. I'd always had a hard time falling asleep as a child and hated naps but the US Army taught me to fall asleep anytime, anywhere and anyplace. They had a name for us and it was ghosts. We were ghosts, never around and never in sight.

Shortly after our arrival some of the guys from jump school decided to quit. Only problem was, you couldn't. They made quitters fall out and stand at parade rest in the hot North Carolina sun for hours upon hours. Eventually, some of them changed their minds and ended up graduating before we left for Vietnam.

It seemed we were to be trained as teachers. We had to teach classes with training aides constructed from waste materials…only. Examples were: the M-60 machine gun or even a simple shovel. We were expected to teach stone aged people how to dig a hole, shit in it and why. And if all else failed, we'd give the bastards blankets, according to one grey haired grinning NCO.

The training was good, the best so far. The place was like a college campus as young men jogged around the brick buildings carrying their mock-up cornflake box radios and tree branch shovels. This is what I had joined the Army for.

A lot of us made our 'cherry' jump (#6) from a C-123 using the T-10 steerable parachute. This piece of equipment had wooden toggles to steer and a cutout in the canopy that had to be positioned or rotated in the air. If you did it right you slowed down and landed into the wind. If you screwed it up you could pick up a lot of ground speed and crash and burn with the wind! I know, I found it hard to turn the chute around on my cherry jump or 'blood jump'. It was hard to figure the wind direction as well and it was really hard when I impacted the ground on Smoke Bomb Hill, I think it was. A jeep raced over to my crash site and they yelled out, "Are you okay!?"

One day in May I saw our names on the list for aggressor detail. It was war games and they always held them up in the mountains north of Fort Bragg. It was moonshine country – the Smokies, Blue Ridge mountain mamas, the real McCoy. Our class was going through its final training up in the mountains but we were just going to be helpers, the bodies needed to operate the cluster fuck. But it was still cloak and dagger work and we wore civilian clothes and carried foreign weapons. One black NCO wore farmer-john Levis and a straw hat. Some of us packed M-16s and a lot of exotic hardware also. Of course, I was issued the heaviest weapon in the armory: the crew-served 30 cal. Browning machine gun, a baby 50 cal. I wanted an M-16. I had to operate the thing sans any crew.

When we got up in the AO we drove around and planted spies in the neighborhood; guys like the black NCO 'farmer' actually took jobs in general stores. We set up a base camp high on a rocky ridge and I slept in a neat crack in the granite that I filled with about 200lbs of sweet maple leaves. Being a gunner, I was called on to patrol in the back of a jeep with a mad NCO and his driver. We raced down the dirt roads trying to trigger enemy ambushes prematurely. The sergeant was a stocky, typical beret with European looks and a name to match. He was our torturer and had a bigger than life reputation for being 'colorful'. He was probably straight up Euro-trash ... kicked out of the French Foreign Legion for murdering somebody. Probably had some Hitler Youth or worse in him as well.

I 'killed' a lot of people that trip and must have fired several thousand rounds of blanks with the baby 50cal. I even did a 'mock execution', a firing squad of one and was awarded a green beret for the effort. But most of the time I fired off blanks on command, off into the trees from the back of the jeep, day or night, rain or shine. Lost a lot of hearing too.

Another time we were forced to stop at a roadblock manned by 'the enemy' – the friendly US forces. Most of us were in the back of a red pickup truck belonging to our contact, a 'good ole boy' named Junior. A GI came over to check us out and Junior hit the gas! I moved for the 30cal. and our famous sergeant yelled, "Open up!"

Brass cartridges and belt links clattered around the truck bed as I sprayed the enemy roadblock soldiers with a barking blast of fire. Almost point blank! It was great, just like a movie.

A few times four of us snuck down from our base camp and descended on a snug little farm house for some real country cooking. I felt just like a blue-belly Yankee during 'the War', but it was some real fine 'grunts!' The lady of the house seemed to enjoy the compliments from us dirty, teenage spies. She knew some of us were bound to die in the far away war, but was loyal to her countrymen, never mind that many of us were from the 'North'.

The big event was the night drop and as aggressors we ran the DZ. We waited for what must have been four hours for the lousy C-130s. I must have been the only stupid fucker standing out in the open, at my post, instead of sleeping in the woods. Finally, the Herks came in over the trees at low level and a cry went up to light our flare pots. I dropped a match into my coffee can of gasoline and sand. 100 men did the same and instantly a gargantuan burning cross exploded across the fields! It was one rough DZ of uneven mountain pastures and 100ft-plus trees choking in all around. A creek ran down the middle of the field and along each side of it were more tall trees. As the last Air Force C-130 passed over, another shout sailed out of the darkness and everyone slapped a shingle down over their flare pots. All went totally dark and quiet, for about ten seconds. I wheeled around as a terrifying crash and scream pierced the night from the woods next to me. Jumpers were going into the trees, crashing down and snapping off branches. Just like the commando drop scene in the movie *The Bridge on the River Kwai*, rifles, helmets and assorted gear splattered and bounced off the ground. Aggressors charged and hillbillys maneuvered in a wild clash; the midnight 'army surplus store' was open for business. I walked up to the road in time to see a paratrooper just miss the power lines then hit, with a sickening smack, the middle of the black top between all the parked pickup trucks. Over shot the DZ a little.

The next day, we abandoned our ridge top camp and moved to the torture camp. In the shadow of tall trees prisoners were brought in and some were worked over by the in-house expert. Sergeant Kawalskihammer, I think his name was, demonstrated mild forms of torture on blindfolded and bound PoWs. His techniques included pouring water down the nose and placing subjects on 4-inch-thick hardwood tree limbs, balancing on their shins. Very interesting … your papers please. Of course, we saw 'nothing!'

Deep in the forest one day, I got lost from my team. Nearby was a stream crossed by fallen logs and littered with boulders and lush tropical-looking brush. Sunlight filtered down in beams and illuminated the gin clear water in places while toadstools clustered beneath ferns. An overgrown wilderness of pristine beauty had me lured into a placid state of mind, but even the garden of Eden had its pitfalls. Danger was, in fact, underfoot. Standing out in the middle of the stream looking for trout, interesting wildlife and things to eat, I looked square into the eyes of a red demon! A powerful rust-colored body with beady root-beer glowing red eyes crouched … ready to strike. And behind him was another holy terror. I'd never seen a Copperhead in the wild but I knew 'em when I saw 'em. They, like an Egyptian asp, were rather short with arrowhead shaped heads and evil little horns above the eyes. These were pit vipers, heat seekers for nourishing their own cold blood. I turned my head slightly to check my footing for a hasty exit and saw to my horror that the creek and its banks were covered with hiding, poisonous, Copperheads, all backed into holes or under rocks and all ready to strike. From their motionless spring-loaded stances they followed my every move. I swear I saw them under water looking up! I broke and ran. Hundreds of eyes watched me book, out of the snake pit!

Back in camp I settled down from my jaunt in the woods. I overheard some of the beret NCOs talking. One said, "Kennedy? Best thing that could have happened … I'm glad."

The NCO looked at me for my reaction, I guess. The date was June 5, 1968 and somebody had shot the attorney general.

About a week later, Winters, MacIntosh … the giant college man, James Maurice with the Dudley Do-Right jaw, myself and a gang of others reported to the dispensary for physicals. Toward the end of the formalities I was informed that if I couldn't read the eye chart without glasses, I would be terminated. Of course, I couldn't and after several tries, I joined my down-in-the-mouth comrades out on the front steps. They had all flunked the physical because like me they all wore lenses. The crux of the matter is we were cheated by the Army and the government into joining for an extra year. Nothing was ever said about a vision requirement for Green Berets. We were screwed. I knew it would happen somehow. One of our crew wore contact lenses and I wanted to pick them off his eyeballs to retest. Talk about a deflated ego. We were sick! We handled it badly.

When my chums from the war games, who were berets already, heard about my termination they were incredulous,

"You're the one who spotted all the snakes."

I had pointed out a mammoth rat snake in a hollow tree over our base camp trail.

Now we had to fallout in a group of twelve terminators and await our fate. Orders for Vietnam were the norm and the name 'The Dirty Dozen' was ours. It was a rotten deal; guys who wanted out couldn't get out, and those that were motivated got canned.

We had all tested separately back in medic school. We were shown a darkened room and I had a bad feeling, back then, I would flunk and my 3 buddies would leave me behind. I answered questions off a tape recorder, very James Bondish. The questions started slowly and sped up to rapid fire; the difficulty increased with the speed. The first one was something about swimming a river above the intended landing area on the far side. The last question had to do with being wounded and crawling towards a missile base, with only a knife, having 3 minutes to disarm a nuclear rocket, with an enemy patrol close behind. More followed. You had a wounded buddy that might bleed to death but the original mission was to blow up a secret fighter parked in a hanger. Explosives were in a truck guarded by a double agent woman spy in the woods. What to do? ... 15 seconds to answer. I'm sure I answered something crazy like: steal the truck, grab the woman, crash through the jet hanger. The questions had come fast and furious, from the machine they were on. I kept trying all the way to the end even though it was necessary to skip many. I just knew I had failed ... but somehow managed a score of 407, good enough for government work. I passed. We all passed. Probably because bodies were needed and we had not given up during the test. We'd seen the Green Beret medics, down from Bragg, who had to fight off the nurses around Fort Sam. We did not want to screw up and not qualify.

But now, at Bragg, us pariahs waited for orders so we could get off the base, take a leave, and go home. Vietnam was almost certain. Screw them, the Green Berets weren't the only elite outfit in-country. However, we were not a happy crew, the possibility of getting killed in some 'leg' infantry unit was suddenly very real.

Still in Green Beret school, they prepared us for war, now. We tested out the M-16, which was a total mystery to me, and saw color movies of crushed faces, and skin all burned off. The faces were missing eyeballs, teeth and total jaw bones, but were shown again after recovery … totally fine and handsome!

While we waited a new movie came out and when it premiered at Bragg, the Dirty Dozen were in the front row. The name of the movie was not the 'Dirty Dozen' but *The Green Berets;* it was not well received. The thing was a piece of garbage and rude noises and demonstrations created a carnival atmosphere in the crowded theatre. The movie was filmed in pine forests and the last scene was the famous John Wayne sunset scene. For years, this piece of drama drew all kinds of flack because 'everyone' *knows* the sun can't possibly set into the ocean off the east coast of Vietnam. Well, to be fair to the director and writer, the popcorn critics and many half-assed writers failed totally to use their meager brains. Vietnam, like Florida, is sort of surrounded with water; it's a peninsula. The country does have a west coast and thus ocean sunsets. Some people never heard of a map, I'm positive.

Well, we weren't 'washed out', we were shipped to war due to the needs of the Army. We all had a critical MOS and perhaps all the medics were dead after the Tet battles. Or some battalion commander with a Special Forces background knew how to get medics for his unit and from where!

On the way home I visited some of our sleepy Southern towns and decided to stop off in Washington DC as well, seeing as how I was all patriotic now. On the way north I met interesting and colorful people and was shown local retreats where popular but dubious social events transpired. One black shop keeper invited me to the rear of his poorly lighted store, I had no idea what he had in mind. He suggested I wait on his couch, left, and a bit later 2 people returned. The old guy introduced me to the local high school queen … if indeed she was even in high school. The room we were in looked like a part of Uncle Tom's cabin, the dusty run down part. Anyway, she sat right down almost on top of me and I swear I've never seen a prettier black girl in my life. She had on a mini-skirt with hula girls and real grass glued on their waists and the charming thing was: I could see no underwear! Up until this time I'd never met ANY black people except the fatherly NCOs in army training schools. We had to import a black girl from Africa in 'our' high school as some sort of training aid ... or cultural awareness, I guess, back in '67. I never even talked to our classmate.

So, I ended up having so much fun in 'Redman' NC I didn't want to leave. Some swell local fellows even invited me out on the town. I remember discussing the finer points of the term 'red neck' when the lights went out. I was really drunk on the nice clear, pleasant, booze in a jar we'd been drinking and the next thing I knew I was being driven out of town by a real nice policeman. He was Andy's deputy Barney in real life ... for sure and when he dropped me off, I swear to God he said,

"You all come back now, you hear ... .and the next time we'll go to my club."

In DC I tried to avoid the mud of 'tent city' and not get any on my jump boots. It was the end of June and a million poor people, mostly blacks, camped out under the cherry trees. One huge, well dressed, black man with concern seemingly all over his face, approached and asked me if I was lost. My new green beret didn't seem to impress anyone and I felt about as welcome as an SS officer at a bar-mitzvah.

Chapter 6

Flying Tigers and Puking Buzzards

July 7, 1968

The longest airplane ride I ever took was the one from Washington State to Vietnam by way of Alaska and then Japan. Steve Winters didn't show up at Fort Lewis when we processed overseas so we lost our friend for good. I heard my name called out twice during one of the formations and saw a taller soldier answer up. This was unusual, Osgood was a damn rare name. I introduced myself to my double and noticed he even looked like me, it was weird.

We flew with Flying Tigers. It was odd going with a crew originally formed of mercenaries or as the Japs would call them, air pirates. Our kind of people. We were on the way to very nearly the same piece of real estate the Tigers flew out of before WWII. We sat together, a bunch of badass Green Beret types, playing cards … for ears. For a while I was winning.

"Well boys, just send mine (ears) to Fort Bragg and I guess the Army will forward them to me," I bluffed. Nobody thought what I said was funny and I do believe they thought I was serious, but hell, it wasn't my idea to play cards. I sure didn't want anybody's parts.

The plane burned and smeared rubber on the runway at Cam Ranh Bay, Vietnam. Shortly, a stewardess cracked the cabin door and heaved it open. She wouldn't look at me for some reason but did manage a, "See you later," or "good luck," or something a little cold and detached. She was young and pretty and the moment was a very dramatic one in my idealistic mind.

Vietnam was pitch dark, hot as hell; there were floodlights in the distance and the sound of generators running. We looked around at the

30

mountains and realized people up in them would like nothing better than to put a bullet through us. The mountains all around looming down on us black ... black ... the color you see when you die.

We processed in that night and filled out a lot of forms. One asked: are you Special Forces qualified? I checked yes. We all checked yes, Maurice, MacIntosh and me. Then the entire room handed in the paperwork we were all hand carrying from the States like good little soldiers.

The next morning, I had to hang around the mess hall after breakfast. The dining room had ice tea and I couldn't get enough. I'd walk out the door, hit the heat, then turn around and go back in for more tea. The heat was driving me crazy for liquid! Going in and out of the screened door, for an hour, I couldn't help notice all the sandbags piled up in a wall around the building. The things came in a wide assortment of greens, browns, and a sort of Indigo color. The old-fashioned cloth sandbag was mainly a shade of bleached brown to white, while the modern plastic woven bag was a dark green. All the buildings had neat walls at least waist high. This was good country for sandbags because that was all that was available. Dirt didn't exist, just white sand. It was everywhere, on the ground, in sandbags and in our hair and clothes. This was the hottest and most uncomfortable place I had ever been.

Later all three of us trudged through the sand and over to the Special Forces office around the back of our barracks. We wanted back in the Green Berets where we figured we belonged. I went in alone.

"Hell yes we can always use medics, are you kidding...?" they told me right off. It didn't matter to them that we hadn't gone through the 91C Green Beret medic school or hadn't completed phase one at Bragg. They would find the three airborne combat medics something to do. A skinny little clerk, with glasses, said, "No problem ... give me your orders and we'll fix you up."

"We turned our orders in last night," I replied.

"Oh ... that's different. It's too late then ... you'll just have to take what you get."

At that very instant I heard our names blast out over the compound from some hidden loudspeaker. A static voice mentioned something about the 101st Airborne. In silence I stared at the clerk and the NCO standing in the background; I stared at the walls, my feet, and back at the clerk.

"The 101st, looks like the 101st Airborne Division," I told the clerk.

"No problem ... that's a good unit," he answered.

"Alright ... ," I replied and walked outside to find the boys.

They were out on the front steps. I was thinking that at least the 101st was a hardcore airborne unit. At least we would be in a paratrooper unit.

"We're going to the 101st. Didn't you hear them call us," I asked them.

"What?" they chorused.

"The 101st, we are to be puking buzzards."

Chapter 7

Jungle School

Transportation in Vietnam was plentiful but confusing. Somehow, we made our way to Bien Hoa airbase and the Division headquarters of the 101st, also known as the 'one oh worst' and sometimes referred to as the puking buzzards. The barracks they stuck us in were dark, wet, smelly, hot, run down and gave off an odor that *was* Vietnam. The smell was of moldy nylon and new space-age material blended with stagnant water, burning shit, insect repellant and a nostril stinging chemical smell of heat tabs burning.

The first morning dawned with an ominous, hot, orange and purple glow. I got roped into working on new wood-framed barracks by a little prick of an NCO who made idiotic slurs about the validity of the jump wings I wore. This 101st has got problems I thought. 80 per cent of the troopers were legs and the lifers seemed to have a thing about wings. Maybe a lot of the new troops awarded themselves wings just because they were assigned into a supposedly paratrooper unit. I couldn't say.

Anyway, it got to the point we'd ghost on over to the EM club instead of working. Screw it, what were they gonna do … send us to Vietnam? One time the lifers did snag us up and we spent the day burning shit, the original shit detail. We went around to the shit houses and pulled cut-down 55-gallon drums out from behind and below the seats. Then we mixed gas into the liquid and solid waste and set it on fire. It was tough, rotten, stinking work but it had to be done. Our surroundings were right out of a Peter Bruegel painting. Fires and plumes of smoke rose everywhere, groups of people were being herded around by other odd little groups of armed characters. The feeling of death hung about the place; it was hell on earth.

For several days we attended classes on map reading, field sanitation, malaria control, radio procedure and the art of the ambush. We went on a patrol at night, crawling over simulated trip wires and booby traps, and during the day shot various weapons. The instructors loved to scare the fucking skin off our hides; blowing a bunch of C-4 right next to our outdoor seats in class guaranteed 100 per cent attention!

Slinging rounds out an M-79 wasn't going to be my job but I enjoyed shooting the 'thump gun'. A burned-out APC was our target and I hit it with the second shell. Next, I fired a LAW and put the rocket through the tracked carrier at about 200 yards. I couldn't hear the instructor yelling, "Damn ... good shot!"

I was stone-cold deaf from the damn thing and I felt like someone had ripped my ear drums out. Days later my ears were still ringing.

At night we drank beer at the EM club and mulled over our private thoughts about dying. The days weren't too bad, if we didn't have to burn shit. The days were kind of enjoyable, kind of exciting. But at night the thought of being a medic with the mobs of legs wasn't pleasant.

One day, during one of the mandatory formations, the corporal in charge decided to make MacIntosh take his wings off. Maurice and I watched as Mac, only slightly inconvenienced looking, thought about the idiot's request. I couldn't believe it and because I was surprised, did not act. Somebody piped up from a row behind us,

"If he earned them ... leave him be."

I guess I was afraid of being sent to some suicide unit if I bucked the tyrant; we should have stuck up for our friend and taken over the formation, mutinied or something. If the corporal had tried to make me strip my wings, I wouldn't have done it. Six months later I would have shot the puke if I could have gotten away with it. Dave did the smart thing, however, and removed the wings, temporarily.

That night the little corporal provoked a fight with the biggest 'shake and bake' (instant sergeant) NCO in our platoon. The formation fell apart and the blows started flying. It was a damn good thing we didn't have our weapons yet.

The next morning we got our hands on the widow makers. We all took possession of new, boxed, Colt M-16s with red plastic flash suppressor covers and rolled paper stuffed down the bores.

Three holes grouped in a tight pattern was the goal for sighting-in our assault weapons. Once you got one good cluster you could adjust the next three rounds if the first three weren't already dead center. An evening of shooting into the berm out on the base perimeter and we were ready. We thought.

The second to last day at jungle school I bumped into a 101st LRP (Long Range Patrol). The little guy wore bleached 'golden' tiger stripes, a black baseball cap with cool looking white 101st arrow-head Recondo patch, and jump wings – the whole nine yards. I asked him about joining up with LRPs. He laughed. The dipshit didn't realize the skinny, four-eyed, beanpole, with the goofy green hat in front of him was a paratrooper combat medic, Green Beret trained and a kind of demonic, gung-ho, warrior.

The last day at Bien Hoa I celebrated by terrorizing the Division area aboard a flat-decked, four-wheeled 'mule'. I tried to slide around corners and spring the front end up into wheelies to impress my friends. They didn't know that I was a race car enthusiast. I loaded up the boys on the mule and was then able to pop giant front-end lift-offs with them in the back.

Finally, our orders came and we lost Dave MacIntosh to some infantry battalion. Dave got wounded shortly after joining his unit and went home. We weren't so lucky.

So, when we left Camp Zinn and jungle school we were down to two men. Steven Winters was sent to the 173rd Airborne Brigade, a hard-charging, fast-moving fire stopper that was most famous for the epic battle at Dak To. He should have been with us and I sure did miss him. Steve's body was carried to a chopper in the arms of a fellow medic after an enemy assault on some fire base early in his tour. It must have been around August or September 1968 when we lost him. Steve was a real hero!

Chapter 8

Black Magic

I had a love affair with the M-16. I thought it was one sexy bitch and wanted it to perform well. Everyone was all the time hearing horror stories about the damn thing jamming and not being able to penetrate the brush and I believe that was true. The weapon was accurate, hard hitting, and made of lightweight aircraft looking materials that stood up to the jungle. It was loud as hell but had an easy kick and the rumor was that the Mattel toy company made all the black plastic parts. I didn't know, but if it was Mattel ... it had to be swell.

Mine was stamped AR-15 and was fully automatic with the selector switch for safe, semi-auto, and full-auto ... rock and roll. The selector switch was activated with the right thumb, for right-handed people, and made a 'click' when flipped up, unless it was squeezed slowly, in which case it was silent.

In jungle school an instructor had leapt onto the stage where we gathered for our initial briefing on our rifles, "Gentlemen ... what you hold there is the finest assault weapon on the face of the earth." The instructor, in his school uniform of black hat and black t-shirt raised his already loud yell to a scream, "Mr Charles does not like black magic. The round travels in excess of 3,000ft a second and makes big holes coming and going! Gentlemen ... you will not ... I repeat, not use the sling in combat with the 101st. Marines and ARVNs and Air Force use slings, the 101st does not. They are too noisy and will snap vines. If you diddy bop around out there with your weapon slung like a toy soldier, Mr. Charles with think you's a Marine or a ARVN or a Airforce and he will zap your ass!"

All our new weapons had a navy-blue sling and adjusting buckles.

"Gentlemen ... your basic combat load will be twenty-one magazines each and eighteen rounds of ammo per magazine."

The 101st used eighteen rounds to help keep the spring strong in the twenty-round magazines that were standard issue in 1968. That was supposed to keep the rifle from jamming.

"Gentlemen ... the Marines had a problem with the M-16. The previous model to yours had a bolt that could be put together two ways, the right way and the Marine way. If the wrong way was selected the weapon would fire once and jam. Gentlemen, this model has been Marine-proofed and will not jam, no matter how the bolt goes in."

The rifles we clutched were new models with cylindrical flash suppressors replacing the three pronged, open, fork type that used to catch brush.

The M-16 was far from a perfect machine and did have flaws, the handle being a minor example. Although this grip gave the weapon a space gun look and housed the rear sight, it was aft of the center of gravity and too thin. Holding the gun by the handle was awkward as the weight pitched forward making the thing always front heavy if you used the grip. The usual method was to slide the right thumb only through the handle and the other fingers out in front of the magazine well, just under where the forward hand grips are the fattest. That was the center of balance.

As time went on, I began to notice a lot of rifles with a ramrod run up inside a little hole cut in the fat part of the handguard. The 3ft cleaning ramrod stuck out of the hole and fitted snug up against the chamber and back on the stock, secured near the butt with an elastic helmet-cover band. This modification looked natural and was hardly noticeable, but I had to ask its purpose. I asked a grunt, "What's the deal with the ramrod stuck up in the handguard?"

"Oh, that's so when you find your cherry ass holding a jammed gun you just might have time to whip it out, stuff it down the barrel, knock out the round from the bore, and fire before some dink out draws you with his AK."

"Oh," I replied.

Years later I read that the problem with the weapon jamming was due to the powder in the cartridge and the company's desire to obtain government contracts. The military wanted a slug with a muzzle velocity in excess of 3,000ft a second, so the Olin manufacturing company used a fast-burning powder to get the required speed. Unfortunately for a lot of soldiers, that powder burned dirty and the result was a thick, choking, carbon deposit that created malfunctions. According to reports, the US Navy, for some mysterious reason, still uses the Olin M-16 rounds.

Chapter 9

Monkey's Uncle

Jumping onto different planes all day made it difficult to tell just exactly how we got to our destination. We toured all over southern South Vietnam. I know we hit Cu Chi and stopped at Phuc Vinh before Maurice and I ended up in the 3/187th, also known as the Rakkasans. They conducted business in the flatland between Bien Hoa, the Hobo Woods and the Parrot's Beak border; VC country. Rakkasan means falling-down umbrella or upside-down umbrella in Japanese. The battalion was to become just about the most bloodied and famous unit of the entire war, and soon. Just our luck.

We got ready to go to the field for the first time. Some medic gave us a one-minute block of instruction on how to use the Albumin serum IVs. As the liquid shot out the end of the needle the class was over, we were ready. Across from the medics' shack where the class was, lived a photographer, with his collection of large black and white glossy photos of dead people. He showed us some new photos of a trepanned head with the brain hanging off to one side. It was a very clean wound, no blood, just grey and white bone and meat with some tuffed up black hair. Very pretty.

The next morning a bulky platoon sergeant and a young lieutenant came for me and told me to get my stuff together as I was going to the field. As they drove me out to the LZ I realized I was through 'getting' somewhere and had in fact finally arrived. This was it, big time, and I was one scared cherry ground pounder. The thing that kept me going was the knowledge that I wouldn't be alone. With me would surely be a couple of guys from California and some debonair experienced stud who would take me under his wing. We probably wouldn't all be killed at once and if we were all rolled up and wiped out … screw it. It would be an honor, a warrior's death.

The helipad was off in some deserted area of the fire base in a flat, sandy, debris scattered corner. We pulled up to a lone figure seated by his gear.

"This is it," the sergeant said as he helped me with my ruck. I carried my equipment over to the GI and set it down. Turning around I saw the lieutenant and the sergeant standing by the jeep, close together watching me like mourners at a funeral. After a while, they drove slowly away.

We weren't the only ones on that lonely piece of real-estate littered with miles of rusted wire, fuel drums and PSP. The short, dazed, timid-looking guy had a monkey sleeping inside his shirt. The soldier neither turned or acknowledged me in any way; he held a smoke grenade in one hand and sat. I took in the countryside and studied the bomb craters stretching to the horizon and the tree line.

"I'm scared," a voice exclaimed. I whirled around and looked at my companion. That was it, I never heard the man say another word. The monkey woke up, crawled out of his nest and started checking me out. The little creep walked up on my chest as I sat in the dirt. He grabbed one side of my shirt and stepped inside. It was truly hot as hell already.

A Huey swung in from the north and my friend popped smoke. A thick purple fog spread from the burning canister. Mr Monkey got nervous and I felt his nasty little hand on my nipple. The chopper eased in and landed. I got up. The downwash from the rotary winged aircraft nearly toppled me to the ground and for a second I lost my balance. Arms tightly around my neck, the nutty primate swung out of my shirt and rode the wind like a hairy scarf. His legs and torso flapped up and down. The shithead hung on screaming and chattering while the pilot in the left seat motioned us on. We climbed in among the boxes of C-rats, glad to be out of the sand storm. The high-pitched whine of the jet engine ended any normal conversation and as our little friend left me and latched onto my talkative buddy, I wondered if I should chamber a round.

The pilots pulled their ship off the ground and nose down, sped off the fire base. We were committed now, I realized, so all I could do was sit back and enjoy the view from the open cabin. The Army aviators cruised the Huey at about 500ft and for a few minutes I was beamed into another world. It was a world of Marco Polo, pirates of the orient, forty thieves, Alexander the Great, war and romantic adventure.

Reality was something else. Outside it was rice paddies, odd squared-off rectangular flooded sections bordered by tall and massive hedgerows or dykes. From the air thousands of bomb craters were visible, some overlapping, all scattered around and through the creeks or clusters of huts.

It was fun flying in the slick. We were cool and free from mosquitoes, plus, every second spent in the air was less time spent at our destination, wherever that was; 300 some odd days left and the clock was ticking.

The door gunners seemed relaxed but I noticed they constantly scanned the horizon. They both looked sinister, dressed in flame-resistant flight gear. With the dark helmet visors down and their green gloves clutching the M-60 at chest level almost in a prayer, they both looked exactly like 200lb praying mantises.

The sling-wing aircraft slowed some and one of the gunners pivoted his gun level, at the ready, so I figured we were about to land. The pilots took us straight in over a row of trees, slowed, and came to a hover at the edge of a large grassy field. I couldn't see anyone around. Touching down, two GIs darted out from the hedgerow and started offloading the C-rats. I bailed out with ruck on and a case of C-rats under my arm. The Huey wasted no time leaving us.

A loose group of soldiers worked around me while others stood nearer the hedgerow. They were hard to pick out, against the foliage, in the bleached and dirty jungle fatigues everyone had on.

I asked for the head medic and was directed to a big Mexican guy who appeared stunned when he realized that the rear had sent him another medic. He shook my offered hand, pointed towards the middle of the field and said, "Your platoon is over there, just do what the medic does."

Christ almighty – I had arrived. I had to go and do what a medic did.

Out in the field, a little to one side, was a clump of bushes and an old broken-off tree sticking up about 12ft. I thought I noticed something move so I pulled the cocking handle back on my rifle and let it fly forward, chambering a tiny .223cal. bullet. All I had to do now was flip the selector switch up, off safe position, and she would fire. Glancing around I started for the old tree, after shouldering my ruck. The closer I got to the clump of bushes the more people I noticed. The whole platoon CP was sitting, resting or hiding in or around a miniature oasis of brush.

"So, you're the new pill pusher, huh?" a brown skinned, slightly older looking guy asked before I noticed the lieutenant's bar on one side of his shirt.

"Yes sir," I replied.

A light rain squall moved through the company position and I stood out in the rain grinning down at another two Latin types grinning back at me from under a dark green rubber poncho. They looked like a freak two-headed turtle. Suddenly a dull 'POP' split through the heat waves. I dropped down on one knee. The Siamese twin-headed turtle vanished under its cover.

"Get down," the lieutenant snarled.

I flopped down prone and my helmet rocked forward smacking my nose and covering my eyes. I heard whispering, then the words,

"Booby trap!"

"Okay CP, let's move out."

Nine men, most I'd not seen, raised and stood, all within 30ft of the CP. They carried radios and rifles. The lieutenant made for the hedgerow bordering the field at a brisk clip. The rest of our group followed the officer and I followed the rest of the group. They slunk through a bamboo wall, walking on a narrow trail.

"Watch where yah go'en, Doc," a voice whispered from somewhere out of the jungle. Doc ... ? Was he talking to me, I wondered? He must have meant me. I was the only one in sight. I liked it ... they called me Doc. In a flash I almost slipped and fell into a punji pit. Dried and hardened needle-sharp bamboo stakes pointed up at me. Overreacting to avoid the pit, I damn near fell to my death in a tunnel opening next to the booby trap. The tunnel mouth looked like something Egyptian kings would build. It was perfectly concealed. The sucker went straight down into a deep shadow and had no tell-tale loose dirt laying around. It was very fresh, new. It was a piece of art completely square, smooth and plumb!

We emerged into another field. A GI stood, bare-chested, letting a medic poke his ribs with a cotton covered stick dipped in Phisohex soap. The wounded soldier had a few little black holes and tiny nicks in his skin.

"Light charge … yeah … a light booby trap," somebody said. I hadn't been in the field fifteen minutes and already we'd taken wounded. Damn!

"Welcome to the boonies … Doc," the haunting voice of one of our RTOs snickered.

Chapter 10

Night of the Living Dead

It was purple heart time for the young soldier as Delta pulled off the resupply LZ and headed out to God knows where. I just tagged along, not realizing that I should have been somewhere near the lieutenant and the CP, or at least in my platoon. It was as hot as it could possibly be and I was confused. It was my first day in the field. Suddenly, an explosion shook the earth. Varoomph! From behind me a shadow raced across the ground in my direction and I cowered down. A smoking body landed 20ft in front of me. Either the guy behind me or I had triggered off another booby trap and sent some poor fucker flying. Instantly, medics were on him, checking his body inside its ripped, holed, and smoldering covering. They held his head and burned black face as he tried to stand and thrash around in a shock-induced panic. It was a white guy with a black face.

"I'm blind, I'm blind, I can't see," he wailed. Rich pulverized black earth had forced its way into his eye cavities and shared the same space as his eyeballs. Grit crumbled out as the medics checked him and the dirt fell onto his chest and then the ground.

"You're okay man ... let me wash the dirt out so ya can see," one of the aidmen told him as I stood outside the cluster of medics.

The company put out security, in the form of a perimeter, for the Dustoff (air ambulance). The guy seemed okay once the crap was sloshed out of his eyes. He had some deep cuts and was badly shaken but that seemed the worst of it.

When the sun started down, I managed to find the platoon CP again. All I really did was to keep walking up the column until I recognized somebody. The platoon medic introduced himself and I remembered seeing him during the action previously. He was from Tahoe City, California, and looked like the typical ski bum / surfer with slightly shaggy blond hair that spilled out from under a floppy boonie hat. We had something in common, we both hung out around the lake during the winter.

"We'll stick together tonight but first we need a fighting position," he said as he handed me an entrenching tool. I was too tired to talk let alone even think about … digging? We dug a two-man hole to the same dimensions as a king-size water bed in the soft ground. In the bottom my new buddy laid both our ponchos,

"We'll sleep between those, you know in case it rains."

I sat huddled in our fighting hole when something that looked like a huge scorpion skittered across the poncho near my hand. Jerking my hand away I turned to my bed mate but he was too busy holding his gut, trying not to laugh, to be of any help. When he finally managed to control himself somewhat, he said, "Fresh water landcrabs, hoo hooie haw ha (choke) ha ha … you've been here half a day and you already got the crabs … hah hah hah hee hee ho ho. God please help me," he managed, doubling over in spasms that twisted his Nordic features. I was exhausted and scared to death but definitely not amused. It was pitch dark and still hot as hell. I figured we would be attacked or overrun at any moment. I was frightened but that didn't stop me from falling into a deep and sudden sleep. Like the living dead. Let 'em come I just didn't care.

Around 0200 the medic woke me up dragging one of the radios into our fox hole.

"Guard duty old buddy," he said as the PRC-25 hissed softly.

"Call the squads once in a while to make sure those ass-holes don't fall asleep … wake me up if something happens goodnight." Great, I said to myself. I spent the whole night trying to communicate, even hearing another voice would have been nice. I couldn't get ahold of anyone, what the fuck was going on, were they all asleep, were they all gutted and slashed from ear to ear? What was I supposed to do, crawl out towards the tree line, where most of the perimeter positions were, and wake 'em up? I knew our hole was inside a protective circle but had no idea really where the squads were set up. If I crawled out somebody would shoot me sure as shit. Was I supposed to sit here all night? I brooded; I didn't even know who to give the radio to. All I knew was I wanted to go back to sleep and forget the nightmare. I fought sleep and stayed up. A couple of times somebody tried to call me and once a voice whispered, "Hey third herd is anybody there?"

"Yeah, I'm here," I said weakly.

"Set rep ... over?" the voice asked.

"Set rep ... ah ... over?" I replied.

"Listen, just stay awake and I'll talk at ya latersss."

The sky slowly lightened and, reaching for a canteen, I found that a drop in the air temperature had lowered the water temperature to a degree that was relatively ... not hot. It was delicious. I quickly learned to cherish that simple pleasure, one of the few distinct joys of the boonie rat.

The hissing static on the radio stopped again,

"Good morning Vietnam ... puck, puck, PUUUCK, it's chicken man, it's chicken man ... heseverywhere, heseverywheressssss." What the hell was that? Somebody was doing chicken imitations on the radio net ... ? It was insane.

Chapter 11

Air Strikes

Gunships came on station. They were C-model Hueys firing rockets, miniguns and 40mm grenades. I was beginning to recognize the sounds. The rockets cracked and whooshed out trailing smoke, while the miniguns sounded like an electric can opener gone wild or canvas ripping. A thump, thump, thump, thump, echoed soon after by crash, crash, crash, crash, while more thump, thump, thumps, overdubbed on the impacting rounds told a story a blind man could understand about the belt-fed grenade launchers.

This was my fourth day out and the heat was killing me; I figured I might make it if I didn't run out of water. The hot afternoon water with the plastic taste running down the back of my throat was beginning to seem like a priceless luxury. It was even starting to taste good.

I wondered what the choppers were shooting at. I kept expecting to be attacked by a large enemy force. When would we get into a fire fight; were the gunships mowing down rows of Viet Cong or what? So far, we hadn't once seen the enemy that was kicking our ass with booby traps. They were winning the war a little at a time. Every day somebody got blown up.

Our platoon CP huddled against a paddy dyke.

"You fellows keep your heads down now, we are going to call in the United States Air Force," the lieutenant warned.

"Hey look at Doc's shits … every theen it brand new," one of the radiomen said, sitting on the dyke like he was at the beach drinking a brew. Everyone was looking at me and my dark green equipment; even my M-16 was fresh from a box. A hand darted out and stuffed a piece of tin foil down the muzzle and over the flash suppressor of my gun.

"Keep the dirt out, Doc," one of the Mexican RTOs offered with a knowing grin.

The smoking oil burners came in low and fast, aimed right for us. They were Phantoms – two-seater fighter bombers with shark-like shaped front ends. We saw them line up miles away and damn, the first guy dove even lower, below the trees! You could see the dirty exhaust until the pilots shoved the throttles forward into slow afterburner burning more of the fuel and spraying less out the rear-end.

They bombed east to west and the target was right in front of us. Lead loomed closer, still behind the trees but clearly visible, and released a bomb. He was a half mile away when the bomb blew off. The Phantoms were flying ammo dumps! Not only did they carry tons of bombs, rockets and cannon shells, many of the day-to-day operating procedures were kicked off with explosives. In a dangerous nest of fuel tanks and howling, horizontal jet-rocket burner cans lurked an amazing and crude store. Shotgun shells forced the bombs off and possibly the fuel tanks as well. The monster could be started up anywhere, using the same internal cartridge system alone. The ejection seat was nothing other than a rocket pack strapped on the pilot. The parachute was even blown out, open and up with an explosive for low-level operation like right on the runway! And of course the machines were supposed to be flying time bombs anyway, with doomsday charges in case of landings at enemy airfields.

The high-drag 250lb bomb unfolded its multi-drag arms and went right for us! The arms made it look like some ghastly spore twirling in from outer space. Both the aircraft and bomb would fly right over us. We hoped. I hadn't the faintest idea what the purpose of the air strike was so I watched stupidly, mouth open, as the jet and HE flew tight formation. The bomb kept pace under its 'mother ship'. The formation of two clipped on over us alright, but you could see that the ordnance was slowly losing altitude. The freaking bomb was really moving and it damn near hit the tree tops around the CP. I'd been ready all along to jump on the west side of the dyke if the fucker looked like it'd plow into the east side. The RTO on top of the paddy wall fell off as the lieutenant shrieked needlessly,

"Unass that position troop or so help me God I'll … !" Everyone hugged the ground and listened to his heart try and tear loose.

WHAAAM … SHREEEEEK!

The rice paddies turned to jello and shook as the explosion was drowned by the roar of twin afterburners, white hot and hissing like giant cutting torches. The pilot peeled away from ground zero to safer airspace. Wing was right behind and he did the same thing, only with napalm. God it was great … turned and BURNED! Shit … I thought to myself, no problem, they missed us.

Later I found out exactly how dangerous the air strike business really was.

After the airshow I stood up and lost all sense of direction. I lost my bearings. The paddies and hedgerows to our front were gone and a blackened landscape from a horror movie greeted us. A charred and smoking framework of a hut was visible in the middle of a field of ash and wisps of smoke.

Chapter 12

ICE

One day a resupply bird came sailing in from the rear and unloaded right in the grass as I stood around and watched, too tired and hot to care much about it. I unloaded my ruck and a couple of us stood in the fluid of the rotor wash in our sweat soaked fatigues. We enjoyed the cool blast, panting like a bunch of sick trout. We were still humping past villages and through hedgerows and over dry rice paddies. We sweated every day and every night from the heat and the terror. Somebody handed me a small, freshly chipped chunk of ice and I plopped it into my canteen cup like everyone else was doing. To the GIs around me, very nearly all of whom suffered beginning stages of heat exhaustion, ice was unbelievable. My sliver of ice was like a pure diamond meteorite landing at my feet, a gift from the fairy godmother. All I could do was stare at the precious thing. I daydreamed I could crawl into the little world of ice and escape all the death and destruction around me.

Some days I just wanted to take off, west, towards Thailand. Other days I just wanted to hide somewhere.

My mind hid in my captured ice palace. A piece of ice in a canteen cup, alas, such a fleeting day dream. A fleeting day dream because soon the ice palace would flood and disappear. I drowned the kingdom with orange soda. The ice would melt but I would have something better, something almost as valuable as blood. I would have a cold cup of soda. Nursing and taking small guzzles that ran down the back of my throat, I wanted nothing else the world had to offer. It was like a cold beer after struggling in the desert for a day. Us drinkers swooned in ecstasy few have ever known and like good sex, were totally content during the act. Like all good things I did not want it to stop. I dreaded stopping.

Chapter 13

Terror in the Grass

July 18, 1968

The company patrolled by a hut and through a small hedgerow. I stopped between the hut and a 20ft wide bomb crater. To my right a hard packed path led into the hut, someone's home. The grass-and-wood house was inside a thicket of trees and brush, making it all but impossible to notice had it not been for the foot path. Here was a beautiful combination of man and nature working together.

A handsome little guy ran out of the hut and stood his ground at the entrance. He appeared to be about 3 years old and I think he had a problem. Something was on his mind. I will never forget him. A brave kid. I'm sure he had never seen many giant, lumbering alien killers who carried guns, knives and explosives before. I got the impression he trusted we would never harm him. I would have dropped any human on earth, anyone, who made a move to hurt that child. With his jaw hanging down I could have sworn he wanted to warn us about something. He looked so concerned. For a minute he stared at me.

BLAMM!

Something big exploded! In a heartbeat the world caved in. Black dirt and things lifted skyward on the other side of the hedgerow behind the hut. I vaulted into the old bomb crater. Would a wave of Viet Cong attack us? Had point triggered another booby trap? Shit, I didn't know. The main thing was I was ready to start shooting and about as protected as possible in the hole.

My little friend vanished into his house.

One of our wise-ass squad leaders nonchalantly walked past and screamed at me,

"Get your fucking ass up there!"

He pointed wildly at the hedgerow ahead and his voice suggested cowardice. The piece of shit just knew something I didn't. But to be fair, this was the first time I really experienced stress … his.

When I reached the ditch that ran through the grass in the hedgerow a GI pointed the way.

"Slow down Doc, take it real easy," he cautioned. "There's booby traps all over this fucking place. Watch for trip wires."

I eased into the grass, terror stricken.

In grass up to my shoulders I flung myself over the ditch and collapsed on the other side. I had landed in a dry rice paddy. To my right a small crowd of soldiers milled around. A body lay motionless at their feet and somebody yelled, "Birds on the way!"

A medic was tending a grunt who sat nearby. The medic had his hand on the guy's head and was trying to calm him down.

"You're ok man. You got the million dollar wound. You're going home!"

The wounded man twisted around like he was looking for something. The aidman's hand slipped off the wound and a geyser of blood spat out on the ground. I lurched forward to help but my partner from Tahoe called me over to the ditch.

Three troopers were clutching at something in the water. My friend was bending over with them.

"It's a bad one," he said.

"Give us a hand will ya? Just turn your head, close your eyes and pull. Whatever ya do … don't look!" They had ahold of a rubber poncho; I closed my eyes and tugged on it. When the load emerged from the water, I opened my eyes and looked. Inside was half a man. He was split length-wise and the poncho was full of red meat and water.

The kid had probably seen the whole thing. He had probably seen a VC patrol and NVA advisors rushing past his home minutes ahead of our formation. He may have watched, through the thicket, as the

VC carried in a dud artillery round. Not understanding, he most likely gawked from his hiding place as the trip wire was rigged. He might have even overheard his countrymen say something like: "Hurry! If the Americans keep coming they must pass here."

We had two dead and several urgent, high priority medivacs. When the Dustoff ship set down I almost lost control. It was madness, sheer madness! A yellow smoke grenade burned fiercely, marking the LZ. The chopper blades beat the air, blending the sickly colored smoke with flying debris, sand, sticks and litter. It was hard to see, talk, hear or even stand. Discarded bloody bandages and plastic wrappers scattered and blew along the ground. The wind whipped the ponchos where human parts were covered. In the branches of a tree a blood soaked fatigue shirt jittered.

Finally, silence closed in on us as the Dustoff pulled out and disappeared over the horizon. Christ almighty, is every day going to be like this? I'm not going to make it if it is, I thought.

Chapter 14

Baby Killers ...

We staggered along in the heat. Where the hell was I supposed to march I wondered again. I still hadn't figured it out. Nothing but strangers all around me; it was my fourth or fifth day in the field. I didn't even know where my platoon was in the file of soldiers snaking around rice paddies and clumps of bamboo. I did know that I was in the company D, 3/187th, 101st.

Stabbing the air with his index finger, some 'bloody wonder' lieutenant pointed towards the horizon as we hobbled by. Next to him was a black soldier with a thump gun.

"Fire em up ... fire em up!" the lieutenant snarled. I watched the grenadier raise his weapon and fire a round off towards the distant line of trees.

Kawump! Chomp!

High explosive 40mm projectiles spit dirt near some water buffalo and what looked like some farmers. The target was a long way off. The line kept moving and we kept walking. I followed the guy in front of me.

Later, still trying to figure out where I was supposed to be, our platoon medic came 'diddy bopping' back, down the file against the flow of grunts.

"Come with me," he said solemnly, humping by. Back where the shooting took place, a group of GIs stood staring at the ground. Two little girls sat in the dust. Next to the babies a couple of mama-sans squatted. A low screech seeped from somewhere deep inside the old crones. The kids, one around 5 the other about 3, were little dolls. They were stiff arms and legs and wide-open eyes like the pink plastic humanoid things found in city dumps. Both girls were dead. Nicks and cuts covered the exposed skin. Their eyes ... open and glazed. Flies buzzed and landed and walked on dry eyeballs. I was almost paralyzed and didn't even want to move. "Check em out, Doc," a voice commanded from behind us. I was afraid of that. I didn't know if this was an everyday occurrence or what, but I couldn't possibly go and touch them. I couldn't take their pulse.

"They're fucking dead you stupid sonofabitch!" our medic screamed. *AWham!* he slammed his helmet to the ground and quickly picked it back up. "God damn this shit!" he hissed as we trotted back up the trail, now with someone from my platoon; at least I felt 'unlost'. I wore my mask, the one for hiding emotions. The feeling of dread and something sinister drawing me towards it was strong in this outfit; was this the way it was supposed to be? This was not war, this was hell. I had images of fierce fire fights and human waves of charging enemy. It was karma. I was seeing the future.

Nightfall found us surrounding a group of huts. We were still in the neighborhood of the killings. Were they an accident? The targets, whatever they were, were a long way away. But why fire with huts all around and farmers working in the fields? I remember seeing white conical civilian peasant hats and water buffalo. Had I missed something, something like armed VC trotting past the farmers and trying to out flank us and maybe get ahead of us to rig another booby trap? I couldn't say. Maybe those kids were just in the way, unseen to us, playing as enemy soldiers snuck past them.

But now, every time I hear some general say he hates war, like they always do, I think of that day. Nothing was worth those children's death. If they had been the only deaths during the entire conflict, the war wouldn't have been any less a tragedy. The old lady at the induction center came back to haunt me, her dead poster children had materialized right in front of me. I'd been warned.

I sat near the entrance to a hut and could see the floor inside lit up with moonlight. The platoon medic squirmed over to my position, along the ground, and whispered, "This is the family's house!"

Oh fuck! Oh great! I thought. Why did he have to go and tell me that? Why are we still here, what are we doing? I wanted to know! I couldn't sleep that night. How could you sleep? You can't sleep in a living nightmare.

Chapter 15

Into the Fire

Soon after, stepping up to the enlisted men's bar back at Bien Hoa, I waved at Maurice to join me. He was back from some fire base where he'd had a jolly old time scoring weed and things while I was out getting my young sweet ass blown up. The rumor was that we were out of the 3/187th and headed up north because of all the medics killed during Tet. I Corp and northern South Vietnam were one bad AO. I couldn't say I was unhappy with the deal. As I sipped a cold one, I thought back to the day before – leaving the boonies and climbing into the resupply log bird, alone. I felt guilty about leaving and as the bird lifted out of the clearing the ski-bum medic flashed the thumbs up sign. The expression on his face said: you are a lucky sonofabitch. I didn't know how lucky. I felt sorry for that hard-luck outfit, they were getting diced up every single day. I felt bad about deserting those guys, but also extremely happy.

Years later I heard that Co. D, 3/187th finally did get overrun one night because everyone was asleep. This unit was not done with me however, it followed me and haunted me closely. In ten months these same guys, the gunners, medics and officers who were still on board, smashed onto Hamburger Hill! Delta 3/187th were the first, the very first, raiders to attack in that most famous deadly battle!

I also learned that the commander of the 2/327th, a Lieutenant Colonel Beckwith, used to trade captured weapons for his pick of new replacements. Whether we were considered worthy candidates for Beckwith's unit I don't know, but as Airborne medics out of Green Beret school we might have been. Anyway, something got us shipped, Shanghaied all the way from Bragg really. But why Maurice and I changed battalions in the 101st was a mystery forever.

After another scenic tour of Vietnam – our plane seemed to stop at every strip in-country – Maurice and I landed at Hue/Phu Bia. Camp Eagle, headquarters for the 1st Brigade 101st, was a couple of miles north-west of the airport, with highway 1 running north and south between them.

When we arrived at the 2/327th, the 'No Slack' battalion, according to the sign at the entrance to the compound, we were ripped off. They took our rifles. We never saw the things again. Mine was sighted in for me and me alone and I wondered if these people knew just who they were fucking with. We were not just 'off the boat'. It was the start of a growing and distinct dislike for the rear areas and the creatures that inhabited them.

Not only did they get our weapons, but we managed to have our wallets lightened when the medical platoon sergeant took off with the slush 'beer' fund he talked us into supporting.

Someone waved us in the direction of our sleeping quarters, which was a tent complete with its own 24-hour-a-day three-ring circus. The canvas tents pitched on a slope were wall to wall craziness. The stinking, damp, crowded, dark, living areas were disasters; the cots sank into the dirt providing lopsided, unstable support. Surrounding the tent was a wall of sand bags, but parts of it had collapsed inwards. This was our protection against rockets and mortars.... From the ground to ceiling a mass of mosquito nets hung from flimsy supports and drooped in tangled disarray over the cots. Piles of rucksacks, C-rat boxes, rifles, hand grenades, and moldy boots lay about, mixed with M-60 belt linked 'gun ammo' and other gear. Bodies littered the scene. Some snored away, some wore boots only and one had nothing on but a single sock. Many lay rolled up in damp, sweat-stained quilted jungle blankets, while others wobbled around, clowning and talking, drunk out of their minds. Some of the jungle soldiers ate and some listened to rock and roll music played at full volume.

Someone handed me a handmade, funny-looking cigarette. I casually got up and walked outside to sit by the back entrance and stare up at the tropical stars. I was ready to smoke my first marijuana joint. What the hell, why not? I couldn't expect to live through the coming year anyway, not the way things had been going. If I became hooked on marijuana, what would it matter?

As I puffed away a feeling of taking part in an exciting, romantic adventure and living life, really living, came over me. The possibilities of really dying, however, just made sitting … breathing in and out, for the moment, a clearer and grander experience. Expecting more from the illegal weed, I flipped the roach away. Focusing on the stars now didn't work, so I stumbled off towards the EM club.

The next day some dude with a boonie hat walked by me like I was a wooden Indian. He stuck out as a member of the recon platoon because they were the only troops allowed to wear the soft French style headgear in the rear. Our platoon sergeant laughed at me when I told him I wanted in the Hawk Recon platoon; the black asshole left me wondering why no one ever took me seriously. It was a recurring problem. I also wondered when we would drink beer from 'our' slush fund. I wanted a beer now.

The day after, Maurice and I were on a chopper, combat loaded, getting a look at the 101st's AO. We snaked up a mountain river, below the ridges, overflying some tough jungle country. Humping down in that seemed impossible.

On Fire Base Brick we walked off the pad and up the hill towards the aid-station. Eucalyptus trees, huge ones just like in California, dominated the knoll – the high feature on the base. The aid-station was dug into the knoll and lay partially underground; exotic jungle trees grew out and around the roof, at odd angles, providing shade. Ammo boxes set in sandbag walls made impressive windows. All you had to do was knock the wood bottoms out. As the tops were already hinged, you just opened and closed the 'window', peeky-boo I see you.

I met all the medics and they were glad to see us. They put us to work right away, filling sandbags; filling sandbags was harder than burning shit and just about as dignified.

The aid-station filled up at night so I slept on the roof, under the stars.

Later the first night explosions and white searing light suddenly registered in the center of my brain. While my body jerked off the ground my eyes flew open. Sparks and fire silhouetted running soldiers – right on top of the medic's bunker! The worst kind of fear, unknown fear, branded my soul. Hugging the sandbagged roof, the explosions looked like muzzle bursts, that were centralized on the north side of the knoll. The noise cut through me; it was the damn booby trap syndrome all over again. Finally, it dawned on me the running figures were mortar crews exposed in the flashes and strobe light effect of their 81mm tubes. A fire mission was pumping – out going. We weren't under attack! I rolled over clutching my ears, squeezing my head like a giant zit!

Chapter 16

D-Day

July 29, 1968

The 2/327th and the 2/502 choppered off Fire Base Brick and stood down at Camp Eagle. Rumors bounced around we were going into the 'valley'.

Maurice, with his concrete jaw and Clark Kent looks and I flew back to Eagle and tried to prepare for whatever was coming. I was miserable. Our days of eating strawberry ice-cream and hot chow up on Brick were over. In the battalion area we endured a madhouse of acid rock and roll warriors swarming around in one big, green, psychedelic cluster fuck again! The young soldiers talked about things we were not part of, things like: AK-47 rounds cutting down men, shoot-outs in bunker complexes and places like the Yellow Brick Road that snaked and weaved all the way down from Hanoi. The Yellow Brick Road, the valley of the Jolly Green Giant, Land of Oz and Hawk Hill were all names for the valley roads or areas in and around the A Shau. This mystic land was said to be 'Over the Rainbow' and was a huge section of the Ho Chi Minh Trail, an NVA staging and storage hide-out with perhaps 45,000 enemy nearby.

I felt kind of lost and wanted to get away from the mob and into a smaller and tighter unit like the battalion recon platoon, someplace a little more organized and hopefully safer. A guy could get killed busting bush with these jokers in the line companies.

"Live for today, for tomorrow you die", seemed to be the motto here; booze and grass were everywhere.

One day Maurice and I were standing around next to the aid-station in a group of veteran medics and hangers-on. One short little blond-haired

60

grunt looked over at me and announced, "Looks like we gotta C-I-D. Yeah CEE-EYE-DEE … look at this puke cherry."

Everyone stopped what they were doing and looked over at me. It got embarrassingly quiet as the blood rushed to my head. I looked over at Maurice for some support and finally asked, "Hey Jim … what's this punk leg calling me anyway?"

Maurice just shrugged his shoulders, he didn't know either. The little shit was high on something. He was referring to the Criminal Investigation Division with his shit-dipped words like I was some kind of narc for the military cops. It must have bolstered his poor self image, pretending to be a big-time drug mover with a 'need to know' attitude. I just blew it off; I had bigger problems.

It started to rain and in a moody funk I decided I was way too young to die. I suddenly realized I never felt more alone in my life. I hadn't even had a real love affair with a real woman. I couldn't die, not yet anyway.

August 2, 1968

Our leader, LTC Charlie (Charging Charlie) Beckwith, affectionally known as 'Charger' to some of the troops in the 2/327th, was preparing for a full sized invasion! Charger was a terror to his officers, with his strutting, battle-scarred body. He was one tough nut – one of the very few to survive a direct hit from a .51/cal AA round through the guts. He got that while flying a rescue mission back in '66 with Project Delta. The very flamboyant Green Beret, French Foreign Legion trained, SAS qualified, paratrooper was our battalion commander! He was known to grab a couple of troopers, four or five LAWs, light anti-tank weapons, and sneak around the A Shau Valley … tank hunting!

Charger's battalion area was crawling with grunts stuffing their rucks with food and combat gear, cleaning weapons or loading aid bags. Squad leaders hurried about passing out grenades, claymore mines, and LAWs – lots of LAWs. I tried to Imagine myself shooting one of the disposable single-shot rocket launchers at a tank. I prayed for a chance.

Yeah, I could see myself firing at a tank alright, but destroying one? The damn rockets just seemed too small. But I had, once already, hit a tracked vehicle ... once.

All we knew for certain was that we were going to the field. In this case the field seemed to be a distant range of ominous looking mountains to the west of Camp Eagle, somewhere over the rainbow?

After a time I had gotten the idea of what to hump and what to leave behind. Combat medics at least had the privilege of pretty much choosing their basic loads. As long as it included the M-5 aid bag. Some of the goofy crap that supply issued was obviously intended for the rear, stuff like mosquito netting and flack jackets. So I decided to forego smoke grenades, radio batteries, machine gun ammo, entrenching tool, claymore mines, bayonet, gas mask, mosquito net, and flack vest, definitely the flack vest! The damn things were too heavy and wouldn't stop a bullet anyway. The 101st troopers didn't wear vests. Marines wore vests. MPs wore vests. Boonie rats almost never, ever touched the things.

My basic combat load consisted of food and water (four one-quart canteens), poncho, camouflage poncho liner, aid bag, mosquito repellent, a pair of spare socks, toothbrush, M-16, and a bandolier of twenty-round clips – eighteen shells per. Later I took to carrying grenades and wore a Colt .45 automatic pistol and a Buck fighting knife, in matching black leather holsters.

We tried to go prepared, we had to. We were told we would live out in the boonies for weeks at a time and needed to pack our shit carefully. Other units went out on nice one-day patrols, but we were going to stay. We were putting together the largest, heaviest rucks of anyone in Vietnam and would be staying out the longest.

We were going deep into virgin mountain rainforest, home of yet undiscovered creatures – big ones! Big ones the natives called the Batutu, similar to a Big Foot!

Our rucksacks weighed in at 50 to 80lbs and sometimes much more after a jungle resupply. Awkward and clumsy, the rucks were not designed to haul our kind of loads. The things became monsters, and field-expedient modifications had to be made. I watched one of our medics – everyone called him Trout – take a discarded C-rat box about the size of a case of beer, only a lot tougher, flatten it out and wedge the cardboard down in between the frame and webbing and pockets of his ruck. With some effort the makeshift devices fitted perfectly and served as a cushion in the space between backbone and pack. A pack bulging with steel cans of food needed a sort of stiff saddle blanket to prevent chafing and sores. When Trout finished screwing around with his gear he came over to me, pulled out a pipe, and shoved it under my nose.

"Here ya go, smell some choice weed, cherry medic."

"I'm not a cherry medic, fuckhead. I was with the 3/187th down around the Iron Triangle."

"Oh my, so ya say, so ya say. Well, that's cool, you look like a freak to me. That's cool."

Well, if I looked like a freak to him, he looked like a hippy with a short haircut to me. The sonofabitch was handsome, in a very odd sort of way, with his shaggy hair, but he was considered something of a nut around the medical platoon. I liked him right-off. He was the medical company artist and covered the daily log-in book with cartoons of every single medic and doctor that showed up with us ... myself included. The cartoons featured fighting and fucking, what else.

Trout split with a couple of other guys, looking back over at me as they departed. Another GI in clean fatigues, sprouting multi-colored ballpoint pens and a matching set of shiny boots, walked up next to me, hesitated a moment and said, "You'll be dead in a week. No way do you want to go out there."

As if to punctuate his point, a machine gun opened up in the distance. He nodded towards the west and smiled. Rain showers were moving through the hills. I was shocked. This fool was giving me advice like I had a choice in the matter. I had to laugh at him because I probably looked green but I had already been out 'there' and had seen sights that would surely make him roll up in his poncho liner and piss on his chest.

Suddenly, the horizon erupted in a crescendo of small arms fire. It seemed to emanate from Fire Base Arsenal, located on a ridge line south-west of us. The entire perimeter was firing down the hill. It reminded me of the battle at Alamo Mission. Grenades exploded amid the constant chatter of gun fire and a thin haze of smoke swirled up over the action, getting thicker by the second.

"See what I mean … here we go again!" croaked my new companion. Only two months earlier Camp Eagle had suffered a large-sized human wave assault. The NVA had breached the outer wire and had set up a perimeter inside the 101st Headquarters area. One of the first casualties was a Bible belonging to Bill Libby, the 1st Brigade Chaplain. It was blown to hell and back.

Just then a big, handsome, black dude, wearing a white foam mustache strode up to us from out of nowhere. Taking a pull from a can of Black Label he shot me a stern look and said, "Man … don't even listen to this asshole. When you get through here, come over to the club with the rest of us medics. By the way … the name's Doc Stewart."

I turned away to get the doomsayer's reaction but he had already split. Likewise the firing on the hill had petered out. They either chain reacted off the machine gun, or it was SOP, or they were just screwing around, checking weapons and blowing off steam. Anyway, Doc Stewart didn't seem to give two fucks about it, so neither did I. He turned to leave, then shook his head and muttered, "Fucking REMFs …." Referring to the pessimistic, 'jerk the clerk', one of the numerous rear echelon motherfuckers, he continued, "Fucking REMFs know nothing about no A Shau Valley!"

With that he spat a trail of beer in the sand towards the west. Suddenly I felt good again. Doc Stewart had made me smile. The guy had a certain warped charm that made you instantly like him.

August 3, 1968

Company A was my new company and the 3rd platoon became my responsibility; the whole platoon! Someone pointed and told me to, "Look for Doc Johnson, he's a black dude and the head medic. He's almost your height, kind of chunky, you can't miss him."

The next day I was still a stranger in a strange land. Oh, I knew Doc Johnson by then and he had pointed out Lieutenant Viney, the 3rd platoon leader to me, but that was it.

"Just follow him," Johnson had said, indicating a rather short officer type.

"If we have a problem, we'll put our heads together. You'll be okay."

I wasn't so sure. Doc Johnson walked off and left me standing. Most of the battalion hoisted themselves and their rucks onto the waiting deuce and a half trucks. We were officially air cavalry that summer ... with the Airborne name too, of course, and like the US cavalry of 1868, were riding out of the fort to engage the enemy on his home turf. A big mistake.

The only difference here was we had a lot more Indians than in the Old West. I even looked for some officer in a black Stetson up in the lead truck to stand up and swing his hand overhead in the famous cavalry sign ... 'forward hooooaa.' No one did. We drove out the back of Camp Eagle in an ignominious, choking, cloud of dust.

The convoy ground west, directly towards the A Shau Valley which was out past the end of Highway 547. Everyone, everywhere, knew we were going in!

The A Shau was less a natural feature of nature than an open graveyard. The floor and mountain-sides were 'aluminum plated' with downed aircraft. One gorge stuffed full of aircraft carcasses was called, oddly: 'the graveyard'! When the 1st Air Cavalry invaded the valley in early '68, they flew into a trap. It was a massacre. Twenty-two helicopters were lost in a single day, not to mention several fighters and a few C-130s from the 315th Air Wing. The Herks had trolled up and down the valley in the fog, at treetop level. Bracketed by AA fire, they burst into funeral pyres as the crew chiefs and loadmasters jumped to their deaths. The 'Valley' was a giant *bitch*! It was full of cobras, bamboo vipers, and flying snakes. Skeletons lay everywhere and one secondary gully was piled with human bones.

Fire Base Birmingham, a hilltop artillery fortress, overlooked a wide place in the highway. Along Highway 547, just under Birmingham's guns, sat one gargantuan airstrip and helipad, the staging area for our invasion. We bailed out of the trucks into the middle of the road and trudged through the powdered dust, off towards the hills on the north side of the LZ. It appeared they didn't want us grunts up on the fire base – wasn't enough room, I guessed. We were to spend the night outside the wire in the boulders and saw grass.

While we trucked out on 547, Les Jasperson, the FO for A Company, was out flying the back seat of an L-19 bird dog, over the valley. Lieutenant Jasperson was famous throughout the 1st Brigade. The 25-year-old, tow-headed 'old man' loved blowing away NVA truck convoys. Convoys not a whole lot unlike the one that just dropped us off. Jasperson had been in a good number of fire-fights and had captured his share of 122mm rocket launchers (six with Alpha – an in-country record). He could walk H&E right up to your perimeter while dodging AK slugs. Les was out in a formation of two spotter planes, one of which flew overhead backup in case the other went down. Suddenly, the FO's plane pitched down as an explosion erupted under the wing. The little high-winger quickly filled with smoke.

"HOLY SHIT!" Les cried out over the radio.

Our famous 'red leg' looked around for a place to set down, and seeing that it was all 200ft trees as far as the horizon in all directions, looked to his pilot for some suggestions. The 'bug smasher' jock turned and with a silly, shit-eating grin and convulsions of apparent glee, gave away the joke. The 'zoomie' officer had fired off a smoke rocket and flown up the smoke trail with the air vents open to scare his passenger.

Yeah, Les was a shit hot FO and was known to key his handset mike while holding it over his head during a firefight – just to give the questioning REMFs at fire control a taste of a live engagement in progress, and yes, the pops and cracks were live rounds singing past, and yes, damn it, keep the shit coming if YOU DON'T MIND!

Third platoon set up in a night laager out in the grass and brush while Lieutenant Viney, his two RTOs, Hart and Moultrie, and myself set up the CP on a patch of fine red gravel. Moultrie was a huge, tall, black man from the deep South. Hart, as tall as his partner but slimmer, came from up North somewhere, around DC or New York. Moultrie was laid back and moved carefully, while Hart was all over the place, talking trash and shooting the shit. They showed me how 'they' set up a hootch. I noticed right away that part of the procedure entailed cutting all the tie-down strings off my new poncho liner. Moultrie explained all this as he happily snipped away ... the tie downs would be used to secure a couple of our rubberized ponchos into a tent or hootch, as most shelters in Vietnam were known. Never mind I could never tie up my poncho liner to dry or use it as a sun tent now. These two RTOs were the very first black men I had ever gotten to know.

My very first patient of the whole war was a big, dirty kid with thick glasses with the nickname Sugar Bear. He pulled up just in time to watch our hootch blow away and sail off in the rotor wash of a Huey that thought our gravel patch would make a passable LZ. When the dust finally settled and the chopper shut down, Bear pulled off his boot and showed me a blister. 'Great' I thought, 'he's got a blister'. Here was something I could diagnose, treat, and probably cure without looking like a beginner. All I had to do was puncture the thing with a syringe needle, drain it, and stick a gauze pad underneath a lamination of Johnson and Johnson adhesive tape.

I finished Sugar Bear's foot and sat back for a second to study the terrain around us. Huge boulders studded the hills around Birmingham. The enemy could have ridden out B-52 strikes between those rocks ... forever.

The RTOs rebuilt the hootch and I wondered why they just didn't tie a couple of corners to the brush and dry branches still growing ... like the old hands at Green Beret school showed us. Take a branch, bend it over, then run it up under the poncho to be a loaded spring that held up the roof. Not enough string I guessed. These two RTOs stuck dead sticks in the ground that barely supported their own weight let alone the added weight of the ponchos.

Hours later I dreamed about the spirit people of the A Shau Valley. I didn't know who they were exactly but the dead Green Berets, the Air Force crews and the Montagnards (many never recovered) waited for us to return, wandering among rusted out battle debris on the air strips at A Shau, Ta Bat, and A Loui.

Suddenly, I heard a scream develop and a motor turn over. I jerked awake. The chopper was departing. I'd forgotten our mysterious visitor. Even before the slick prepared to take off, our hootch blew off its mooring for parts never discovered, exposing us to the starlight and a horrible blend of deafening noise, grit, small stones, and dust. In an instant, Moultrie, Hart and I were coated with grime and spitting sand from between our teeth. Then it started to rain, hard! That was the Boonie Rat experience, one we lived twenty-four hours a day, seven days a week, for our entire tour.

Earlier that day, Captain 'Wild Bill' Meacham of Bravo Company 101st Aviation Group, refused to fly us into the valley. He turned down the mission and walked out of the briefing. After all, he was going on R&R in a couple of days and did not want to miss that event. If he was shot in, say the foot, how could he go?

'Wild Bill' said later: "Yeah, I refused to fly the mission, or at least that's what I said at the time. Of course the CO had other ideas. It rained on and off that night and about 0400 the next morning I got up to make a weather check as usual. I was already up so I ended up grabbing my co-pilot, Jim Thompson, aka Lord Jim, to fly a recon of the valley ... alone. We launched before first light and immediately ran into a wall of clouds, ringing the entire valley. Inside the clouds were some serious 'Cumulus Granitus'. I found a break in one of the passes and crossed a saddle at 4,700ft. Slipping down into a hole we just squeaked under the slop and dropped down. As we flew by Ta Bat in the middle of the valley, I was shocked to see, you know the field runs south to north and that road (548) on the east side of the strip, well, it was covered with fresh tank tracks. You could see them in the mud from the recent rain. Bits of dark mud and sand splattered around the tracks still fresh and wet."

August 4, 1968

In the morning Company A shook itself awake and after the sun rose, snaked down the hillside to the road. As the grim crew stumbled back through the brush the first choppers hovered in. They arrived in groups of five. On board were Mermite containers of hot chow. More slicks landed and parked in long rows on either side of the highway. All of a sudden, an F-4 Phantom materialized out of nowhere over our position and quickly dipped a wing at us like cavalier fly-boys will. Vapor trails shot off both wing tips just like the Blue Angels. He was almost out of sight before his engine howl and slip stream roar caught up to us. Out of sight over the top of the ridge we had camped by, we could still hear the jet as it dove on a bombing run. A second or two later, it popped up into view above the shredded air … in full afterburner! The earth shook! A cloud of black smoke and dirt billowed and mushroomed up from the horizon.

CRACK…BBLAAAAM! The ground trembled and lurched under foot. The fighter returned and continued pulverizing the unseen enemy not more than a mile away. I wondered if we were going to the other side of that ridge. Knowing we were going to the A Shau didn't mean I knew where it was. I didn't have a map and no one bothered to show us one. The F-4 kept coming in from different points on the compass, making passes and pounding his target. We'd been told that the terrain would be softened up with air strikes and artillery just before our arrival and later they'd blow a path in front of our point elements.

Chow was just like basic training as the cooks with their gear lined up for us. Beckwith didn't miss the classic old paratrooper tradition of feeding the boys a good, hot meal before a 'jump'. To us youngsters it seemed more like the last super for the condemned.

Later, someone assigned us to a bird and we all flopped down around it. In 1968 the 101st never put more than five fully loaded grunts in a Huey on CAs. I tried to locate Lieutenant Viney and the RTOs – but shit … they were 'lost' again. Rushed around all morning to get ready and then we had to sit in the dirt and wait and sweat. Viney knew where we were going. He'd been in the valley before; his dad was a Green Beret in one of the camps back in 1966.

"Hurry up and wait … that's all this fucking army knows," a grunt gunner with an M-60 sitting next to me cursed.

'Wild Bill' Meacham was up about four ships from us with his crew and would be in the first lift of five, last ship, serial# 16121. It was trimmed out with white paint on the skids and stinger, identifying it as a 2nd platoon bird. Lieutenant Les Jasperson was in the very first Huey, up front where all the action would be. Captain Cope and the Alpha Company CP had to be up in the first lift near Jasperson.

The pilots milled around with their own kind, talking in small groups. Some of these guys, these aviators, didn't look old enough to drive a car, let alone a jet powered Huey with a crew of two pilots and two gunners. The first ten choppers were the Kingsmen, the 101st Aviation Group (assault helicopter battalion) Co.B. You could tell a Kingsman a mile away. They all had huge black spades painted on the front of the nose of their aircraft which looked wicked as hell.

Somewhere with that mob was crew chief Frank Sloan, my high school friend and fellow Soquel Knight student ... now a Kingsman once again.

Kingsman 'two five', Meacham's call sign, had a Snoopy painted on the pilots' doors depicting the dog shooting a machine gun and wearing a flying helmet, scarf, and clenching a pipe between his bared teeth. The name of the machine, 'The Dog', kind of screamed at you in red letters near the nose art. 'The Dog' was a famous helicopter. Martha Raye left her autograph behind the left seat on the inside cabin wall. Touring VIPs were not the only ones familiar with 'The Dog'. Extra sharp NVA troops, assigned to special killer teams that tracked our recon and LRP units, had more than once noticed the big-nosed pooch. They even had a bounty for Snoopy's butt.

'The Dog' would, like a mad and tortured junkyard mutt, die a terrible and fiery death on March 9, 1969.

But for now, while we waited, I daydreamed about our chances. All along, Maurice, who was going out with Bravo Company, and I were nagged by self-promoted statisticians, in-the-know, who claimed a combat medic's life expectancy was common everyday knowledge. They had told most of us in basic training, "Oh ... gonna be a medic huh ... ? Yeah, the life expectancy in combat is ten minutes."

This annoying spiel followed us … it was a curse. It was *always* the same shit, the time frame some ridiculously low figure. At jump school it was five minutes, at Green Beret school we'd been told we could expect to live no more than sixty seconds … *tops*! Jesus H. Christ, I fretted, what was the life span of the lucky old timers, on the long side, the really salty, hardcore, grunt medics who'd been around? I wondered just who the hell was considered 'seasoned'. If we survived half an hour, a whole day, a week, would that be unusual? Screw it, I thought, that shit can't be right. Could it? If it was, no medic would be left alive in the whole stinking country! Bunch of rubbish!

But it wasn't rubbish. Not at all. In combat, against standard Army practice, many medics took it upon themselves to crawl after the wounded under fire. Heroes. The medic's job was to stay alive to treat the wounded and dying, but over 2,000 medics and corpsman would die in SEA. Hundreds would die in the first seconds of battle.

The sun climbed higher and we kept waiting. Someone had a beat-up transistor radio playing full blast. Rock and roll lyrics drifted on the heat waves around our gaggle of war birds.

"GooooooD morning Vietnam!" an armed forces radio disc jockey yelled before finishing up his intro by howling, "It's Chicken Man, it's Chicken Man … he's everywhere … he's everywhere … !"

I never did figure out just what that meant, but suspected it had something to do with the 101st eagle patch. I think some people called us chicken men. I'm sure the locals did.

At the ship behind us, a group posed for a cameraman and his 104 Kodak Instamatic, the camera of choice for us boonie rats.

Our gunner, with the Mohawk-airborne haircut and a nice case of purple acne, said,

"Yeah, Doc, ya know the life expectancy of your airborne medic is fifteen seconds in a fire fight."

"Right … I heard." I wanted to scream: Who the fuck told you that crap … numbnuts?

I pulled my helmet down over my eyes. I snuggled deeper into the dust and rested my head on the skid of the chopper – that way they

71

couldn't leave without me. I didn't notice, but up at the front of parked slicks, with a fist beating the air over his head, the flight leader signaled 'saddle up', just like a cavalry guy. Our pilots and gunners eased up and into our bird, kind of cool-like, not wishing to startle their human cargo. The Rolling Stones song *Paint it Black* was on the transistor. While electric motors whined, engaged and turned the main rotors of the lead ships up where Meacham was, our crew pulled on their two-toned flight gloves and donned their helmets and body armor. Bill Grant, Kingsman one-eight, slipped into and under his shoulder harness and lap belt. Then plugged the cord and jack from the back of his helmet into an intercom outlet fitting. Grant and his buddy Meacham were both all-American looking studs who reminded me of older brothers. The kind of guys who knew everything about cars and chicks.

We rucked up, staggered a bit and climbed aboard. Mr Grant, our A/C, hit the starter switch on the stick and watched the rpm needle come to life. The tail and main rotor turned. When the rpm was up, the pilots watched the engine temperature gauge with extreme interest. Then Grant torched an internal mixture of jet fuel and a shower of sparks – fuel from nozzles and fire from the igniters.

WWWWHHHHoooooosssssssshhhhhhHHHHH!

We had ignition; we were jet powered. The turbine hissed and whined and compressed the air, ready to unleash full power. I sat in the door behind Grant. Both my legs hung out in the fashion of the bad-ass air cavalryman I thought I was. My right hand clutched the bulkhead on the forward edge of the cargo bay.

Meacham and Jasperson took off the strip in the lead birds and turned north. Grant eased the collective up and the power increased automatically in our ship. The Huey, #16348, became light on the skids. Grant's skids were tipped in yellow, for first platoon. As we lifted off the sensation of flight began to grab hold. It was hard to tell just when we broke ground though. Vibrations through the deck and a slight yawing back and forth of the nose, as the pilots adjusted for torque with the foot pedals, indicated a hover. The machine stopped its tail wagging

'Huey Shuffle'. During this transition period of lifting off, the vibrations running through my rear-end relayed a kind of unsure feeling. We seemed to be off the ground but the far hills and ridges sat motionless. The commander eased the stick forward, the nose dipped down and the ground began slipping by, slowly at first.

The unmistakable feeling of forward momentum grabbed us by the balls. We were airborne! The deck angle tilted forward some more and our flight of five picked up speed. Damn, this was exciting ... screw all that humping. This is the way to fight a war, I thought. No bugs, no heat, and no walking involved here.

To the south, other flights orbited, waiting their turn on the strip for the pickups. The sky was full of aircraft in formations of five. It was a major CA, that was for certain. At least fifty slicks were flying our battalion to battle, and that didn't include the C&C birds, gunships, the fixed-wing FACs or the fighter bombers. Freelance, Army and wire service photo journalists darted about taking flicks. Other shutter-heads rode out with us.

One Japanese photographer, Shunsuke Ataksuka, was famous for going out with the 101st. The guy spent more time out with the Hawk Recon than did some of us GIs. You gotta love war, it makes us all friends in the end....

Weeks afterwards, newspapers around the world published large action photos depicting a sky jammed with helicopters stacked up behind one another in long formations. The Black Spades of the various 101 aviation units, some painted on white silhouettes of giant spiders, made a wonderful contrast any art lover would well ... love. A little less obvious but mixing well in the melee, were the white or black clubs identifying 2/327th troops or equipment. Like the 1949 movie *Battle Ground* with Van Johnson – about the 101st surrounded by Germans – we too wore white shamrocks on our rifles and helmets. We didn't know the history behind them, we just knew the symbol was ours.

CH-47 'shit hooks' circled us in the outer CH-47 traffic pattern set at 400ft. We entered the slick pattern, also 400ft, looping around the pick-up zone, re-arm pad, troop staging area, gunship fuel pit and part of the

Hub Trach River. The gunships had to sneak in under us, along the river, at an absolute altitude of 50 feet, to reload.

Chaplain Bill Liddy was going out with the 2/502(Strike Force); the 1st Brigade sky pilot remembers in his own words:

"The 2/327th camped right next to us and at 0830 Sunday morning we were told to get our packs on. At 0900 came the biggest collection of choppers I have ever seen. About fifteen to twenty gunships, for protection, and several medavacs just stood by. I'd say at least sixty troop ships were on the strip at any one time."

As our chopper turned at about 50ft altitude, a gaggle of five behind us lifted off the road. Dirt flew out along the ground like shock waves, kicked up by their rotor blast. We had launched our happy mission! Below and behind us the gunners and crew chiefs in the tail flights stood up – alert, nervously looking around checking the tail clearances and other traffic. The danger now was mid-air collisions.

Like WW1 airmen, most of the aviators looked rather dashing – sporting lavender, pink, black or yellow scarves that trailed snapping in the breeze. Rather! Smashing! Top drawer! The scarves identified flights and flavored the already electric atmosphere like some medieval joust to the death!

By then 'Charger' and the Division commanding general, General Melvin Zais, were buzzing over the central A Shau looking at the socked-in LZs. Both officers could have passed for modern-day legionnaire officers in their starched fatigues and fancy Roman-looking gold belt buckles on shiny black leather. Their handsome and determined grimaces added to the effect. However Beckwith didn't much care for Zais and felt restricted under the watchful Division Commander.

Like the flying monkeys in the Wizard of Oz, we made like the air cavalry and charged! My perch was a magic carpet ride to hell. "Look ma, … no door" – just thin air and a long fall. But as the saying went, it's not the fall that hurts, it's the sudden impact!

The slipstream snatched at my legs as our speed increased. I felt it wanted to suck me out. I pulled back in and sat Indian style right on the edge. I was grooving on everything. I was high on WAR!

By then we were 1,000ft above the river valley leading past Bastogne. The valley provided the flat surface for Highway 547 until it passed the fire base.

The crew chiefs had removed the doors and we could see almost as far as North Vietnam. The air was actually cooler, so we relaxed, letting the deck take the weight of the rucks. For every 1,000ft of altitude gained the temperature dropped almost 2 degrees.

The mountains rose to greet us!

Our whirly bird was a green on the outside, grey in the inside aluminum tin can. Kind of like a beer can full of gasoline, and a large dry-cell battery tied on with lots of bare copper wire and tape and then heaved out of a speeding car. What could go wrong with that? Another mass of moving parts crept up alongside. The new wing-man climbed and dropped gently in formation. The troops inside nodded and flashed us peace signs.

Jumbled together inside our chopper, helmets askew, we were five indifferent killers jetting along at over 100 miles an hour. We kept our weapons pointed out the door so we could back up the door gunners 60s. They told us to keep the rifles pointed out the door for safety, but most of the time safety was not practical. After a time you got used to weapons pointed at your face. After all, it wasn't a Boy Scout hunting course we were on. No magazines in the 16s was another rule we broke. Shit, we did one better, everyone in our bird had a round jacked into the chamber!

LTC Beckwith received word that his choppers were on the way and one of history's largest airborne assault raids was on! At the last minute the insertion order was changed. Zais put the 2/502 into A Loui slightly before we were to land at Ta Bat. As we rode, Ta Bat still had some fog cover. The 1,500ft hard clay surface made an ideal NVA artillery practice range target.

It was certainly no typical rice paddy insertion, more like a rotary-winged armada attacking a mountain fortress and NVA R&R center. NVA gunners were ready, they knew what was coming. They had already plastered the 1st Cav earlier in the year. They wanted another massacre. It would be like shooting carp in a barrel.

Our invasion force entered the mountains. John Wolfgang, going in with Bravo, sat in the middle of his ship, watching the ridges drift past. An empty pack of Kools and a OD book of matches crushed flat against his steel pot beneath the elastic helmet band. John worried about crashing. The bird made him nervous and wet with sweat. He'd fumbled around and chain-smoked waiting for take-off and wasn't much better aboard. John had dreams about dying in a Huey crash, taking an RPG round and crashing into NVA positions. His dream ended with him trying to crawl with a broken back and the co-pilot thrashing around with his ribs sticking through his chest.

The warbirds beat their way over fog and mist-filled saddles and 5,000ft elevations. We skimmed the trees and dodged dead snags. Small waterfalls, idyllic pools and mountain streams glimmered behind the huge ferns and tangled vines choking the rain forest. It was bloody breathtaking, my wildest and best dream come to life.

I glanced at my leather and canvas jungle boots that used to be black but were now a sandblasted cream, almost white. I shifted my focus to the throat of the grunt next to me. He had decorated his neck with at least twenty-five plastic Madonnas, each on its own knotted string necklace. The wind blew his black hair into his eyes. I starred at the wad of religious doodads beneath his web gear and gun ammo. Pancho Villa would have been proud of the young assistant gunner with the hundreds of belt-linked .30/cal. machine gun rounds crisscrossed over his chest and around his waist. Tastefully placed among the mass were several grenades.

Trees seemed to blur past the door as we descended through a pass. The 101st had learned from the 1st Cav's mistakes, or at least tried to. The 1st Cav had been shot out of the sky, flying at altitude over the valley. Our plan of attack was to go in at low level. Low-level hell.

The valley ran about thirty miles north-west to south-east along the border of Laos. It was a prehistoric lost world that had survived to modern times. It hunkered between surrounding 6,000ft peaks of the Annamite Range. The valley was scary ... recon teams simply vanished and so did their rescuers. SOG teams were forever on the missing list. It was a miniature Dien Bien Phu, just a smaller version of Khe Sanh; our for-real Marine out-post last-stand Alamo. All three: the A Shau, Khe Sanh and Dien Bien Phu had airstrips in a valley surrounded with enemy gunners and 'strong points', or friendly, forward observation bunkers. The A Shau Special Forces, during the overrunning of the three Green Beret camps, likewise suffered N.V.A. trenches dug right up to their wire.

Brigade had established two different corridors from Birmingham into the LZs. A north route and a south route; we were on the southern one, over fire base Veghel. These were race track circuits, an almost endless pick up and delivery, then turn around for more.

We hugged the trees and then our runaway elevator to a world of hurt dropped us into the pit. The pilots nervously scanned the high terrain that was all around us for signs of AA fire. In front of us a shot-up Phantom F-4 fuselage burned and exploded inside its own crater. It was hidden from the world. Engulfed and closed over with triple layers of trees and brush, the heat at the F-4 site charred black the leaves surrounding the ungodly hole. Bits of tail and wing, however, none larger than a basketball, more than made up for their lack of size by littering the countryside with an incredible amount of debris. It looked like your county dump back home.

Enemy crews manned their equipment and waited for a shot at us. AA gunners on 37mm. portable cannons, that pumped out ten rounds of double detonating explosive heads a second, heard the helicopters and watched from hidden clearings amid giant trees. All around, an Army waited, waited to open fire into us. An army of 51cal. AA guns, radar-controlled heavy machine guns, tracked vehicles, sampans, long-range artillery, motor cycles, trucks, scout cars, rocket launchers (sometimes used as mini SAM missiles) and aircraft, including helicopters and giant Antonov-2 bi-planes was cocking and locking. The local fauna hushed and bent ears to the rumbling of idling light tanks. The usual morning serenity was destroyed.

'Wild Bill', whose specialty was out of country LRP and Special Forces SOG insertions and extractions, felt like a shooting gallery target. He, like my buddy from school Frank Sloan, were not used to clustered-up formations. But little did we know, we were already shooting gallery targets. Targets...like you know for bullets! In fact, as we crested the main east ridge, Bill's crew chief, checking his camera, saw a flash and explosion down on the highway. Some hero from Hanoi had just fired a B-40 rocket at the flight. The crew chief took his picture!

At the head of the slicks Captain John Soars escorted us in. He was up on the left side of the formation, over the valley. Larry Clark was flying behind us on this first assault wave in a C-model Huey gunship. Clark, bumped from a command seat into the co-pilot position was trying to link up with Soars, his team leader. Soars was the platoon leader of the 'Spider' gunships and flew a 'Hog'. Hog ships went heavy with rockets (48) and carried no mini-guns.

When Clark and his A/C took off from their fueling strip near LZ Sally, they were 400lbs over gross weight. On board was maybe half a ton of jet fuel and they had to slide on the skids and bounce down the runway to takeoff. The thing wouldn't hover. As Spider 55 (Clark) topped the A Shau Valley's eastern ridge they pulled in alongside us. Overloaded, their machine felt like a flying slug and couldn't gain much altitude.

Our forward view, from the hold, was restricted, but drawing closer the valley floor swung into sight from around the nose. Almost time! The bottom of the valley was all saw grass, bomb craters, and scattered, torn, broken, burned, tree trunks. Some of the snags looked like decapitated and tortured scarecrows, crucified and left as warnings. Tons of yellow dirt and sand in 20ft piles marked B-52 craters and ringed the flooded holes that floated bits of pulverized vegetation. They were fresh – from that morning! Haze and lingering ground fog still obscured the north end of Hell's Valley.

Already over the valley gunships patrolled and braced for the first sign of tracers roping down from the gun sites. The Spiders, Lancers, Hogs, Frogs and Black Widows were all over the place trying to protect the Kingsman slicks. Heavy radio chatter rode the common air frequency. The gunnies prowled along the roads looking for camouflaged trucks, AA sites ... anything. While keeping an eye out for AA sites mainly, the rotor jocks jabbered away in a kind of ominous banter. You could stab the tension with a gook AK-47 bayonet. But out of the confusion and chaos a clear and true voice rang out; it was Wild Bill.

"What in the fuck are we doing?"

Meacham's voice had that Western twang or slight Southern ring that matched well his all-American good looks. Whatever it was he was trying to convey, it worked to break up the foreboding atmosphere … some.

To the north of most everyone, Tom Holcombe was riding herd in his C-model gunship, guarding a stick of slicks and their load of paratroopers.

Holcombe's overall mission with the 160th AVN GRP, the Lancers, Co. D, was to guide and protect the lifts coming over the mountains and advise the other gunships where to hose down the gooner hot spots. He planned to expend one half of his ammo prepping the LZ and the other half on enemy positions.

Tom felt his ship responding well through Nomex and leather gloves; the fog was clearing and it looked like a good day to fly. Tom and another gunnie, with two colonels flying, went into a donut-shaped orbit around the LZ at A Loui. As the Lancer commander looked out the right window, he guessed the swarm of slicks to be near the 100 mark. They poured over the horizon, coming his way.

Suddenly, out of nowhere, AA fire snapped out and down from a gun site and tracers started into Holcombe's troop ships! The colonel's bird was hit also. The windshield exploded into the cockpit, slashing the A/C's face. Holcombe dove his helicopter between the slicks and the fire and was immediately struck with five 51cal rounds. The bullets tore through major structural 'hard points', destroying the machine and exploding the battery. The bird filled with smoke and shook up and down, slamming up in the air as if hit repeatedly by a large sledge hammer. The co-pilot, on his first mission ever, had a bad helmet mic and sat terrified – mute to all the action but painfully aware of the danger. His ringside seat guaranteed that he would be the first to the scene of the accident, along with Holcombe of course. Holcombe took the time to scream and narrate the major events of the aerial adventure as they happened, concerned that the second pilot wasn't getting the picture.

With every warning light blaring for attention, the gunship went down into the valley of death. Before they hit the ground however, Holcombe was able to shoot a full ration of rockets and mini-gun ammo into the enemy positions. At the same time, one door gunner shot it out with one of the AA crews. The gunner gritted his teeth, squeezed the butterfly trigger and walked his tracers into the enemy flashes. M-60 rounds peppered the armor shield and struck the weapon, taking it out. Holcombe wrestled control and managed a forced landing, successfully.

Meanwhile, I watched our door gunner on my side, lavender scarf flying, clutch the M-60 like a waist gunner on a B-17. He swept the thing back and forth following his line of sight at all times. His eyes blinked and jerked, scanning his area of responsibility – namely out the left door and 180 degrees of the port-side airspace, high, low, fore and aft. We felt the ship slow. Closer to the ground the valley didn't appear so flat. It turned out to be a series of gullies, steep banks and some smooth places, possibly overgrown rice paddies. We crossed a sluggish stream and lined up with the old strip. In the distance small trees and clumps of brush followed more creeks. I imagined the hedgerows full of AK-47s and RPGs pointed right at us. I wondered if we would hit booby traps.

Our choppers turned north onto a long final approach into Ta Bat airfield. Soars in the 'Hog' made a left-hand turn of 360 degrees as Clark, now flying alongside the Spiders' leader, covered us. Clark and his A/C took the over weighted bird as high as it would go, raised the nose, and started lobbing rockets in the general direction of our LZ. Clark assumed the H&E hit somewhere near the target in front of the slicks. WO Clark, the electronic wizard, suddenly realized the gook gunners were trying to lock on to some of the invasion force with radar-controlled guns. As radar swept his ship the squelch on his FM receiver broke and produced a tone. Clark immediately turned and dove away.

Soars wasn't so lucky. As the Spider captain swung around in his turn to follow us, he was hit with heavy machine gun fire from west of the LZ. Old #471, with the name 'Climax' on the doors, was struck in the right rocket pod and started to burn. Something in the rockets was on fire. Soars had seen the AA site that got him and attacked. He dove on the target for a bombing run. As he closed on the trees surrounding the site he punched off the rocket pods on both sides, jettisoning them down on the enemy gunners. The pods missed the gun crew but were close enough to mark it with brilliant burning high explosive smoke and flames. In what may have been the 101st aviation group's first bombing mission ... all was not lost. It's something ... scaring the gunners half to death and then marking the target for the gunnies close on Captain Soars's tail. Old 'Climax' limped back to a 1st Cav fire base where the commander quickly made a deal and was re-armed with another set of rocket pods. Soars had traded promised booze for the folding fin rockets, something the Cav could well afford.

'Climax' survived the battle but on September 4 1968, Captain Soars flew her into typhoon Bess; old 'Climax' was destroyed.

Closing on Ta Bat, Meacham was monitoring at least five radio conversations. Gunships from the 101st aviation group: Killer 3-6, 3-0, 3-3, 8,6, (all Spiders) and Gunner 1-5 were in the area discussing places to check out and hunt gooks. The Spiders used the call sign 'Killer' for the CA.

"Three zero ... three three ...?"

"This is three zero ... go ...."

"We're just north of the LZ coming in on the west side ...."

"Roger, well come on down south here ... you might get something, it's all quiet up there ... over ...."

"Roger ...."

The CO of the Spiders had just ordered two light fire teams (lites) to head south as they might be needed south of the LZ. The four armed attack choppers captained by Gaskins, Wheeler, Wollard and one other, turned to the south and flew straight into a flack trap. They were engaged with 51cal and 37mm AA air bursts. The wingman of the 1st fire team (Clark/Gaskins) and the lead of the 2nd fire team (Wheeler) were hit hard.

Suddenly over the radio a warning call blared out in a crescendo of confusion.

"Killer eight is receiving fire!"

"Killer eight is receiving fire!"

"Who is receiving fire?"

The young voice of Harry Kim, Clark's crew chief, screamed: "We're on fire ... we're on fire ... go down ... FAST ... FAST ...!"

Gaskins calmly announced: "Killer eight is on fire ... we're going in!"

Other pilots commented: "Put it on the ground ... put it on the ground ...!"

In a southern twang: "He's shot up now ... sssquawckkksss ...."

Clark, the ex-machinist from Burbank, California, had, seconds before, slammed an audio cassette tape into a recorder of his own. Following that he jammed a little mic under his helmet and into the ear cup. Clark recorded for history, on audio tape, the sounds of AA rounds dicing up his Huey. Spider 5-5 was shot through the engine and fuel cells. It burst into flames.

Paul Wheeler and his wingman Claud Wollard saw tracers chew into Clark's chopper. Wheeler saw flashes on the ground and only had to turn 10 degrees to his right to engage his enemy. Before Wheeler could get one rocket launched his cockpit caved in from the impact of burning tracers. Wollard was horrified to witness half the fire teams shot to shit, burning, and going down.

Clark's UH-1C filled with smoke that made it hard to see. He reached over and pulled the emergency door release handle. The door peeled off and fluttered into the jungle valley. Curt Gaskins the A/C, Larry Clark the co-pilot, Harry Kim the crew chief and Bob Burton the gunner were in deep shit! Flames started pouring into the cabin, sucked in by the slipstream. Gaskins frantically started searching for a clearing ... whipping his head back and forth. As the flames started to engulf the aircraft both crew climbed out on the gun mounts and skids.

'Wild Bill' Meacham later recalled what he saw from our position: "I was flying north-west on long final. I heard this guy on the radio, first. We were real busy along about then with a bunch of troops in the cargo deck. We had to look around and see where he was. We had no idea, of course, he could have been anywhere. Then I looked down and saw, all I could see was a fireball and a rotor mast going north-east right under us! The gunner and the chief were both out on the skids, hanging on, trying to get away from the fire."

Gaskins reduced power, he'd already dropped his rockets, away, off the sides and was trying to get the bird down. He had to crab the ship so he could look out the side window and autorotate in as well as lose altitude. Another gunship broadcast his intentions to rescue:

"Killer 1-5 is going over to the downed ship ...."

Gaskins undid his 4-point safety harness for some reason (probably fearing being tangled in a burning wreck). The aircraft commander picked his field and tried to come around into the wind. On short final the Huey clipped some treetops on the edge of the 'clear' spot as Gaskins started the autorotation procedure. Just as he started to flare the tail let go, burning off in a shower of molten aluminum. The nose immediately dropped and as the aircraft started to nose in, the gunner dropped off. Kim tried to jump but couldn't. Something was terribly wrong. The slipstream beat Kim's clothes and the fire burned his hair. He'd forgotten to unhook the 'monkey strap' – the lifeline designed to keep the airmen in the fuselage at steep angles of bank. Kim yanked frantically on his tether – but was snagged. What was left of the bird slammed in, hit and bounced, catapulting Gaskins out the greenhouse overhead window. The last thing Gaskins saw was a ball of burning jet fuel flying through the air around him. The last thing Clark remembers was the terrain contacting the front windshield. They made the 'field' and landed in 8ft elephant grass. Kim was dragged under the chopper!

Holy shit; seconds later our gunners opened up without warning. The gun next to me jumped and surged on its mount as shells and disintegrating belt links choked the canvas brass catcher. Was someone shooting at us? This was my first CA and hell, I didn't know what was going on.

By then the troops from the 2/502 were on the ground and converging on Holcombe's aircraft. But, as N.V.A. AA fire still flew through the air and searched for targets, Holcombe's crew climbed on top of their winged chariot to pose for pictures. Holcombe, suddenly aware he was alone stomping off towards the rescuing cavalry, wheeled around to see his men playing grab-ass and posing in the middle of a battle. Hollywood warriors in a Hollywood war – that was Holcombe's boys.

As our flight flared to land one of the guys in the other door climbed out and down to stand on the skid. I followed his lead. Even though we would have fallen to certain death it was quite a rush … literally. Holding on with my right hand, I balanced on the black no-slip surface of the skid. My sweaty left hand wrapped around the forward grip of the M-16. I figured the idea was to get away from the chopper before we were all blown out of the sky. My pulse and heart were running away, wild, and I wondered if we were to survive this landing, would we be fighting, trying to kill people or what? It was so noisy and confusing with the downwash whipping the elephant grass, it was a bitch trying to tell if in fact we were being shot at. I stopped worrying about it and reasoned we'd know soon enough. I only hoped that bullets smacking across my chest wouldn't be the first clue we were in contact. A sucking chest wound would have been Mother Nature's way of saying, "Surprise … you're in a firefight!"

I was ready for anything. I was ready for N.V.A. in human waves to pop up out of the grass and charge us from across the airfield. I was ready to die I guess. I didn't think I was going to, but I was ready, just in case.

5ft above the rusted PSP we bailed out and hit the ground. My right knee smashed into my teeth a split second before the ruck yanked me back and dumped me on my ass. Stars swirled and blinked as I scampered and struggled to my feet, waving my arms, trying for balance. Double timing off the strip away from the helicopters some of us took care not to walk into a tail rotor. Walk around the front of any bird was the procedure.

At first, we hid out in the grass like a bunch of fish in seaweed. The M-60 gunner next to me stuck his head up out of the elephant grass. He looked around with a funny smirk, as if to say, where the fuck is everybody?

Gaskins woke up not knowing where he was for a second. Laying out in the dirt, a smell of mowed grass and plowed earth didn't quite seem right.

Larry Clark woke up and stared straight up at the overhead switches. Clark's head was twisted back and as he opened his eyes he noticed that the whole overhead panel was burning. That was definitely not right. He jumped out the door and took off. Someone yelled. Clark returned to the ship and looked for crewmen. A horrible scream sounded from somewhere in the back compartment. Boiling flames and intense heat beat Clark away from the wreckage when he tried clawing inside. The gun ammo started cooking off and the co-pilot shagged ass. Clark promptly bumped into his gunner who'd survived the jump. Harry Kim, the warrior crew chief from Hawaii perished in the flames.

With a big bleeding gash, torn ankle, severe burns and cuts, Clark and the gunner skyed up. Unknown to them, Gaskins was looking for them on the other side of the wrecked aircraft in tall grass. The pilot and gunner headed east and heard a firefight to the south east. They turned to their left and went north crossing a trail with fresh tracks. Clark looked for a place to hide out.

Our lift birds absolutely lost no time in lifting off, another flight was thirty seconds behind them. A storm of dust and confusion almost kept me from spotting Lieutenant Viney and Hart over on the opposite side of the runway, up to their ears in grass. Some of us trotted back across to form up with 3rd platoon and when we did, it sounded like someone was firing off in the distance.

thud, thud, thud, thud, thud.....!

A tracer hit the ground, skipped and shot straight up – burning out. From out of the west a heavy machine gun position instantly sawed into the battalion. We were taking heavy fire into the LZ. But before anybody was hit, what was left of the Spiders ... pounced – just like real spiders. They spotted the threat immediately and banked into the flashes, straight on. It wasn't the approved method but it was the most direct. One of the pilots floated his Nomex covered left hand over the arming panel on the left side of the control pedestal. He flipped the arming toggle to 'armed' and checked: 1) amber indicator light illuminated, 2) armament selector switch on center position (2.75 rockets), 3) rockets remaining pointer showing: some rockets remaining. Next he identified and located the target through the sight assembly group hanging in front of his face from the roof. As he pumped the trigger switch on the cyclic stick he grinned and tracked his missiles to impact!

The assault gunships did their job.

Viney and his RTOs were up on the bank, overlooking the runway and general area. I eased into the grass next to the lieutenant and watched the next slicks land. I still couldn't tell who was firing, was it the door gunners or what, I wondered. I didn't know we were taking fire at that time. Viney's face contorted into a mass of stress lines as he screamed into the radio handset. We were taking fire!

Next came a shock! The other shot-up Spider, the leader of the 2nd fire team, Paul Wheeler, overflew our position coming from west to east at about 200ft. The fucker was on fire and burning like an engulfed Winnebago full of tar paper rolls, going over the rail of the Golden Gate bridge!

The pilots didn't need the reminder from the frightening fire warning lights – they could feel and smell the heat! Wheeler raised the flip up guard on his armament panel to get at the launcher jettison switch. He had to get rid of the rockets. The gun ammo was stored onboard but the rockets could be dropped off. He punched the switch ON.

Nothing happened!

Remembering the old drill, he immediately grabbed the manual jettison handle that looked all the world like a VW gear shifter, and jerked rearward. All the rocket pods released from their eyelet mounts and tumbled off.

I jerked around to watch the ship burn and noticed the door gunner was missing from the starboard side. In fact I couldn't see any crew at all. Richard Lappin was up near the point element of company A and saw the ship come over and watched in horror as an Army aviator leapt from one of the Hueys.

Freepost Plus RTKE-RGRJ-KTTX
Pen & Sword Books Ltd
47 Church Street
BARNSLEY
S70 2AS

✂ DISCOVER MORE ABOUT PEN & SWORD BOOKS

Pen & Sword Books have over 4000 books currently available, our imprints include; Aviation, Naval, Military, Archaeology, Transport, Frontline, Seaforth and the Battleground series, and we cover all periods of history on land, sea and air.

Can we stay in touch? From time to time we'd like to send you our latest catalogues, promotions and special offers by post. If you would prefer not to receive these, please tick this box. ☐

We also think you'd enjoy some of the latest products and offers by post from our trusted partners: companies operating in the clothing, collectables, food & wine, gardening, gadgets & entertainment, health & beauty, household goods, and home interiors categories. If you would like to receive these by post, please tick this box. ☐

We respect your privacy. We use personal information you provide us with to send you information about our products, maintain records and for marketing purposes. For more information explaining how we use your information please see our privacy policy at www.pen-and-sword.co.uk/privacy. You can opt out of our mailing list at any time via our website or by calling 01226 734222.

Mr/Mrs/Ms ....

Address ....

Postcode.......................... Email address...

Website: www.pen-and-sword.co.uk Email: enquiries@pen-and-sword.co.uk

Telephone: 01226 734555 Fax: 01226 734438

Stay in touch : facebook.com/penandswordbooks or follow us on Twitter @penswordbooks

An intense fire, trailing black smoke and debris burned and belched from the belly where the tail joined the engine compartment. I stared in fascination and my jaw dropped. Tracer bullets floated down out of the mountains and ate their way through the stricken aircraft. Bits of metal and Plexiglass spat out and dropped off.

"Get your damn head down ... Doc!" Viney screeched.

I couldn't do it, I had to watch. The fire burned and ate through a steel support and the whole tail boom, tail rotor still doing its job, melted and sagged down about 30 degrees. Get it on the ground, get it on the ground, get the sonofabitch on the ground, I ranted to myself through clenched teeth. They kept flying.

While this was going on, LTC Beckwith stood his ground on a grass-covered bank and watched the battle. He too saw the choppers go down. At least four impacted the earth, two of them burning, between Ta Bat and A Loui, two miles to the north. The after-action reports state that no troop-carrying birds were lost, just gunships, one light observation chopper and the F-4. Other reports indicate twenty-one birds forced down or crashed on the first two days of the operation. Les Jasperson saw six go in. In Shelby Stanton's book, *The Rise and Fall of an American Army*, he says seven troop ships were heavily damaged and another four gunships hit or forced down. Added to that were the F-4, loach, and possibly four more Huey C-model gunships.

John Wolfgang, a Steve McQueen look-alike, felt slugs pierce his bird like it was tissue paper. A tick and the flying machine would shudder slightly. When they were on final, Wolf realized the pilots had shut the power down. Things got real quiet inside with the engine shot out! The 2nd pilot read off the emergency auto-rotation check list to the number 1 pilot but, the drill was already done. The A/C was just making sure he had enough room, straight ahead, on the airfield to skid to a stop. Lappin saw Wolf's chopper auto-rotate, hit hard, skid along the orange earth and the crew unass their mount. As Wolf staggered out under his gargantuan load – out across the LZ he passed the fresh carcass of a loach – a Hughes 500 scout ship. The red trimmed tail fins and boom were planted in the dirt like an abandoned plow at the end of its final furrow. The wiring and cabin and transmission, twisted out and spewed along the LZ. It looked a lot like a deer drug by a semi-truck and tangled up in its own guts. As a gunship dove on targets in the hills, Wolf stopped for a second, looked around, and snapped a photo of the wreck and A company unloading from the slicks!

At 100ft the burning Huey that over flew us, banked away to the north, looking for any place to land quickly. Nothing but gullies, trees and gashed-out craters and creek beds were available. I strained on tiptoes to keep sight of them. Jesus Christ it looked bad … finally they turned back towards us again, trying to lose airspeed and altitude enough to set down. They were now lined up with our strip and headed right for us. Keep it coming, keep it coming, *keep it coming*, I pleaded. Less than a mile away they crashed. The machine smacked the ground, heaving a bow wave of dirt, like a beaching destroyer. They'd come in with way too much airspeed. The sagging tail dragged for a while then broke off. Crap flew off both sides of the nose and the airmen were on the toboggan ride off their lives. The aluminum sled hit a log with one skid which swung them around and into a series of rolls like a stock car. They toppled to a halt, seeming in one piece – except for the tail; the crash snuffed the fire out. We saw no movement and no explosion. My reaction was to go over and check the crew. I imagined NVA crawling over the wreckage and I worried about trapped men and fire. I yelled at Viney, pleading, "Lieutenant, let's go get those guys."

Viney whipped around and scowled sharply at me; his features distorted and his short light hair stuck out from under his helmet like a wet bird.

"Jesus Doc … don't move … we're all standing in a minefield!"

A minefield. My brain hit red line!

It seemed the French or just as likely the Green Berets had long ago mined our side of the runway. We had walked across the old Special Forces airstrip, compound, perimeter wire, fields of fire and right into the minefield. Nothing left but the airstrip/road and mines.

Despite the efforts of our dog handler and his German Shepherd sniffing out many of the mines, someone near the point was blown away.

The 101st point man, the human mine detector; just like down in the fucking Iron Triangle.

While I'd watched the Huey crash and burn, shockwaves whipped bits of grass and soil skyward in the familiar pattern of some kind of booby trap. The rifleman flopped back on the ground, hard.

"Hey Doc, they want you up front … be careful," Viney said.

But what about the chopper crew? I brooded. They were right off the strip close to us. Still, no one had flown over and checked the crash site out. What about them? I thought to myself, I could still see dust or some smoke in the air. It didn't matter, my responsibility was to A Company, 3rd platoon, 2/327th, 101, and I had no choice.

Meanwhile Spider 55 was on its own. They'd crashed north of us somewhere. The idea to take to the woods by Clark and his badly burned gunner was a mistake. They started out busting brush armed with one .38 service revolver and five rounds. Their E&E tactics (escape and evasion tactics) were okay; they just should have stayed near the wreck. Gaskins got himself picked up within minutes after the shoot down.

The new boonie rat aircrew almost walked into an enemy AA site but stopped short to gaze up at a circling bird dog. The NVA hated the spotter planes and decided to duel it out with the aircraft.

BBBAAABOOM! BBAABOOM! SSHHOOOWWACKABOOOOM!

The North Vietnamese opened up, scaring the living shit out of the novice ground pounders. The O-1 ducked into the clouds retaliating with a rain of shells from somebody he'd directed into the AA site, but this actually threatened the two Spiders as well. Clark and his crew beat feet out of the area.

Later, the men tried to flag down a light fire team, but all they got for their efforts was a burst of mini-gun and a couple of near-miss rockets.

All the ordnance slinging through the jungle did have one advantage noticed by the two Americans – the NVA patrols that had up to that time been whistling and signaling and looking for them, split.

Finally, as it started to rain, and the young WO sat watching leeches attack his still oozing wounds, Clark made a command decision. He'd had about enough of the grunt trail-blazing bullshit. They attempted to return to their burned-up chopper.

Back on Ta Bat they called me to go up front and help out. Only one problem, I had to walk past some very nervous looking GIs and right in the minefield too. Down a bank I dropped, then over a little creek and back up a cliff – with steps pounded in by thirty pairs of boots. Finally, out into the open of an old rice paddy, I hustled along passing the grunts frozen in place. I gaited up the trail in the short grass they had made. I remember thinking that I was becoming an old hand at this unseen explosive terror shit! The trouble was, I had to step off the trail and into the mined turf to get around each trooper. Fuck it, drive on, I told myself.

Each guy whispered encouragement or some suggestion as I passed:

"Be cool Doc," Sugar Bear said.
"Watch where ya going Doc," Lappin exclaimed.
"Sorry about that, Doc", from Rebel.

Up ahead at the front of the queue, a small group of soldiers stooped, crouched or stood around … something. The scout dog and the handler were on the site. As I passed another soldier he simply pointed to the side of the path. Right by my feet, 2ft away, were a couple of sheets of shit paper stuck in the dew, in the grass.

Oh fuck me … how my heart sank; I knew the paper marked mines. The dog handler had dropped markers. The sight of those little squares of toilet paper put the fear of God in me and literally terrorized my soul beyond the point I thought possible. The grunts stared at me, gauging my reactions, as I forced myself on. I felt the eyes of thirty scared humans on the back of my neck.

Luckily, Doc Johnson was already at work. He was true to his word. The chief medic was helping my man after things exploded to hell.

I gratefully dropped my ruck where I'd just walked in and felt a cool rush of air on my back where it was sopping wet. If my rucksack set off a mine, well, so be it.

The pointman was laying on his back and staring at his right foot; his face had already turned white.

The foot was nearly gone.

His jungle boot was lunched, but somehow had remained all in one squashed piece. The foot itself was exposed, a mass of splintered, twisted, white meat and bone, intermingled with sections of leather and nylon boot. It looked as though someone had worked out on a uncooked plucked chicken with a roofing hammer. The heel was out of place and the toes pointed backwards, but what really surprised me: no blood. Just a few drops and specks were splattered in the grass.

I knew this guy had to be in pain, or would be shortly. Doc Johnson told me to give him a shot. I went for my little green box of morphine syrettes . Actually, then, I didn't think he *was* from my platoon, but used my morphine on him. I'd hoped Doc Johnson would use his.

After extracting the pack from my breast pocket, I separated one of the syrettes, broke the seal, pushed the wire plug in first and then pulled it out of the needle barrel. Next, I plunged the sharp steel into the boonie rat's thigh, right through his pants! Finishing the job entailed squeezing the mini toothpaste-looking-tube dry of dope.

Doc Johnson and I, after a couple of tries, got the ungainly, mess wrapped; the wound was so distorted it made the effort awkward and we'd had to start over.

Shortly, a Dustoff landed right in the minefield with us. I wondered if anybody had bothered to tell them they were setting down in a nest of corroded hair-trigger mines? A pink smoke grenade burned fiercely, fanned by the departing prop wash. It billowed out horizontally to the ground. It smelled like burning chalk – powdery, pungent. Pieces of litter and bandages skittered across the minefield.

After the Dustoff sailed away, Alpha Company eased out of the open paddy land and into the jungle, to the west, towards the highest mountains around, without further mishap. To our north stood a fantastic rock cliff, plugging the valley, like a desert mesa in the jungle, at least 1,000ft high and straight 90 degrees from summit to valley floor. What a hideout; what an observation post…!

Late in the afternoon out in the jungle, Clark and the gunner waved down a loach with some aggressive body language. Finally a scout ship crew chief-gunner spotted them and directed the two towards elements of the 2/327th. One of our medics patched them up and another gunship took the flyers out before dark. The Hawks or somebody had found what looked like a tape recorder thrown out of Spider 5-5's hulk. The 'no slackers' threw it onboard with the worn out aviators.

Later I had plenty of time to think about the battle, but mostly I thought about the guy in the minefield. It would be a miracle if he hadn't lost the foot. But the guy was lucky … in a way. He didn't have to hump the bush anymore and he didn't have to endure being sweaty, dirty, or living in a damp, uncomfortable, hot, leech and mosquito-filled, hostile, jungle environment. He was free from the terror and uncertainty of minefields and crashing, burning, aircraft. He was free from worrying about all the everyday things a boonie rat worries about. Little things, like being suffocated and burned to death by our own bombs and napalm. Little things, like getting shot by your own men or getting blown away at the end of your claymore or having a trip flare accidentally ignite on your web gear and burning the living crap out of you before anyone can unsnag it. Shit like that … the guy was free from all that stinking bullshit. He didn't have to worry about being captured, tortured, or waking up dead, with his dick in his mouth. He was alive! He could not be shot or blown up anymore. Yeah, he was just plain lucky.

We set up 3rd platoon's CP right next to the paddy in thick, thick, brush. As it started to rain, I started to dig. The platoon sergeant noticed what I was doing and approached the hole.

"Atta boy, Doc, that'll make a fricking good garbage sump. Needs to be a bit deeper, don't cha think … ?"

I stood up straight, dropped the entrenching tool, and as I looked him in the eye, my face turned a deadly gray. In a flash I dropped my pants and grabbed my socks, in front of the startled sergeant, and as he stumbled backwards, I blew a goodly yield of diarrhea into the hole. I had to work fast because of the swarms of mosquitoes mostly. I suffered what the experts call an excessive discharge and evacuation of overly watery feces, right in front of God, the platoon sergeant and everybody. Laughter from unseen hiding humanoids could be heard. The almost speechless NCO made for the safety of the thicker plant life mumbling, "Combat will do that to ya, combat will do that … happens every time."

It was true, I'd actually had the crap scared out of me and although I'd be frightened again, I'd never poop my guts out again.

It was dark, clammy and almost cold by the time I finished attempting to string my new hammock and finally got it tied up at both ends. What a day!

About 0400 in the morning somebody shook me awake. It was still dark and still raining. The brush was so dense I didn't know or care where everyone else was and couldn't imagine where this annoying person had just crawled from. I'd spent the entire night sitting upright in my miserable hammock that had become a sling, legs dangling to the soaked ground. The brush was so thick that no room existed for a proper hammock, so it merely hung from too thin branches in a cramped little space among the leaves, like a child's swing. A dark hulk crouched in the wet vines and creepers behind me. Suddenly, a voice, with a Latin accent, hissed out to greet the dawn … it was Timoteo Benovidez, one of the grenadiers.

"Good morning Vieeetnom. Hey Doc … can ju deeg it? 2nd squad needs some malaria tabs."

Later we broke camp and headed out on a course to the north-west. I never heard what happened to the Huey that crashed almost at our feet. I did notice one of the platoon sergeants, an older man who looked as tough as dried shark entrails, wearing a new pair of pilot gloves stained with flecks of blood.

We rucked up directly towards the mountain called Dong Ap Bia.

Chapter 17

Dead Fall

The entire battalion was spread out, hiding and maneuvering in thick jungle around Ta Bat. Two days after the assault the 'no slackers' went on the offensive in a reconnaissance in force, cutting west directly towards the Dong Ap Bia ridge. A and C companies were on the north side of the Rao Lao River. B and D struck out on the south side, with the Hawk Recon platoon protecting their flank.

Prior to this I had humped an aid bag through some rough, hot terrain, but nothing like this. Three days later A Company had moved only two and one half klicks to a spot 518 meters high. We were in another world – a world we peered into and hesitantly entered as competitors for top dog in the food chain.

The Annamite Range forms the backbone of Vietnam as the mountains run the length of the country along the western or back border looking a bit like a human backbone. Just like a corpse. This terrain was serious stuff, all steep elevation except for the valley floor. The entire place was dark, forbidding and eerie. We prowled the creeks and small waterfalls, and explored among the giant, 30-ft high ferns. Creepers and vine-choked bamboo thickets blotted out the sun in our new home. But the real inhabitants were the tigers, elephants, monkeys, giant dragonflies and the isolated pockets of prehistoric-looking critters like the dwarf albino Java rhinos. (Incredibly, a story circulated throughout South East Asia of Big Foot monsters that tore the heads off GIs. We were reminded we were not alone.)

We took a break and I studied the shadow world in which we trespassed. I lay in the cool dirt. Out in the thick wood, Tarzan-vines and long, pointed leaves, I noticed a strange shape. Something was wrong here. The thing looked like a bushman's corral section, or a picket fence. Two rows of strong, straight, sticks were shoved into the ground. The rows ran parallel to one another. Overall, about 5ft long, the rows sat 4 inches apart with the sticks close together, almost like a cage.

Something moved to my front. Something was coming my way. Something made the leaves crackle and flip over in the air. I raised my rifle and tried to draw a bead on the intruder.

My eyes began to adjust to the darker areas, and I noticed several more contraptions out of the corners of my eyes. Some were old and rotten, others were new but someone had fitted a heavy log snugly between each two rows of sticks. Some of the newer logs were jacked up 45 degrees from one end with the opposite end in the dirt, blocking one entrance between the rows. In most of the older devices, the log simply lay flat on the ground, imprisoned with waist-high sticks.

A rat or grand-daddy field mouse poked his face into my sights. He hesitated for only a second, then darted down the passage between a particularly large and fresh 'corral'. The little, chubby-cheeked fuzzball ran, down to the end of the rows and began to sniff around. A log end blocked the exit where the rodent started digging. The opposite log end was suspended and deadly!

SQUICK!

A dark shadow dropped like a guillotine, as leaves exploded upward, and lay among the rows. I shrugged out of my ruck and carefully approached the scene of the crime. Along the path the jungle rat used between the sticks, a log now lay. I knew the animal was underneath, flat as a tortilla, stuck in what I later figured to be a Pacho Montagnard deadfall.

It was so simple, so efficient. I walked over and told Lieutenant Viney that the forest was full of the things.

The forest stretched clear across Asia and here in this valley, hiding at the end of Ho Chi Minh's trail, the enemy was all around. Day after day, our column snaked by openings of ravines. Out of the high country-ridges and gullies, were man traps – narrow, deep, ridges and ravines.

Inside some were gook base camps with fortified and camouflaged bunkers facing each other from opposite sides of the canyon.

The ridges and fingers of earth were perfect protection for the fighting positions, kitchens and living areas. They would have survived a B-52 strike any day! Once we tried to sneak up on a camp, but by the time our ungainly swarm entered the mouth of the fortress the NVA had split. It was spooky as hell anyway, up under the tall trees with the fighting trenches all around. I tried to burn down a living area, but the roof only smoldered and wouldn't burn properly as it was still damp from the rain.

We humped down wide established trails replete with bamboo steps, other trails we had to cut ourselves. Our daily routine was typical of a tour of duty with the 101st in I Corps. Almost every day a column of over-weighted GIs stood around on some nameless animal trail, much of the time in heavy rain with visibility measured in inches, waiting to move another hundred feet or so, not knowing for a second where they were, or even when the move would begin again. What a bitch.

Later, the Hawk Recon platoon camped out in a wide ivy-covered flat spot next to a good sized creek. In between the creek and the old tree-covered bank, they had made their night laager. Late the next morning, they were gathering up their gear and making motions to move out when A Company intruded through a corner of the Hawk's perimeter.

As we tromped past the recon men, we walked a little taller and the weight of our rucks slackened some. The Hawks looked pretty darn cool, wearing soft hats and sporting commando M-16s, AKs, and the occasional Tokarev pistol or Smith and Wesson revolver. The Hawks leader was some dashing English Royal Marine lieutenant that had ended up in the US Army with us.

We waded the creek and marched uphill.

The NVA stored gear all over the valley, their biggest base camp in South Vietnam. A week later we found a 'truck park' with twenty or so Russian Lil trucks. The truck motors were stashed somewhere, probably buried nearby. Unexploded 1,000 lb bombs lay in a dry brook with small trees mixed among the neat rows of waiting vehicles nearby. The NVA probably used creeks for roads, as the rocks in the stream beds offered usable traction. Plus the mostly treeless waterways were just not obvious thoroughfares.

We set up in the area and after dark a couple of combat engineers who'd been tagging along with us invited me over to their position. They'd already fired up a bowl of fresh Southeast Asian dew. One of our medics had made a hookah pipe by stuffing a canteen full of surgical tubing and water. We all passed the war pipe, even Lieutenant Jasperson took a hit. The smoke was real cool, but when I got up to go, I couldn't.

I couldn't find my gear, rifle, aid bag, CP or anything familiar. Actually, I soon realized I had my rifle in my hand and the aid bag over my shoulders. I was crawling around, feeling sticks and branches and wondering why the shit seemed to be growing horizontal to the ground and not up like regular shit.

Knowing I was wasted, even though I secretly didn't believe it, didn't help one bit. I'd never really been stoned before. One thing was for sure, I didn't have to be told to never, ever, do that again … talk about a bummer!

Chapter 18

One Head is Better than None

On August 10, 1968 Delta Company, 2/327th, 101st was wiped off the face of the earth.

August 9 found the Delta 'dogs' beating up hills so steep the map contour lines looked stacked. Jim Scales and his buddies, Paul Mather and Howard Baldwin, could have made careers as high dollar fashion models or maybe even movie stars. They'd posed proudly in a group photo, which, had it not been for the filthy clothes, multiple bandoliers and cocked M-16s, could have been mistaken for a team captains' reunion at Harvard. Scales, a rugged looking Montanan, who'd been in the Company since May 20, remembers what happened:

"It was late into the afternoon and Doc Stewart was helping several of us up to the top of a hill. He was out of smokes and I gave him some cigarettes. Stewart was a well thought of troop.

Stewart was tall, muscular and yeah he was a handsome dude. He was supposed to be gone, home; he was past his DEROS date. We had racial tension in the battalion; blacks stayed with blacks – whites with whites but, with Doc Stewart, we had none of that.

Sergeant Garcia, our famous buck sergeant, was supposed to be gone also. He was the coolest of the cool. He used to slug officers who had a problem with young, Latin NCOs.

Anyway, we hit contact and some SSG or buck E-5 got hit right away. He took a burst across the chest. His name was 'Danny' something. He was point for Delta. We fired up NVA on a bluff right to our front. We stayed put all night. The CO., Diest, kept us in front of those (two) hills, where the fire came from. He called an air strike in the next morning, August 10, 1968.

98

Our perimeter took a blast from the air strike, right in front of us! Luckily we were dug in pretty good. The air was full of dust and dark, hazy. There was a lot of secondary. Like a clock face, our platoon faced the hills from about 11 o'clock to 3 o'clock. Another platoon was in place from 3 o'clock to about 7 and another platoon covered and was connected from 7 to 11. The jets came by like from east to west and I think they adjusted to the right. On the return pass from west to east they may have dropped to the right of the FAC's smoke, which was the wrong way and right into us. They might have been confused like that. Should have bombed left on the return swipe. "

We in A Company were clomping down a narrow ridge. I noticed that the brush was not too thick under the trees. You could see off both sides at other ridges and peaks all around.

Word came back up the line to lay low, an air strike was on the way. I remember a lot of urgency, about the strike, coming from our platoon CP. I started worrying about the white smoke, red smoke code (white for friend and red for grease 'em) and hoped they had marked our position properly. Something was said about bringing 'it' in close. We had no protection at all and I was frightened. Something wasn't right, I could sense it. And I especially didn't trust the higher ups with our lives.

A jet came right over us. You could see him close behind the treetops. I didn't know who was getting the air strike but they dropped close to us at first. We stayed put, laying in the dirt with no cover, all morning. By then I was sure something was wrong.

Scales remembered: "The other two Delta platoons got hit bad, back behind us around 7 o'clock. They just got it bad! They weren't dug in and got caught in the open. I know there are books that say we got hit with rockets, mini-guns and … but I heard the blast and felt and saw dirt fly everywhere. After the bomb landed in front of us, I heard the screaming. I wasn't sure what was going on. I got up and ran around a bush and found out right away. Doc Stewart was the first thing I saw, he was on his back, head in the lap of one young white medic; I forget his name. One leg was shredded like a mop, all stringy. I could see … he was almost gone. We got a collection of dressings and took them down to the other two platoons. Somebody said, "Other two platoons got hit, need dressings." I took some down to them.

The Hawks came over and stayed with us for about a week. The CO told me choppers were coming in with, I guess, Doc Herron, and all the medics he could get his hands on. Doc Herron, known to Charlie Beckwith as my 'Christmas Elf', really did look like the chubby cheeked bright-eyed country boy he was. I don't think Beckwith came out at all. We had ten to twelve KIAs including at least half the medics dead and about fifty wounded. It took most of the day to fly out bodies, parts, wounded, etc. They brought out replacements from the rear, cooks and stuff. Like three out of nine available cooks – rucked up. They 'cleared out' the rear. During the evacuation of casualties, Beckwith called for enough choppers to evac SIX football teams! "

John Wolfgang remembers moving to Delta's position and stacking bodies and limbs like cord wood.

Doctor Herron recognized a head belonging to someone he knew then realized it was the head of the ... 'chief' medic of Delta Company. Doc got it sent home and it became, perhaps, a bit of a challenge to some small town mortician.

Jim Scales talked to one of the Hawks, the head medic, a black guy named Doc Smitty. Doc Smitty had a shaved head, was kind of short and stocky and looked like one tough hombre. Smitty was a character. He was always yacking about something – a great guy.

As the dust settled from the last Dustoff ships, Doc Smitty bummed a cigarette from Scales. The NCO handed over some cancer sticks to the medic. Doc Smitty said, "The lord loves a cheerful giver."

Scales thought, what a thing to say. Smitty was always saying how popular the recon platoon was back home and how they were always getting care-packages.

Napalm horror (naphthalene palmitate salt) was another air sucking killer. Once before, George Meyers, on his last days with the Hawks, remembers approaching a conflagration and finding a hand melted onto the forward barrel assembly of an M-16.

Another time, Walter Smith on an Air Force forward combat control team saw a large number of 101st soldiers burned to death. His team was working the fast movers that did it.

Six days had gone by since our little invasion and Company A had been spared most of the crap the other companies were going through. Our turn would come.

Chapter 19

A Walk in the Jungle

The business end of the M-16 rested on the toe of my right boot. We stood in the trail that point had slashed out. My upper body was supported over the butt of the rifle; the ruck was gouging the shit out of my shoulders as usual. I dabbed at my face with the green towel around my neck and watched drops of sweat stain my jungle jacket front. I gazed down at my top left pocket which contained a Boy Scout steel mirror, my last-ditch heart armor. A length of surgical tubing, for an instant tourniquet, and a white spoon stuck out of the slot along the top of the pocket. My shirt front was already soaked with sweat so the drops from my head were readily sucked up and absorbed.

Plants, high trees, vines, creepers, lianas and brush walled us in and roofed us over. The sun was high but visibility was still only a couple of yards through the vegetation.

A leech did a tightrope act along a vine trying to get me. Moving like an inchworm, bunching his translucent body up into a loop before thrusting head forward into each step, the little blood sucker tracked. The little vampire paused and waved his head excitedly, sensing, feeling, groping-blind, up and down and side to side. He smelled blood. But what he got was a thin stream of clear liquid cascading over his body that left him thrashing and dying in a puddle of poison. His body and head stung and he wriggled and withered in excruciating pain, tying himself in knots, like a snake sliced in half. I put my white bottle of insect repellent back into my fatigue pants pocket-and smiled. I was learning.

Next I had to decide whether to sit down, with the possibility of having to just stagger upright again in an energy draining exercise, or stand the biting ruck straps. It was a major decision. It looked like we would pause awhile and as the pack was fully loaded and as it was deforming my back I took a step forward to make room to flop down. Something jerked me back. A wait-a-minute vine had snagged my gear.

"God damn things. I hate these fucking things," I muttered. My temper flared and I put all my weight against the evil horned plant, knowing I couldn't win. Twisting, I tried to rip free, but the vine, with its thorns, simply tore the fabric and equipment on my back. Surging forward gave me slack. I hit the ground in a cloud of dust which puffed out like brimstone. The vine, still intact and still in place, in a loop clutching the ruck was a human snare.

"Fuck it. Don't mean nothin'," I cursed. All I cared about was the weight off my shoulders. I felt like the idiot who beat his head with a hammer because it felt so good to stop.

I noticed Joe Mann sitting off in the shade, one foot out in the trail and sun. His head was cocked sideways and he seemed to be studying the shadows behind the nearest trees. He was frozen.

"What is it?" I whispered. We always whispered. Twenty-four hours a day, seven days a week, our voices never rose above a hiss.

"Listening," Mann said with his handsome wise-guy smile.

"What?"

"I hear 'em listening ... they're out there, listening."

Listening? He was listening to them listen. Sounded about right. In fact trail watchers and unit followers were undoubtedly watching us at that very moment. I just hoped none of them had me in their sights.

"I don't hear anything ... in fact it's unusually quiet ... too quiet. Nope, ain't nothin' but us chickens around here cowboy. Ain't nothin' at all ... except maybe the wind ... or Indians!" I whispered in my best John Wayne imitation.

"Shut up, Doc."

Suddenly I caught sight of movement down the trail. I whipped my head around. Sergeant Rock, the third squad team leader was tapping his lips with his fist, on the thumb, (the probably time enough to eat signal). Good. I shrugged out of my pack, pulled out my parachute rigger knife and attacked the wait-a-minute vine. I killed the shit out of the sorry bitch and freed my gear. It was like cutting wire. That chore done, I loosened the ruck's two main compartment straps and got at the tie at the mouth of the waterproof bag that lined the inside of the large storage sack. The C-rat cans were still cool from the night before, I noticed, as I fished around for some pears. I debated a couple of seconds if I should eat my favorite C-rat entree now or later. Fuck it. I might be dead later, I thought. Might as well enjoy it while you can was my motto. With the P-38 can opener, next to the dog tags on my parachute cord necklace, I cut the top off the container of fruit. The clear syrup was cold in contrast to the afternoon heat as my spoon cut into the greenish white meat of the pears. It was heavenly. Fruit in the heavy syrup was the all time prized meal of boonie rats.

A figure with an M-16 trudged through the heat waves, floating its way up the resting column of grunts.

"Fuck this humping, drive on, drive on, no slack shit," he muttered.

The man stopped where I sat and said, "Doc, yah gotta give me something, I need something for this humping. It's killing me. Gimmie something ... Doc"

"Like what?"

The tall, sharp-featured man thought for a second.

"Hell, I don't know, Doc. You're the pill pusher. Just give me something, anything, as long as it's Darvon. Drove on with Darvon, Doc ... gotta drive on with Darvon...."

"I can't give ya Darvon for that ...!"

"Well, what are the fuckers for then, Doc?"

"Headaches mostly."

"Doc ... Doc, listen, I got a headache bad. Yeah ... I forgot to tell yah ... bad. Give me a Darvon Doc, I'm just dying here!"

"Jeeze man, why didn't you say so ... I got just the thing."

The aid-bag was already off my ruck so I unzipped it, opened a pill bottle and handed him a couple of pink and grey capsuled Darvons, the analgesic artificial morphine substitute related to methadone.

"Here ya go, try some Darvons," I said.

He was so happy I thought he'd fall down on his face. Bubbling with joy and goodwill he bounced around and extended his fist for the boonie rats 'dap', in thanks and fond farewell. After the brief ceremonies he whispered, "Thanks, Doc. Yeah … the no slack quack. Right on, man!"

He turned to go and I said, "Any old time, but remember…."

He stopped, turned again and with a worried look, mouth and jaw sagging, "Yeah?" he asked hesitantly.

"Remember … to drive on with Darvon."

It was getting dark by the time our section of the column wound its way inside the perimeter. We were setting up in a flat area among a thick grove of trees. Troopers dug in for the night. Artillery rounds screamed overhead. The company commander was probably lost and trying to locate us with marker rounds. Either that or the FO was pre-plotting the area around us getting ready for the night and possible attack!

An air burst of 'willy peter' exploded damn near on top of us it seemed. Damn it was close. Surely, they had our position now … I prayed. The cloud of white phosphorus smoke from the round shot out a million tiny comets of burning orange, each one pulling an ugly pure white smoke trail. The cloud turned into what looked like a huge singed white spider, dancing and kicking across the sky.

Every couple of minutes a HE round impacted somewhere close. The shrapnel whined off in all directions. Fuck, I hated that sound. It was like the phony ricochet sound effects from an old western:

PPpinnngggggggggGGG!

Mysteriously, the sound echoed in all around. It was impossible to tell accurately in what direction it was all going. I imagined fist size, razor sharp, raw steel pieces, slinging head high towards my face. The stuff sounded like it was flying through our position.

WHHAMM. A round detonated.

PPinnGG. Metal whizzed out, then … THoccKKK. Something smacked into bamboo or tree trunks.

Many of the trees were scared with deep wounds of pulpy fiber and splinters.

As I approached our platoon CP another one hit.

WWHAMM,

pinnnnnngg,

whop,

whack,

whack,

thock...!

Metal showered out into the trees. Jesus Christ, the shit was definitely getting on my nerves.

Out of the darkening grove, a lanky black kid with short hair approached me holding his head. Blood ran down his neck.

"Say, Doc, ya got a minute? It ain't bad at all, just a little cut."

"God damn ... look at this shit!" I exploded. "What the fuck is going on here?!"

Lieutenant Viney, the platoon sergeant, Lieutenant Jasperson and the rest of the CP turned to look at me like I was crazy or something.

"Are we being attacked by our own artillery or what?" I pleaded. "It's not enough we gotta hump all fucking day long. Nooo! We gotta go get shot up and dodge artillery rounds too. Our shit!"

"Hey, Doc, it's okay ... I just—" the patient started.

"No, it ain't okay," I grabbed my aid bag, furious.

"No, really, Doc ... I just...."

"Tell 'em to knock that shit off, NOW, we're getting that stuff in here, in case you haven't noticed. What the fucks the matter with 'em," I croaked, looking at Viney, Jasperson, Hart and Moultrie accusingly. They continued to stand around like nothing was happening.

Examining the guy's head, I continued, "If somebody else gets hit I'm gonna freak out, gonna fucking FREAK!"

Just then another grunt arrived on the scene and with a laid back witty style, addressed me in a pleasant manner.

"Hey, Doc, how's the patient? What ya say about this cherry, ghosten' muthafucka here, hittin' himself clean up side the head with his own entrenching tool? T-R-Y-I-N-G to dig a fox hole ... did he scalp himself or what?"

I looked at the injured boonie rat wearing a new, guilty smile and turned away.

"Doc, I was trying to tell yah," the injured GI continued. The others in the CP turned back to whatever it was they were doing, not trying to hide their silly grins. Fuck it anyway, it still sucked having to dig in because of our own artillery.

Around 0100 I bolted up out of another nightmare. Again artillery rounds shredded the air. Les Jasperson was next to me talking on the radio. What the hell was it … was he calling up a fire mission? Les put the handset down.

"Say, Doc, you want this shit in close or it won't do you any good. Trust me … it always sounds a hundred times closer than it is."

Oh, God. It sounded like it was coming through the trees again. The noise was terrible, like small meteors of exotic cosmic ore smashing the speed of sound and clipping through the tree tops ahead of sonic booms. The sound penetrated my body and soul. I was terrorized beyond my sickest imagination.

SSSSSHHHRRRRRIIEEEEEEEEEEEEEEEEEKKKKKKKKKKK …

Like a million children boiling in oil! I wanted to crawl up my ass hole and die.

On August 12 we got sprayed. I looked over at Lappin while he cocked his head slightly in a funny kind of way. Suddenly a formation of C-123 Providers, aka flying boxcars, pounced on us. They were on us before you could scream 'liver cancer!' Just like the time up on Fire Base Brick, a fine mist of greasy chemicals filled the sky and coated our skin. This time, in heavy jungle, Lappin was standing in a small opening gawking, and as the last of the Fairchilds bore a hole through the air over us, one of the crew standing in the jump door waved.

Chapter 20

AMBUSH!

August 14, 1968

We sat in the trail and cramming crackers and fruit down our throats, tried to eat a quick lunch. Hot as a motherfucker and no clouds!

After a long pause, the grunts up ahead at the front of the column struggled to their feet. When my turn came I strained forward and wobbled around trying to keep my balance. I hadn't wanted to get up at all. What would these fuckers do if I just refused this bullshit. I knew some of us considered just taking a heading west towards Thailand. Ah, sweet dreams.

The rucksack straps bit into my shoulders. Funny things rucksacks. You could never get both hands under both straps at once, like when Heide goes hiking in the Alps. Because, one hand always held a weapon. You learned to slide one hand at a time under one strap, move the damn thing off the raw spot and redistribute the weight somewhere else. Then repeat second strap with the same hand. We tripped off down the trail which was covered with roots. Unknown to any of us we were now no more than a klick from the top of Dong Ap Bia Mountain!

Word came back up the column that we were going to cross a 'blue feature' (stream or river shown blue on the maps). They told us not to stop for water. We slid down some steep banks and dropped off a vertical ledge about 10ft into the creek bed. It was the kind of creek my brother and I used to fish for trout back in California. It flowed resin clear, 12ft across, 2ft deep, with an occasional deeper pool.

Lieutenant Viney, up ahead of us with the first squad, radioed back to put out security up and down the 'blue', but it was already too late.

A number of NVA regulars were a few feet upstream with us in their sights.

The NVA must have been waiting for more Americans to emerge down the trail and cross the water. A couple of us dropped our equipment and I set my rifle down and walked directly towards the enemy soldiers holding AKs on us. The North Vietnamese pushed the AKs' selector levers down with their right thumbs to full automatic or single fire.

The NVA might have been bathing, filling canteens, and relaxing. They might have just been glad to be away from their base camp, their lifer officers, and their war. These soldiers were probably the front line defense of a large camp atop the nearby mountain later known as Hamburger Hill.

The NVA might have been trying to probe Alpha's perimeter being set up on the ridge above the stream and bumped into our inbound column. They could have been following us all along.

They could have just been bait, but they did have the drop on us.

I couldn't resist; I needed water now. After dumping my ruck on the rocks and laying my '16 on top of it, I approached the water with two empty canteens. Fuck it, I'm a medic, I operate differently, and I might need the water for someone, I argued to myself. I stooped down on one knee and held a plastic container under water. I turned to look at something, a figure upstream? Suddenly an M-16 barrel exploded in my face – the muzzle was right at eye level, a foot away! Flame shot out the flash suppressor as the gun barked. Hart fired up the creek and the explosions left my ears ringing. What the fuck is happening? my mind screamed. I remembered Hart dropping his ruck and going for water. Now his muscular back submerged in the small rapids as he took cover. He lay in the water in front of me. The fucking gooks were only about 20ft upstream!

Like crocodiles they had watched us. Point had probably surprised them and they had dropped down, no time to hide. Maybe they were trying to count us … and just got too close. All they could do was slink down into the pool, like Hart was doing. About the time I came along and started filling canteens, they probably panicked. They rose up like creatures from some black lagoon. Water poured off their battle gear, the red stars and belt buckles shining in the sun. They opened up with AKs, point blank, at Hart and me. Later I thought that maybe they saw I was unarmed and tried to shoot the others behind me first. Seemed like it. As Hart pumped bursts back at them, water spattered off one's chest from the impact of high velocity .223 rounds. Return fire whizzed by a fraction of an inch past my head and face while other slugs streaked between my legs. I collapsed back over my ruck scrambling to get away from the firing and out of the middle of the exposed creek bed. I kicked and slid back, up against the bank, still unarmed – like a dream in slow motion. Somehow my '16 was now out in the stream.

Platoon Sergeant Attwood, the tall skinny wolfman of an NCO, yelled for a fire team. He liked the nickname Wolf but we called him granny behind his back most of the time. Chief, our gunner, started up the creek firing his M-60 from the hip. The only trouble was he was behind me, downstream. M-60 tracer bullets flew past me going upstream like deadly red laser beams. I was caught in a crossfire as streams of burning steel tore past me going both ways. Granny huddled over the radio next to Moultrie and screamed into the handset, "Fire mission ... Over!"

Jasperson's RTO, Dennis Portlance, for some insane reason low-crawled upstream past me. I asked him to throw me my '16.

"I hit one of 'em, Man, I know I hit one of 'em!" Hart was jabbering away.

An artillery shell ripped the air. It shrieked overhead and hit about 75ft away.

WWWWWHHHHAAAAAMMM!!

Mother Earth rock and fucking rolled! The sky turned from blue to black with a mushrooming spray of pulverized soil and vegetation. It literally rained dirt and debris. I was scared shitless! They were cutting it way too close and I couldn't handle the unseen incoming shells.

"Add one hundred!" Granny, screamed again into the handset to the artillery boss. The next rounds landed further upstream as the platoon sergeant walked them up the blue to track the fleeing gooners.

A minute later, Lieutenant Viney took a squad of five men to go with the gunner. The chase was on! Viney tried to out-flank them by busting brush and dropping onto the creek in front of the NVA. Viney and the rest disappeared from view.

If I had walked a few feet further up stream I would have stepped on the ambushers gotten shot or both! I didn't remember hearing them fire, possibly due to Hart's M-16 blasting in my face.

After unloading half a clip of ammo and seeing the GIs fall and scatter, the NVA turned to run the only way possible … upstream.

"MEDIC … MEDIC…!"

Someone hollered from right behind me. I wheeled around and saw a body laying on the rocks downstream. A crimson tinted geyser of blood spurted from his neck! Oh God, somebody was hit! It was a young all-American-looking kid with black hair – some new guy. It was Bulmer. In an instant I was crouching over him trying to stop the blood. The blood was so dark, almost black. It looked as though an AK round had hit dead center and gone clear through. His neck looked broken. The eyes and tongue were bulging. His breathing shallowed. The blood flow slowed. I covered his mouth with mine and felt his cold tongue and two-day beard. I blew air in, but it sputtered out his neck through the open wound. CPR was useless. I knew the man was going to die. I felt totally ignorant and totally helpless. I really didn't know what to do. I felt like shit and that it was my fault. Maybe if I had finished Green Beret medic school like I was supposed to, I could have laid his neck open with a scalpel, which I had, and closed off the blood vessel with a hemostat, which I carried. I could have splinted the neck, set up an IV solution and then given CPR. But what if the bullet hole was through the windpipe? What if the bullet had cut the spinal cord? I just couldn't handle it. The guy died on the rocks of some nameless little shitty creek in the Western A Shau Mountains – half a world away from his home and all I could do was … watch. I tried to convince myself that the massive shock could have killed him anyway.

Later, years later, I ordered the KIA report, the 'deceased file' on Bulmer and saw he'd been shot in the chest as well. I never knew it.

Our squad chased the enemy for a bit. A nice blood trail gave away the enemy riflemen. Pursued uphill through dense undergrowth the NVA soldiers turned and fired back. Grenades bounced down and exploded near the GIs. Benovidez took a hit to his hand. Viney's first impression was that they were being hit with mortars.

At first, the NVA had a head start. But one was probably bleeding from a horrible wound. He was most likely shot through the chest several times but ran like a scalded jack rabbit … for a while. Finally, down to the last grenade, the infantryman heard the Americans moving closer on their trail. He pitched the wooden handled pineapple type grenade down the slope.

Benovidez shifted the weight of the radio on his back. His hand was throbbing and the bandage was a bloody mess. He wasn't used to carrying a radio and he wasn't used to chasing NVA soldiers through jungle. The Chicom grenade hit him square on the head.

Everyone hit the deck. Nothing happened. The dud only made a small dent in his steel pot. Damn, what next? he thought, stunned. The grenade lay at his feet and in a sudden fit of rage he kicked it off and away from him. As it disappeared up and through the leaves and to the R.T.O.s utter amazement-it exploded! Steel bit into his face…his second grenade wound of the day! Later that evening I looked at a wound directly below his right eye. Lucky! I slapped on a band-aid.

Meanwhile, some of the pursurers thought Viney will probably get us ambushed. The gooks were probably setting up waiting for the bait to lead Viney into some bunker complex. Viney listened to somebody higher up the chain of command tell him to continue pursuing.

"Sssssssss … okay, Viney … get me a body count, Viney, over … .sssss."

But Lieutenant Viney must have thought to himself, fuck this shit, crazy shit, and answered:

"Sssss Roger … yes, sir, we'll keep it going here some more, … out sss."

He threw the handset at Benovidez, then motioned for his team to sit. Viney flopped his short frame down, removed his helmet, wiped his forehead with a sleeve and with his commando CAR-15 cradled in his lap, silently studied the jungle. The jungle covered them in all directions, 365 degrees up and down and all around. The Lieutenant tapped his mouth with his fist several times. They want a body count, well they can go and get their own bloody body count, the West Pointer reasoned.

Surviving my baptism of fire, I sat back waiting, and watching the poncho-covered corpse at the ambush site.. Flies ran back and forth on the sun-warmed, rubber-coated nylon poncho. Stupidly, I had tried to stop the blood flow with my fatigue jacket, like some dumb Boy Scout first aid stunt. I had a battle dressing right on my pistol belt still unused. I sat in a daze, bare chested, holding my blood-soaked shirt. I didn't know what I was doing. I was deeply depressed and yet happy at the same time. I was alive!

Finally, Captain Cope, with his RTO dogging his heels, slid down the bank. As I rinsed my jungle jacket in the water, the college boy captain with Buddy Holly glasses took a step over the body, tripped, and almost fell on his face. His boot had snagged the poncho and exposed the dead grunt.

"What's this? Get this thing covered up and outta here!" He snapped.

With a disgusted look the officer stormed off dragging his RTO behind by the coiled radio handset cord connecting them.

Two paratroopers cut down a couple of small trees with machetes. They seemed to know just what to do. In seconds the trees became poles (boonie rat craftsmanship) slicker than snot. They laid the poles parallel to the body. They grabbed a poncho from Bulmer's gear and snapped the 'snaps' along the long sides together, making a sleeve tube of the fabric with the poles inside. The poncho became a litter. Litter? Bodybag with handles was more like it. At least they hadn't tied his feet and hands to a pole, hog tied, like a bunch of cannibals hauling a big pig to supper.

After slinging the cadaver and shouldering the ends of the jungle bodybag 'stretcher', they bore him away. Legs with jungle boots hung out the end of the poncho. The boots dragged and bounced off the rocks, doing a sickening little tap dance shuffle-kind of dangling like. The jungle chirped, squeaked, groaned, creaked, whistled, popped and clicked in the afternoon heat.

Chapter 21

Bamboo Vipers

Like an idiot, I almost threw my jungle jacket away, but instead I decided to wash it out some more. I remember sitting by the steam clutching the bloody thing, and someone saying, "Come on, Doc, you better hang on to that … you'll need it."

Most of the company had already set up on the ridge above the stream and, like Rich Lappin, heard the whole fight. Parts of 3rd platoon, myself included, staggered into the perimeter and I was greeted with sharp words and encouragement. Eisenhower, the company clown, a very witty, slick, black guy with a shaved head and a big mouth, opened up on me.

"Yeah Doc, the no-slack quack finally got himself his CMB. God damn, all right, Doc, get some … get down wow-who-iee-shit, OK, cool, Doc … dig it…!"

His energy was infectious, but out of respect for the dead I just stared at him like he was crazy. I realized I had very nearly been killed, but in doing so had earned the special silver combat medic badge.

The next thing I remember was Lieutenant Viney violently shaking my arm and sputtering, "Wake up … God damn it … Doc!"

I felt around, feeling tension on my arm and the coiled black snake of the radio cord around my sleeve. The radio handset rested in my lap. It was the middle of the night and the only thing visible was the phosphorous on the leaves around me. I'd fallen asleep on guard duty. I was exhausted. Oh shit, I was in trouble now, I thought. It was the first time it had ever really happened to me. Still, somebody was always falling asleep and I hadn't heard of any executions for dereliction of duty, so maybe I'd skate for my infraction.

The next morning faded in with thick 'crackin' A Shau Valley fog (named by the French). The kind of fog that could kill you as sure as zero air cover would. My poncho liner was soaked, and the dew covered everything. Drops of water dripped from every leaf, twig and vine, as I rolled over to study the machine gun nest and its crew just behind me. I pitied Lone Dog and his A/G. They hunkered down in the mud of the trail, weapon pointed out, covering the path. They lay on an air mattress in a hollow of bushes, maybe 3ft high, that was part of the game trail. They'd spent a miserable night, guarding their section of the perimeter. We in the platoon CP were hardly any more comfortable, but at least we hadn't had to stare off into enemy territory all night like they did. We were back from the perimeter by 15ft, back from the 'edge', back in American-held terrain, such as it was.

Lone Dog reached for his malaria tabs that I held out and all hell broke loose. It seemed like the whole perimeter ripped loose with everything they had. It was time to get down to business. A body flopped down next to me and swore, "Oh shit, here we go!"

I knew they were going after us in the fog. I looked around for targets and noticed people over in the company CP standing around with their thumbs up their asses.

"Cease fire … cease fire … cease fire … cease fire … CEASE FIRE!" The ones in the know screamed. The 'old man', Captain Cope, had apparently decided that everyone should fire his weapon this morning, for a very good reason, I was sure. The only problem was, 3rd platoon didn't know about it until it was over. It was called a mad-minute, and the way they did it guaranteed you'd believe an enemy suicide charge was in progress. Really smart … and funny too. Funny like a fragging. Thanks for the warning! Damn, somebody could have been shot taking a shit outside the perimeter.

Later I was to witness, but not conspire in, the great snake massacre. It was just awful! A dozen grown men in a tight circle thrashing the earth with machetes and entrenching tools. Little sticks and bits of wildlife flew up out of the circle. A very dead piece of meat was soon shoved my way on the tip of a machete.

"Bamboo viper, Doc … ain't it?"

Now as an amateur herpetologist, I could safely say the specimen had definitely been alive a moment ago and may have even been green, but anything more than that would have been really grabbing.

Chapter 22

Murder Wasps

The next day.

We were up to our necks in rugged brush and humping up and down in the usual heavy timber and jungle. I had no idea where we were going. I assumed we were humping north as the sun crossed our path right to left at least most of the time. Actually A Company was due south of the hills in the Dong Ap Bia cluster. Hill 800, 900, and 937 were close. An order came back up the column to take 'ten', so we sat in place. Of course, no sooner had I gotten comfortable, I heard a call. It was for me. It was Mother Nature and she said it was time to take a screaming bowl movement and I needed to hurry.

I squirmed out of my ruck, M-16 in hand, and walked off. A few steps later I turned and could not see a thing of my comrades resting nearby. The brush was too thick. Behind me was a ravine, sloping 50ft down to a dry bottom, offering a likely spot. I propped the rifle against a tree trunk. Grabbing the trunk, I squatted and let it all hang out towards the bottom of the ravine. That's when I noticed the bees. Wasps or giant bees, it was hard to tell, but whatever they were, they were 2 inches long, yellow and orange, and looked as mean as starving piranhas. The things had a hive not more than a foot away from my hand that I hadn't noticed. This same hand was supporting my weight and keeping me from falling back into the gorge. The bastards buzzed in and out of the small slit in the tree. I froze. Right away, they noticed something was wrong and started milling around the hive opening. One of the nasty insects walked over and crawled onto my hand like he was king shit of the bees. The thing to do was hold tight, avoid being stung and they would buzz off ... right? The old Boy Scout solution.

Wrong!

Out of nowhere an incoming wasp hovered in my face. I felt its terrible little wings brush my cheek and could tell he was agitated beyond his norm. God help me! I had always heard the thing to do was to sit still. Other bees were swarming and looking interested in my head. One landed on my nose. All I could do was close my eyes.

"Please don't sting my eyes," I pleaded.

I had three others closely inspecting my face, crawling over me with tiny, dry, rasping feet and one even tried to pry its way into my mouth! I was helpless and only a few feet from my buddies. I wanted to scream. I wanted to die.

What I did was freak out! I couldn't take it anymore, so I let loose of my grip and fell back, down the bank, sliding along with the M-16 as it rattled and bounced over the rocks. I did not care. Screw it, anything is better than sticking your face in a hornet's nest, I thought. I frantically beat the air around my head. I will kill you all, your eggs, your larva, the pupa and the whole fucking nasty bunch, I promised! And the Queen I will kill her first!

"You bastards, you cock sucking bastards," I spat.

Damn, I was pissed! My body piled into a heap at the bottom and miraculously I wasn't stung. Bitten maybe, but not stung. I think the one that tried to get into my mouth bit me because later my lip swelled up.

Making my way back to our stopping point, I found the whole company gone! They left me behind. I was alone in enemy territory. I was pretty new and they must have forgotten about their medic. I almost missed my ruck on the way back, but it was laying right where I'd left it. For a second I had to stop and listen for the sound of men moving off through brush before catching up. Fuck it. Nature's call would have to wait.

The Dayglow Forest

I began to really feel at home in the jungle, despite the rumors. We knew the NVA bivouacked in these mountains. Always the rumor of a battalion or two in our AO floated among us. They weren't far away!

I loved laying in my hammock at night, warm and seemingly secure. Rolled up in my jungle blanket, wearing my sporty jungle sweater over my jungle jacket, tucked into my jungle pants, tucked into my jungle boots, I was comfortable. With a hot dinner of dehydrated spaghetti and meatballs in my gut, I listened to the pitter-patter of rain on the vinyl poncho stretched above me. My M-16 leaned against the trees by my head. My blood system pumped anti-malaria solutions, and I wore the special jungle perfume – the best insect repellent (bug juice) in the world. My medic's bag lay under me.

The trick to keep the mosquitoes off was to cover up in the poncho liner and smear the repellent all over your chin and nose. Then, pull the liner over your head, clutching it under your chin so that you could still breath. This didn't keep the little vampires from swarming around your head, but it sure as hell kept them from landing. The repellent worked for me, it stung and it burned if it got in your eyes or a cut, but it did the job. Occasionally, I'd lie in the hammock and drink a beer. If I was in the right frame of mind, and often I was, I could actually enjoy the warm brew. If I drank it fast enough, I could even cop a goodly buzz.

I slept above the ground when I could find the right trees. You had to stay clear of the 'fuck-you' lizards and the dreaded 'two-step bamboo vipers'. The two-step viper was a horror story often told around the cook stoves. The crux of the tale was that, if bitten, you could expect to run about two steps before falling on your face, stone dead!

A light show went on every night among the rotten leaves that littered the jungle floor. Phosphorus organisms gave off bright green light almost like the street lamps in a gremlin's village. I'd grab a particularly bright one, dust it off and hold up a whole and perfect outline of a hand-sized leaf – in radium green. An atomic leaf! You could actually read by its light.

Dropping into a deep sleep, I'd often dream about little men with big guns and sharp long knives searching for us. The infamous 'fuck-you' lizard would begin his sorry two-note song.

Fuck you, fuckyou, fuckyou, fuckyou, fuckyou, fuckyou … FUCK YOU!

Chapter 23

Two Heads are Better than One

A couple of days later, the platoon set up for the night on the top of a hill. We moved into some old fighting positions we found. We ran patrols out from our NDP across the Rao Nai, a fair-sized river. Our hide was in a truly awesome stand of teak trees. To the north of the position a 300ft cliff ruled the river in a spectacular scene right out of the *The Bridge On The River Kwai*. Trees were growing out of the side of the cliff and their roots splayed out, anchoring gigantic boulders that would have long ago joined others of their kind in the river. When we first dug-in I dropped my ruck, grabbed my boonie hat and '16 and went for a look. As I pulled up to the cliff's edge a leopard launched out in a frantic dive. From her perch on the cliff face she flung her sleek, black-spotted, cammo-patterned body off into a dark, green, pool. Underwater, her ears pinned back as the current took her, she clawed for the north shore. Without stopping to shake off, the cloud leopard streaked up the rocky bank and just vanished into the jungle. A darting shadow, she never even looked back.

The next day, coming back to our hilltop, through an area hit with what looked like a B-52 strike, the brush and trees were blasted back all around and several craters were in evidence, point found a skeleton. Curious, I walked over and looked. A pile of bones, a rotted uniform and a rusted-up AK-47 were strewn around. Some black hair, looking surprisingly good as new, sat on a skull that grinned back at us.

After fording the river and walking halfway back to the NDP, I decided to go back for the skull. I was poking around looking for a place to enter the water, for the third time, when 'BoBo' came bopping down the bank on the far side carrying his M-79 and 'my' skull. I yelled across the river, "Hey, BoBo! Bring me that skull would ya?"

Red-haired Gary, BoBo to his friends, started hopping and skipping and balancing off the boulders trying to keep his 115lb, 5' 6" body out of the water. He called out cheerfully, "Sure thing, Doc I was just going to blow his mind on these rocks."

He raised the head above the river and waved it menacingly above the boulders.

I carried that thing around for months. After all, I was a sort of doctor and doctors have those kinds of things ... right? It gave me a sort of professional look, I thought. Or maybe it was the jungle headhunter aura I enjoyed. In camp at night I gave it the place of honor, usually tied above my hammock on a tree and wearing my boonie hat to help camouflage the white bone. Like a headhunter's totem pole, it watched over me as I slept. In the morning I lashed it to the top of my ruck, strapped down, tied through the cheek bones. It sat looking backwards, right behind my head, guarding my six. Just what I needed out in the jungle: eyes in the back of my head.

After a while the company got used to the sight of me trudging along with a monster ruck and the head perched up on top. But I got a lot of funny looks from the chopper crews. I never once got the feeling this head was some evil JuJu stabbing me with bad karma.

We all thought the NVA soldier had died from a B-52 arc-light, but later we came to the conclusion, after much debate and lengthy discussion, that he died from chronic overbite, the worst case we ever saw.

Once, I met a dude who carried a head. He was in the 'Herd', the 173rd Airborne, and he lugged a whole human head around with him in a sandbag. He was a medic, and one time he just decapitated a freshly killed VC. He explained to me that he wanted to study it. He said it stunk.

The Herd medic wanted to be a 'real' doctor and, I guess, get a jump on medical school. He founded his own self-taught medical program, complete with plenty of free cadavers. I think he called his little classes, Human Dissection/Autopsy 101 with Gross Anatomy 173.

I do know some members of our recon platoon carried fresh heads as, well, 'souvenirs'. I saw the photos, but it was before my time.

Chapter 24

The FO

I hated to carry a lot of sodas and beer. Our loads were too much as it was. Les Jasperson was different. He tells the story:

"I don't remember Beckwith leading the battalion into the A Shau. We were lucky enough to have been led by the new S-3, Denny Frasche. What impressed me the most was the way he introduced himself to me after Beckwith sent him out with Alpha to see how we operated. He walked up, stuck out his hand and said, "Hi, I'm Denny Fransche. I understand you're the FO"

Not, I'm Major Fransche. He went out with the C&C of course, and when I unrolled my poncho liner the first night he was with us, he saw 5 or 6 beers. He knew grunts traveled light and asked if I had a whole six pack. I opened up my ruck for him to see and said, "No. A case."

After the worst days out in the field I would let water drip over a can of beer so the evaporation might get the temperature down to 65 degrees or so.

Chapter 25

Wolves and Apemen

I heard what happened over in Bravo Company not long after we found the trucks. John Wolfgang was sitting up in their company's perimeter one freaking dark night grooving on the jungle. Bravo was south of the Lao Rao and this was a new experience for the new 'shake and bake' NCO. It was raining lightly and big snowballing drops of water collected, joined forces and spattered down from the triple canopy. He couldn't believe it was so dark under the trees, so weird, so eerie. John contemplated the seat of his pants, which were wet, along with most of his fatigues except for the areas under his arms and the upper crotch. Those areas seemed to actually dry out as the night wore on.

Suddenly, a twig snapped and a quick thrashing noise and commotion sounded out in the front of his position.

Wolf groped for a grenade and readied the thing by prying the cotter pin straight; at the same time he ran his thumb over the trigger on the claymore again. Our young paratrooper was ready to defend himself and his company, without giving away his position, just as he'd been trained to do at NCO school. Like a child's worst nightmare the noise flared up, sounding closer this time, and John knew NVA sappers were moving on him. He threw the grenade.

Bravo woke up and went to 100 percent alert as Wolf's radio hissed, sputtered and demanded info. The cherry boy sergeant duly reported, "Movement out here, sir," he whispered.

"Okay, Okay ... be cool, be cool," was all John's platoon leader could say. The mood of the unit was not happy, they had to try and go back to sleep in the rain. But that was not to be.

The noises quickly started up again and movement through the brush continued, bolstering John's fear that Charlie was making a last probe before moving in for the kill. Incredibly, someone was standing or crawling only a few feet away, it was so close John heard it breathing; it was human breathing for sure.

However, SEA mountains were the home of some mighty weird creatures. Scientists from around the world agree that Neanderthals still roam the outback of China. Snowmen in the jungle they are called.

Tropical Asia is reported home for many types of Yeti relatives. Massive giant orangutans 40 per cent larger than the modern species strutted through Vietnam. Their teeth, called 'Dragon's Teeth', are sold as magical implements (potions). The animal's scientific name: Gigantopithecus.

Violently, a trip flare popped ... SMACCCKKK! ... HHISSSS! a brilliant yellow and white light burned behind black tree trunk silhouettes. A human form stood up and ran like a wild man. John thought more were in front of the running thing. He unloaded two grenades, rapidly, and as their fuses burned, he blew his claymore.

The explosions were simultaneous and shredded the jungle growth with steel. The company flipped out. They returned to full alert until after the sky gave way to grey.

As the men around John reeled in their claymore wires sans the claymores, they noticed the bodies. A death mask grinned up with its almost human head, eyes and lips horribly drawn back in a frozen scream. Three, so called 'rock apes' had given their all, messing around the paratroopers' NDP looking for food. John Wolfgang was no longer the 'Wolf'. He was Ape Man.

Earlier that year Gary Linderer and his team from F Company 58th, 101st LRPs actually saw a large wild man. A damn monster from the wilderness. Gary, one of the LRPs, told me the story:

"We were laugered in up south of the Nui Ky mountain over-looking the Perfume River. The terrain was so steep we had to tie ourselves to trees to keep from falling down into the void during the night. I was on one of my first missions and the next morning some of us were eating. A large grove of bamboo was up slope from us like a big wall or fence. Suddenly we all heard busting brush and breaking branches; something big was coming our way and we got ready to engage. No claymores were out because of the slope and brush. Suddenly we watched the bamboo shake and vibrate and about 5 meters away a 6ft tall, at least, red-colored humanoid steps out and stares at us. It was covered with long reddish brown hair, had very long arms and a hairless almost human type face. It didn't seem afraid of us at all, just curious, with intelligent eyes. It raised its left arm but just stood its ground for about ten seconds then split without a word or sound.

"We didn't discuss the meeting until returning to base as we were on high alert as usual in the boonies. I don't think any of us believed what we saw that morning was an orangutan or any other kind of ape. I would never forget that face."

Chapter 26

Murder Incorporated

Back in Bravo Company John Wolfgang had gotten off to a bad start in the 2/327th. He became one bad-ass M-60 toting, death-dealing, rock and roll jungle cowboy. But it took a while.

When Wolf had first come to the A Shau he'd humped just about everything supply had issued him. The result was that he'd fallen out, three times, with near heat stroke. The last time Charger himself had raced to the rear of the formation and jumped dead into Wolf's shit. Charger snatched Wolf's M-16, popped the magazine out and left the junior NCO with a single round. The idea was to leave malingerers, which Wolf wasn't, behind to bite the bullet, I guess. This bit of psychological counseling was a mistake. It almost cost the rowdy battalion commander his life.

Humiliated and shamed, Wolf thumbed the safety off his cocked rifle and drew down on the officer's neck. A couple of grunts who'd been ordered to hold Wolf's bandoliers tried to give them back to him but seeing the mad man prepare to fire, stopped. The colonel was almost out of sight, up the trail, and they all knew it was now or never. The shot never came. Wolf had had a clear picture of a sweaty group of working neck muscles in front of his peep sight and definitely 'no slack' on the fucking trigger, but fortunately the madness drained.

Chapter 27

Extraction

I think Charger had wanted A Company to continue north and swarm over hills 800, 900, and 937. We were so close. However, possibly due to a bad weather forecast, General Zais pulled the battalion out of the western A Shau mountains.

Near the place I saw the leopard the word went around that the Hawks were taking volunteers. It was dusk when I heard, and 3rd platoon went nuts. Lieutenant Viney was running around or talking on the radio or taking names. Some of the guys wanted out of A Company and into the recon platoon, bad. Joe Mann was one and I was another. It was hard to tell if Viney was trying to get rid of people from his platoon or seeding the Hawks with good troops. Joe Mann, Richard Lappin and Gary 'BoBo' left; they were a little green but becoming more jungle smart every day. It was funny, because if he was dumping undesirables (a common lifer trip) Viney got dumped right along with them as the brand new Hawk Recon platoon leader. He left A Company on the 18th.

I told Viney I wanted out of A Company platoon and all he did was ignore me. He had no power to make a switch as I was officially in HHC and would have to be reassigned from A to E company by headquarters. I wanted into the Hawk Recon; they had a tough guy reputation. They had walked right into Charlie after unknowingly camping within just feet of the enemy's own NDP ... killing eleven NVA. They, like Tiger Force, were rumored to take ears and other parts of the head. I never saw or even heard about crap like that during my tour, but as I spent most of my time in or near the CP. I wasn't considered trustworthy with information of that kind I'm sure. To be honest, I do know that a couple of Hawks had the head of some Asian and took parts of it to 'make' their own gook. But this was long before my time.

126

EXTRACTION

On the 18th LTC Beckwith started extracting the battalion. It was no easy feat. Special choppers and hand-picked crews came in pumping oil into their exhaust systems for smoke screens. As walls of white smoke settled through the trees towering around the LZ, the slicks, right behind the 'smokeys', made the pick ups.

3rd platoon, higher up in the trees, went out without the smoke cover. All during the pull out, General Zais rode Beckwith's ass giving advice over the command net and infuriating our battalion commander.

Zais probably ordered Beckwith to pull out just before we walked onto Dong Ap Bia or hill 900 or 800 or were engaged in a battle that Charlie Beckwith surely wanted. Lucky us! Charlie Beckwith didn't get along with Generals all that well and Zais was no exception.

We'd been out 2 weeks, straight, breaking brush in wilderness mountains right in the middle of Ho Chi Minh's trail, an unheard of task for most units in the war. But it was nothing for Charging Charlie and his Merrill's Marauders style. I'm sure Charlie was highly pissed and frustrated not being allowed to push us into a battle that might have prevented the Hamburger Hill grinder in 1969.

Before we left the boonies that morning, and while we waited for our lift, the area was boiling with activity! A F.A.C. had called in a napalm air strike nearby, a Kingsmen log bird flew into our growing P.Z. probably with Pathfinders and somebody had assigned hunter-killer 'pink' and 'white' Saber teams to us directly. Most likely the 2/17th Air Cav. At first we got Saber team #18, a white team.

The Saber teams were Loach scout ships followed by gunships. They buzzed around all morning and Saber team #25 spotted trails with recent heavy, heavy use and NVA moving South toward us! They saw 4 NVA moving within a couple hundred meters of the P.Z. Later, Saber Team #27 attached to A Co. (us) spotted 3 NVA carrying ammo boxes close to our position. They killed 2 and got a secondary explosion using white phosphorus rockets! Just to our North. We had been aimed at a real hornet's nest; why else were we heading north towards the highest hill around ever since leaving Ta Bat air field? Ta Bat was the logical choice if we were to assault Dong Ap Bia.

The Pathfinders had cut and mashed a large LZ on the side of a mountain. It was startling to see after living and humping in thick cover for two weeks. Stepping out onto that LZ was like opening a door and stepping out onto Broadway, naked. In no time smoke grenades flew out into the center of the clearing and the unforgettable sound of rotor wings saturated the air.

The ride was real short.

They dumped us right back in the valley next to a fire base where we spent the night and got a bath. We also got a cherry new platoon leader.

I flopped down in 2ft of jewel-like creek water. I took a real bath using an extra bottle of Phisohex soap. It was fine. Nothing like a bath after two weeks of not so much as one good hand washing. Laying around in the sun, with a view of the fire base through the trees wasn't too bad either. I even had enough energy and desire to sketch and draw.

Our new lieutenant introduced himself and seemed pretty sensible and low key, even if he did look like a giant version of Lassie's pal, Timmy. He said, "My name is Lieutenant George Wood and I'm here with you all to learn and keep you from getting killed!"

We liked him right away.

The next day we rotored off the valley floor, flying east out of that deathtrap and onto Fire Base Zon. From Zon we caught a CH-47 'shit hook' for Fire Base Veghel.

The 'shit hook' spooked the shit out of everyone because it was so dark inside and we were trapped. The cargo ramp sealed up and we had no windows. Unassing the big Boeing twin prop was like unloading onto a vulture's nest on top of the Empire State building. The horrible machine slowed, we could all feel that, but as the rear cargo door whined down a 2,000ft drop into the mountains was all we could see. Blue sky and green mountains, that was it. The enlisted gunner waved us towards the ramp and 3rd platoon started jumping out! Sonofabitch ... not until the last second did I see the narrow patch of red earth under us. Had anyone jumped to the right he would have sailed out and off a near cliff, tearing into tree stumps and concertina wire and out of the base perimeter. A left turn landed you on a thin ridge line covered with sandbagged bunkers overlooking an eye-popping vista of jungle and mountain tops.

EXTRACTION

Plowing up the ridge with my rucksack and gook skull kicking my ass, I noticed HHC had an aid-station dug into the hill. GIs from the mortar platoon, commo section and 105 howitzer crews sat back and watched us climb the slope; they stared silently. They would probably never know how it was outside the wire and probably never wanted to know.

All our clothes and gear matched perfectly, a bleached and dirty blend of OD. Dust puffed up from our tracks. The day was as hot as a 'bowl of fuck' as usual.

Later Bravo company flew in and I stole a couple of almost-cold beers. Maurice was on the north side of the main ridge with the rest of Bravo. He was in the mood for an almost-cold beer and while he swilled it, began to tell me about shooting up some NVA. I told him my stories and we enjoyed the day, glad that we were both still alive. Above us the shadow of Fire Base Eagle's Nest, the 101's highest artillery base, cast darkness on lesser peaks under the clouds. It was one heady sensation, ogling the magic landscape in shades of browns, reds and greens.

After A Company left Veghel, NVA rocket teams laid several 122mm rockets into the exposed ridge line, hitting Wolfgang in the wrist with shrapnel. Maurice and Wolfgang posed for a photo to record the event for a possible purple heart in case anybody gave a shit enough to award one. As Maurice slapped a neat bandage around Wolf's wound and a cameraman jockeyed for position, the medic looked over his shoulder for any more missiles.

Chapter 28

Wind in the Burning Willows

Alpha humped off the fire base towards the east, with our new 'fearless' leader, Captain Colgrove. Colgrove packed some weight. He was a big old boy who looked like your typical college football offensive guard. We spent the whole day slipping down the mountain side, mostly on our rear ends. Our rucks were so heavy and the terrain so steep and muddy, that it was just one mad scene. You had to grab onto small branches and trees to keep from picking up momentum and flying totally out of control. Strung out in column formation, without any branches in reach, it was easy to lose it and come sliding down on top of the guy in front of you like a 200lb mud ball. The only course of action in that situation, was to flop on your butt and try to dig your heels in. It was a 'fun' day.

A few days later, after humping through some incredibly beautiful jungle with large limestone boulders and gin-clear, cold mountain streams, 'A' Company reached the badlands. We were still patrolling somewhere near the bottom of the mountain that supported the fire base. This new area seemed dead, devoid of life.

That evening our leaders decided to NDP on the side of a nearby hill in the middle of a defoliated forest. Bad move! All the trees were stripped of leaves and either dead or dying. It was a skeleton forest. Air Force 'ranch hands' in their C-123s, spraying agent orange, blue, white, or other Godforsaken chemicals, had defoliated huge sections of the country.

As I sat on a log eating chow, I looked around and noticed that the large limbs and fallen trees laying about would provide good cover in a fire fight. The Asian forests seemed mostly of hard woods and the dense, solid logs would stop damn near any kind of small-arms fire.

A light breeze was blowing as I went to sleep in our great little pocket of safety. Forest fires smoldered on the mountain nearby, across the narrow valley from us adding to the nightmare effect of the badlands. Some of the dead brush and tree limbs had caught fire and red lines of glowing coals and small fires worked slowly with the wind.

About 0200 we were jerked from sleep by a terrible 'CCCCRAAASSSHHHH!'

Startled, I woke to Hell on earth! A nuclear device appeared to have detonated in the naked creek bottom down the hill from our position. The light breeze was now up to hurricane force. Bits of wood and dust flew through the air. Someone screamed. The wind had come up during the night and was snapping limbs off the trees, high above our fighting perimeter. Pieces of wood, bark and clouds of dirt would, unseen, smack us in the face. 1,000lb limbs were dropping into our positions. It was as bad as a rocket attack or mortar barrage and the odds of dying were similar.

Word came over the radio to stay put. We were taking casualties, but no one was to move. Crap, where could anybody go in the middle of a forest that was trying to kill you?

I crawled over and pushed my head under a nearby log and, by hugging the dirt, managed to jam my entire torso in too. Hour after hour, trees blew apart and rained down on us! All I could do was flinch with each crash, wait for the next impact and listen for screams from our company area. It would mean I would have to disobey orders, 'oh my', and grope around in the dark for the dead or wounded. Sometime during the morning I drifted back off to sleep. Nobody near me was injured.

At first light a chopper landed with the battalion medical officer, Doc Herron. He ducked down and double-timed it out from under the rotor disk, carrying his aid bag. Herron looked like a doctor in charge of a bunch of rasty paratroopers. He was a stud, good looking, a jumper, and well liked by most of the medics. He even seemed to enjoy coming out to the field as long as he didn't have to spend the night. He was frank and said, "I really don't like it out in the bushes. I always returned to the firebase but my job was to go out and be a 'cleaner'...I had to go out and clean up the messes!"

The dawn was sweet, still, warm and cloudless – just another typical dry season day in I Corps. As Doc Herron walked by our platoon, our company comedian, flopped on his back, kicked up his heels over-head and offered his posterior to the chief medic. As clouds of dust billowed out from under him, the grunt (he looked like Sammy Davis with a shaved head) moaned, "Give it to me, Doc, give it to me."

He slid his pants down to his ankles, exposing a pair of OD boxer shorts. He continued the frantic bicycling exercise with kicking feet and butt wiggling at the sky.

Doc Herron, grinning, glanced down at the disgusting spectacle, and said, "Hello, Eisenhower, I see you have survived our little treatments for your numerous love diseases," never missing a step.

Eisenhower continued swiveling his ass around to follow the good doctor, leering at the departing chief surgeon.

"Doc, Doc ... oh wait for me ... oh ... oh stick it to me ... Doc ... Doc ... hey Doc ... are you listening?"

God damn it was funny. Funniest thing I ever saw! I fell off my log, I laughed so hard! It was pure madness.

No one had died that night, but the attack of the 'Killer Trees' left us with six wounded; one trooper with a bad head injury flew out with the doctor, our 'Christmas Elf'. No one in 3rd platoon had been hit.

I could just imagine the award ceremony: "... and to trooper Pervous Hardcore for wounds received in action in the Republic of South Vietnam, against botanical wave assaults of killer trees ... the Purple Heart."

Jesus, what a war! Mother Nature had won another round. She came after us for killing her forests. It was as simple as that!

Of course, the curses and poisons went on for years ... for everyone ...

Thank you, big business! Thank you, Dow Chemical.

Chapter 29

Yellow Slime

After the battle with the killer trees, Alpha slogged northeast through a lot of dead jungle and at night we sought out healthy growth to hole up in. At least we tried to stay out of the big trees.

One afternoon Sergeant Rock and White Boy came over to my position to show me some bad cases of boils. The things were hideous. These infections started out with a gradual swelling and ended up titanic ingrown pimples with volcanic red knobs that were topped with ugly quarter-sized puss openings or heads. So much pressure backed up that often times when I stuck a syringe needle in an explosive spray of greenish, pea soup or off-yellow slime would burst out and sometimes get me in the eye or mouth.

Whiteboy, a big tow-headed kid, had a history of boils and now his squad leader, Sergeant Rock, the short, energetic, competition diver from San Jose, California had one. I started on Whiteboy by just touching his forearm. It was so painful that the gental giant gnashed his teeth to choke a whimper. His arm was at least twice its normal size and looked like a good case of Elephantitus. The damn thing was blown up and felt brittle as glass; the skin was drawn tight.

I knew that draining the thing would immediately relieve the pain. Gently supporting his infected limb left hand prints where the diseased skin failed to rebound normally from my fingertips. After picking through the transparent skin on the head, we got a half pint of the ghastly goop, at least half a pint. The shit came out like yellow jello. You'd start near the elbow and sort of squeeze and milk the crud out of the cavities between the muscle. Like cement from a truck's hose.

When we finished, a deep hole exactly like a large caliber bullet hole stared back and you could look deep into the wound via the eyeless socket. The sucker seemed bottomless when I stuffed in the gauze packing with my ten inch metal probe. I'd pack away with the probe or sometimes I used the wooden stick cotton-tipped applicators.

After a day or so I'd pull out the packing, reapply a bandage and the thing would heal over (I packed over forty bad cases and they all did okay).

Rock's boil (or really cellulitis) was up the crack of his ass and extremely painful. I made him drop his pants and turn around while a sorry crew of curious rubberneckers started milling around, some smirking and grinning.

"Get outta here, I'm operating," I commanded.

I grabbed ahold of hot infected gluteus-maximus ass. The boil head was off center from the anal canal opening, but real close, so I had to slide my thumb almost up his ass hole to squeeze the pus out, but I managed it. This was the worst boil I had ever seen and what came out was the phlegm from an exorcism; split pea green, nectar from hell.

The last persistent gawker slipped behind me, bent down for a closer look and exclaimed, "God damn, Doc, what's all that shit coming out of the Rock's ass hole?" The little rectal inspector, without a shirt, turned his face into mine and smiled a silly grin. Rock cranked his head around and snarled,

"Beat it, butt-breath!" and the whole perimeter erupted in muffled laughter. But Rock's antagonist knew he had the upper hand in the delicate situation; so had the last word, "Yowie ... Doc's tearing Rock some kinda new asshole ain't he ... wooiee!"

Boils were weird. Some people got them and some didn't, simple as that. The poor slobs that did would heal up and in a few days get another one. We all lived the same, ate the same and bathed about the same so it was kind of strange. For some reason I never got one. In fact, my six-year-old case of athlete's foot even went away. And I wore socks, usually damp, and boots twenty-four hours a day seven days a week!

Some would gamely suffer the boils and more than once I sent them into the rear. I told them, "And don't come back or I'll lose your shot card!" That threat seemed to work even though I had nothing to do with shot cards out in the bush.

Some guys wanted to come back and some guys had to be talked into coming back. I did my part and nobody could stop me, I got them out of the field. The medics in the rear knew better than to send anybody back out with a bad case of cellulitis.

Chapter 30

Bastogne

Finally, our merry band topped another torn-apart ridge line and the sight of an ocean of defoliated trees greeted our tired eyes. In the middle of this decay sat the fortress – fire base Bastogne. We walked in.

A Company waded the creek and strode into the fire base as water poured from our gear. The creek was part of the western perimeter and over the years had eaten 25ft down into the dark earth. As we went across the base's water point and bathing area, I was knocked out by the beauty here. Martini clear water in big pools lay back in grottos of mammoth rocks and overhanding banks. Sunlight danced on the cliffs and banks in net shaped patterns of light that pulsated in time to the wind and water. I couldn't wait to get back down to wash and swim.

They put us on two side-by-side ridges, a gulley between them, covered with fallen logs and no shade in sight. We didn't care. We threw up ponchos between all the crisscrossed logs and made spiffy shelters, strong windproof shelters.

Granny came over and suggested I build a shitter for 3rd platoon, one that could be serviced and the shit burned. I told him that I wasn't an engineer, I was a medic – I didn't make house calls or shitters. But then I remembered all the drawings in our books at Ft. Sam, drawings of slit trenches and mass latrines so I figured, why not, it would beat digging cat holes on top of cat holes every day.

In about three hours 3rd platoon had the best shitter on the hill. No sooner was it done and the new sign hung in place, declaring the contraption the private property of our platoon, the old man, Captain Colgrove, came charging down off his ridge, jumping and dodging blown down logs, armed with a roll of toilet paper and a determined grimace.

I'd found a cut down 55-gallon drum and built up around it. On each side I laid a 3ft wall of sand bags and wooden ammo boxes. Across the walls I dropped a 6' 12' x 12' beam to sit on and over the whole affair I secured a poncho, sun shade parasol. The drum could be pulled in and out between the walls and under the beam. It was a pretty nice structure, the first bathroom I ever made. Only one problem, no one wanted to burn the shit. They refused my request. I built the thing – why did I have to take care of its operation? We changed locations before I had to face the indignity of becoming a bathroom attendant. Well, it was all sort of a medic's job, the sanitation and building part anyway. I guess I could have taken the job more seriously. I could have stood by the shit hole and handed out shit paper and maybe condoms, breath mints, cigars, and soaps if I'd had them. Like a pro-attendant in some big city.

The next day they moved us higher up the hill and 3rd platoon C.P. got three walls and a roof, kind of a half-assed bunker, but of course we lost the crapper. I hung my gook hammock off the tree trunk beams that supported the roof and made myself comfortable. And I was comfy, until about 0100. Something exploded and the concussion dumped me out onto the ground. At least it felt like the shockwave slapped me out of bed. I thought a grenade had gone off in the bunker and broke out in a heavy sweat; I looked around for the lieutenant or Moultrie or Smart. They were tossing around on the floor snoring!

The stars proved a beautiful night and I dusted myself off and looked outside. Funny, all seemed quiet.

No sooner was I back in the sack, eyes getting heavy, when a white light seared across my eyelids and another blast rattled me to the bone.

"God damn, what the fuck … over?" I moaned.

"Artillery, Doc … outgoing … " I heard a voice croak. It turned out we were right across from some heavy artillery battery that started a harassment and interdiction mission. They were harassing everyone on our side of the fire base. Every three minutes a 155 shell tore off into space. It was torture. It would have been much better firing constantly or even spaced out more but as it was my terrorized and shell-shocked mind knew a blast was due and tried to anticipate the explosion by counting backwards. I was sweating again, wasn't enough time to fall asleep between shots, that was part of the problem. About a minute before the next round blew, my mind would reel. I was going to have a breakdown. I couldn't take this. I lay on my back, eyes screwed tight, nervous system ready to explode and body rigid with fear. I started counting, I didn't want to but couldn't help it: 45, 44, 43, WHAAMM! Shit, I misjudged the interval, that was the worst thing: a bad surprise. My body jerked, startled beyond belief – it was the nightmare of the booby traps again.

I don't think anybody slept that night, not in 3rd platoon anyway. The 155 rounds were supposed to land near some enemy camp or activity and scare them, or at least keep them from resting, but it was us that got the worst of it.

Chapter 31

Rat Attack, Tat

Life around Bastogne was pretty good except, of course, for the fire missions, or walking behind the engineers as they swung metal detectors back and forth over the ground in front of our detail squad as we cleared Route 547 of mines. Lieutenant Wood led us down the dirt highway.

Doc Herron had time enough to wander around taking wildlife photos with his little instamatic camera like many of us had. His favorite subject was one of the million 'dead' trees still standing around the base. Well, this dead tree still had a lot of green leaves on it, but it was the only one. Colonel Beckwith himself liked to strut around with his shirt off and sometimes helped us fill sandbags. With his shirt off everyone could see his 'zipper' – the infamous, ugly, scar snaking across his belly. The wound that left him for dead.

About this time, Charger took Doc Herron in under his wing and told the doctor to get rid of the 'piece of shit' .45 pistol on his hip. But Herron didn't even know how to clean the M-16 he got, so was reluctant to ever fire the rifle and never parted with the .45.

Once we ran down to the chopper pad and jumped on a bird to go help out the 82nd Airborne. When we got to the crash site, dust still hung in the air and a slightly dinged-up Huey sat half-in and half-out of the tree line. 3rd platoon put out security around the crash while another team hooked up a sling to lift the machine out.

Then we climbed back into our ship.

We took off while our door gunners sprayed the tree line just after the crippled bird was yanked off the ground by a flying crane.

Another time we combat assaulted out of Bastogne, following the creeks and gullies in the higher terrain towards the west. We flew below the ridge tops in the rain. Large drops streaked down the huge windscreen.

Our platoon, after landing, humped up an old trail on a narrow little ridge when suddenly I was startled to see Sergeant Rock and Granny breaking brush off the ridge. They had dropped all their gear, even their weapons. About ten minutes later they were back, out of breath, covered with twigs, leaves, cuts and scratches.

I never could figure out who kicked ass on who. It was age and toughness against youth and strength, probably a draw. Although Rock confided in me later that Granny had fought unfairly.

The next day I sat around bullshitting with some of the squad leaders and they all started giving me an extra ration of shit – they grilled me about my jump wings.

"Hey doc, when did you go to jump school?" one asked.

Another one chimed in, "Well Doc, what company were you in anyway?"

I had to explain and describe everything from the cracks in the benches at Stewart Hall to the location of the 'animal farm', but when I reminisced about the frost-coated plastic pitchers full of beer at the snack bar near our barracks, some of the wise-guy paratroopers around me began to accept my airborne qualifications ... some.

In the afternoon we humped back down into the grassy flat ground and got resupplied.

The log birds pounded their way to our position and threw out or unloaded beer, soda, towels, fatigue pants and shirts, ammo, smoke grenades, radio batteries, medical supplies, new guys, TV cameramen, mail, shovels, a chaplain, Doc Herron, hand grenades, claymore mines, trip flares, canned food, dehydrated instant meals, cigarettes, coffee, cigars, writing stationary, boots, socks, heat tabs, C-4 plastic explosives, mortar rounds, rain gear, poncho liners, ponchos, waterproof bags, salt tablets, malaria pills, machetes, tooth powder, water blivets, halazone water purification pills, shit paper and insect repellant; but no ice. Unlike the 3/187th, the 2/327th never had ice on resupply day. Maybe once – the year I was with them.

Supply day was a time for strange rituals. Sometimes we all took our clothes off and stood around with our dongs hanging down. We simply discarded our dirty fatigues into a pile and grabbed clean ones from another. Rock picked his way into the new clothes with a weird sort of determined grin plastered all over his face. The short, lean, bundle of muscle had just made sergeant and he was looking for something. Something in particular. Rock's eyes suddenly slammed wide open. It was right where he knew it would be, he had found it: a jungle jacket with buck sergeant stripes. The stripes were the old style, yellow, non-camouflaged, stacked chevrons. Three of them on each sleeve. No sooner had Rock donned his new shirt, he was jumped by the lieutenant and Granny.

Now Granny looked every day of 50, with a gray crew cut, and large flabby chest muscles on his otherwise tall and lanky frame. However, to his lasting credit, he was humping the sticks – outdoing some of us youngsters. The attackers grabbed the young buck sergeant and poured warm beer over the stripes, shirt, head and face of the surprised soldier. Beer exploded out of the beer cans that were pressed onto his chest and shoulder. Rocky stood and took it like a man. We watched the apes clowning around, wordlessly acting out parts in the initiation. Had to be some sort of Army tradition for new NCOs I thought to myself. Ah … war, ain't it grand?

All the grab-assing didn't impress us much. Nothing grand about any of it. In fact, it was a bunch of bullshit. The glamour of a combat paratrooper that I'd expected had somehow eluded me. Where was the glamour in this? Did someone say something about glamour? Glamour, glamour, who said anything about glamour, did they forget our glamour on the supply ship again. DID YOU SEE ANY … glamour? I didn't see any glamour. All we saw was a bunch of grunts drinking beer and standing around naked, trying to dry out their jungle rotted skin.

Guys wrote letters or stood guard duty. We usually had time to write a quick letter home. Stamps were never a problem, at least. We just wrote 'free' in the upper right-hand corner of the envelope in lieu of a stamp. Later a bird would come back to pick up the 'DXed' clothing, the mail, people going on R&R, people going home, visitors and anybody else that didn't have to stay with us. For some strange reason the doctors, Herron included, chaplains and assorted REMFs never seemed to want to spend too much time with us, let alone the whole night. They didn't like the dark and nasty old jungle. They seemed to get nervous, almost as soon as they arrived, that they'd miss the last slick out. We loved it when, due to unavailability of aircraft or the weather, these strangers from the rear were forced to spend the night. We wanted them with us. It really made our day to see them miserable. We wanted them to suffer along with us. As for the line company resupply and beer-bust crap, you could have it. I wanted out and into a recon unit.

Back at Bastogne we went swimming and I tried to learn how to shoot my new .45 cal. pistol. I got a new box of shells but couldn't hit a 55-gallon drum at 40ft. The weapon was designed to shoot people in the head ... point blank. I could use it.

The Hawks showed up one day and settled into the fire base type of 'trench' warfare. We were overrun with rats. "These damn rats are big enough to fuck a chicken flat footed!" Beckwith said. Wolfgang spent nights working on the rat problem. He scrounged up a coffee can and a claymore detonating system (wire, clacker and cap) and set up his own little chamber of horrors to repay the rats, whose idea of fun was to sit on your face in the middle of the night. Wolf would bait the can with food ... usually C-rats (for rats of course) and either use a small wad of C-4 or lacking that, the cap itself. While Wolf pulled guard, he'd listen for the scampering of little feet in the can then squeeze off the mini-mine. Sayonara mini-mouse!

Our platoon got a new platoon sergeant. His name was SFC Louis Solivan. Solivan looked 35 at least, was compact in stature, and had Latin features for the most part. He'd been in the Army for nearly twenty years and with us he quickly became excepted as 'cool'. Unlike Drill Sergeant Maybry back at Fort Lewis, our sergeant was out humping the field along with us and doing the job he was trained to do, which entailed keeping us youngsters alive. One favorable aspect of the US Army in Vietnam, was the career NCOs that took us kids under their wings. It seemed that the more combat time and the more flamboyant these old paratroopers were, the better we liked them, usually. They didn't give a damn if we smoked weed in the rear, hated the Army, lifers in general and tended to wear our hair long. They understood us. They knew we'd perform when the shit hit the fan.

Solivan helped me with my .45. "Doc, the .45 is a strange animal," he told me. "Ya gotta just do three things with her ... practice, practice, practice."

Chapter 32

Fizzies

While Alpha Company was getting ready to go back to Eagle from Bastogne the Hawk Recon platoon explored out in the A Shau again. They'd been out awhile.

Spanky, Doc Smitty, Wolfgang, Cowboy, Fellows and others along with Lieutenant Viney were starving. There'd been no food or resupply for days. They couldn't find any water either! Someone broke open a saline solution IV bottle and passed it around complete with a couple of Fizzies (candy drink mixes) bubbling away inside. No one could drink it of course.

Later with the sound of falling water, wearing and cascading through boulders, echoing in the trees, Wolf readied a team for a water run. Wolf told his team to be sure and bring plenty of grenades, he had a plan to put meat on the table, or at least in a canteen cup.

Viney somehow got word of the fishing expedition so when Wolf passed by him before disappearing off down the mountain side he said, "Sergeant Wolfgang, just get water and don't screw around wasting grenades."

"But sir, we're damn near starving to death up here. We gotta try sumpin ... some of the men are sick from eating lizards and that stinking monkey," Wolf argued.

"Forget it, Sergeant. You'll give our position away ... no way ... got it?"

"Right," Wolf answered.

A giant carp rushed the buzzing animal it thought was hurt and vulnerable. But before he could even open his mouth, he was dead. The grenade concussion killed every fish in the pool.

The fire team couldn't conceal their joy and triumph in performing the ancient art of the hunt, returning with meat. Viney was furious and later collared Wolfgang informing him that formal charges would be brought up – for disobeying an order.

But the fish were big ... whoppers in fact. The GIs swooned with pleasure, eating boiled fish and hot sauce washed down with H_2O, or even the hoarded and very scarce beer or – so help me God – a cherished and shared soda!

Wolfgang's and Viney's relationship was never quite the same after the fishing trip and in fact, it got worse.

Chapter 33

Low Lifes in the Lowlands

Back at Camp Eagle, the home of the 2/327th, our flight touched down and dropped us off right in the battalion area. The battalion motto was 'no slack', which was our emergency password also. We unassed the choppers and walked down the hill from the pad in the noonday sun. Hippy looking Doc James, the filthy, longhaired medic from 1st platoon, walked at my side as we began to notice a lot of faces staring out from the doors and windows of our new headquarters' buildings.

"Lousy fucking pussies," James sneered.

I was stunned at his new attitude; so cruel, so cold, so unlike a real flower child.

"Well, at least the lousy fucking pussies built us some wood barracks and some showers," I said with a smile. Gone were the tents we used to sleep in. I strode along, M-16 in hand, the NVA skull covering my rear from its perch as it looked backwards from the top of the now seemingly weightless, almost empty pack. We were looking good, standing tall and feeling mean. The theme from *The Good, the Bad and the Ugly* played somewhere in the back of my mind.

Ta, Da, Daa, Da, Da Daa, Da.

Yeah, no slack, that was us. Had to showboat for the barrack boys. Some blacks asked about Doc Stewart. "Hadn't seen him," we said. He was in another company, Delta we thought.

The next day the First Sergeant of A Company called us all together out front in the road. Our 'first shirt' or 'top' was a bundle of energy with a crew cut. He yelled, "Okay, you girls are all gonna get a hair cut here. No exceptions. The barber shop will be open all day here. Now, another thing ... I don't want no dope smoking, no cases of your veenaireel

146

Above: Oil painting by author of August 4, 1968, "Into The A Shau Valley".

Right: Richard Lappin and author ambush site and shoot out. The author cleaning his M16. Photo is on sand spit, a high-speed enemy trail.

Platoon Sgt. Oliver reading the paper, always ready. Osgood cleaning next to ruck and aid bag. Sniper in hills behind opens up at us on the spit. The year before I spotted NVA platoon on spit as we camped in the hills.

Doc Osgood on the morning after ambush with his new AK-47!

Company A medics on return from A Shau. Just back to company area from bloody battle, Charlie Beckwith commanding. Our ambulance and aid station behind.

Author next to bunker and bridge near Phu Loc on Highway 1. .45 and M-16 ready to go.

Zinger and Rossi giving the Hawk Recon salute. The M-16 is named: Flower Power!

Zinger and Rossi with knives and pipes, a Hawk trademark.

Rossi with carbine
and an unknown
soldier with
12-gauge trench
sweeper in front of
our mail room with
battalion motto.

Doc White or
Doc Ramsey, with
Jim Fellows in
the center, and
Bollinger at Camp
Eagle in Phu Bia.
Fellows joined the
LURPs, airborne
rangers.

Cline and Tick.
Tick is holding
a thumper M-79
grenade launcher.

Rossi gets war paint on Hawk Hill, July 1968.

Sgt. John Wolfgang and medic Doc White or Doc Ramsey.

Walter Jackson: Ranger, Lurp. A California boy from Fort Bragg, this Hawk left the service as a major.

Above: Munson, Chavez, Rick Knight, Azzolino, Zinger and Yargats relaxing in a grave with peace pipes.

Left: Fighting medic Doc Brown, aka 'Voodoo', on Hawk Hill.

Pee Wee Dobbs on Hawk Hill. 11 NVA bodies taken.

Above: Doc Osgood boarding choppers as Chico starts map reading.

Below left: Commander Talbot. Gotta be a good pilot with beard AND love beads...far out man!

Below right: Sgt. John Wolfgang at Camp Eagle 2/327th rear area.

Triplet and J.J. Smith in a bomb crater by the Ho Chi Minh Trail.

Gunship pilot Clark with 'The Dog'.

Rick Knight Hawk RTO with new SKS on Hawk Hill.

Above: Hawks on the move, hunting. Spanky, then John Wolfgang, then medic, Smitty.

Right: The Hawks and 3/187th headquarters (Fire Base Berchtesgaden) during battle of Hamburger Hill, May 1969. Hawks moved off into the trees during huge battle at night.

MY HOME MARCH-JUNE 1969 - WOUNDED HERE IN ALL NITE FIGHT 13-14 JUNE

FIRE BASE BERCHESGADEN - 3D BDE C.P. ASHAU

Jo Jo Biliter in his grave with siege gear on in Fire Base Berchtesgaden during attacks where we were allowed to sleep during midday only.

Gunship pilots, not models or Parker pen salesmen! Dean Murphy, Loren Bryant, Clark, Claude Woolard and Curt Gaskins

Left: 326th Medical Eagle Dust-off crew member...air ambulance.

Below: Hawk Recon group photo.

Right: Bill Meacham...SOG LURP pilot flew 'The Dog'!

Below left: Fritz with rolling paper 'guy' art on helmet. Ready to jump out and grab a beer! Fritz was killed in battles near the DMZ.

Below right: Eagle Dust-off mission in action. 'Fly United' mating ducks on helmet. Flying over the Perfume River.

Captain Torba in an unarmed ambulance. It would later be hit by an RPG by some 'hero' of Hanoi. All except Torba, including the patients, were killed.

Dipboye, Talbot and Speer at Khe Sanh, flying Eagle Dust-off. Talbot sported love beads.

Left: Crew Chief Eagle Dust-off Larry Wagoner showing off AK-47 wound. Note that fly boys had furniture, fans, and travel posters, and rooms, too! We had one blanket.

Below: Rare photo taken in the middle of combat of a gunship diving on targets as we unload birds. Scout ship parts litter the airfield at Ta Bat in the A Shau Valley, 1968. Like Custer's last stand!

Jim Scales, Paul Mather, unknown, and kneeling in front is Howard Baldwin. Delta company bombing survivors, NOT movie stars.

A grunt cooking c-rats – not ready to serve – using a heat tab stove.

Col. Charlie A. Beckwith aka 'Charger' was the author's commander.

Map 1968 shootout. 1969 ambush map.

Left: Drawing by Combat Medic Dave Trout of a "Typical" Medic.

Below: Jungle map. Follow eagles clockwise from Ta Bat airfield and end in Dong Ap Bia, Hamburger Hill battle area. This was my route of march on August 4, 1968. Upper left eagle position is Delta, 3/187th,101 in 1969. First in!

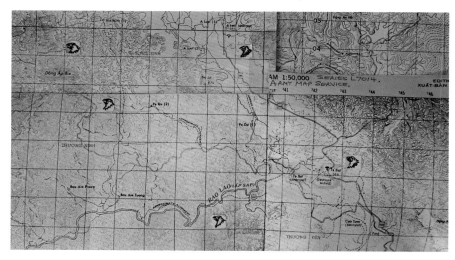

Above left: Author's painting of John Wolfgang, Hawk team leader.

Above right: Author's painting of August 4, 1968, "Into The A Shau Valley."

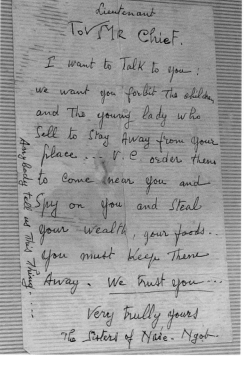

Above: Boonie hat with Hawk Recon scroll, 101st Airborne patch, as well as Jump Wings on a Special Forces background of blue and gold, Combat Medic's Badge.

Right: Nun Letter…A note written to Hawk Recon warning them of Viet Cong spies.

Above left: Benovidez…Timoteo Benovidez near A Shau Valley with grenade wound under right eye! He was part of the 3rd Herd, A Company.

Above right: Sergeant Arnold…Sgt. Arnold was a Green Beret before joining the 101st. He would earn a Purple Heart after being shot by an arrow.

Jack E. Henry Jr. (middle) on Lang Co bridge, 3rd Herd, A Company.

Jack Henry and Thomas Rebel Odom with Kit Carson Scouts when we were in 3rd platoon, A Co. 2/327, 101st.

dezeeeses, and for God's sake, don't murder nobody while you're here under my command here in the rear. Now, I'm gonna turn you over to the Air Force here and I want you to pay attention to what they have to say here."

A couple of pilots, both wearing jump wings under aviator wings, attempted to explain why a bomb landed square on the heads of Delta company, eventually killing twelve and just about wiping out the entire unit. Almost sixty were wounded. The 'peccadillo' was in all the papers back in the world, but of course we, in the same unit, had never heard a thing about it until now. Oh sure we knew something happened that time we waited around most of the day and were told to keep our heads down and lay behind trees. We'd heard explosions and even felt the earth shake, but that was it. One of the dead was Sergeant Antonio Garcia, a good soldier who was well known and loved for punching some battalion staff officer in the face.

The flight officers in their dark flight glasses and flight suits told a tale of remorse and sorrow and added that the FAC had marked the target wrong, missed the target, or otherwise overshot somehow. Maybe it was a combination of human errors, maybe the location of Delta wasn't clear due to the tree cover hiding the smoke grenades used to verify friendly positions to the FAC. The trees were often so fucking high that by the time the smoke finally wound its way above the branches it was too thin to see. For whatever reason, a fighter bomber made his pass the wrong way and dropped on us.

I left my skull with A Company, and went to Eagle Beach for the day. I even got to body surf some waves with a pair of USO dive fins. Afterwards we joined the other 'no slackers' running around smoking dope off in the old bunkers, old tombs or boozing it at the club, back at Eagle.

After a few days of partying and watching porno flicks, we received our ration of Trojan rubbers and loaded onto trucks. The battalion was changing AOs and we were to ride down Highway 1 into the lowlands along the South China Sea, the operating areas of the Viet Cong. A lot of 'contact' with civilians was expected and we were ready for them. We carried protection; the toughest, thickest, seemingly strongest prophylactic known to man: the Trojan workhorse – the plain, unlubricated, non-reservoir, white, heavy-duty style rubber. Visions of a German Shepherd mating with a woman in some ancient dirty movie we saw one night played across my daydreams as we headed south in the rain. Doggie style, they did it doggie style, naturally. War is such a 'dignified' influence on youth. Such a character builder … what a crock of shit.

One night before we left, we watched "The Sand Pebbles" with Steve McQueen. Our big old company commander: Leslie H. Colgrove, drinking beers and Jack Daniels along with his boys, got into some disagreement with the battalion Sgt. Major who was on hand. The result was an ugly beating of Colgrove by this NCO.

The next morning early, Capt. Colgrove called the entire company A outside for formation. He told us we were leaving for the Lowlands. No more Ho Chi Minh trail.

But first he walked over to the battalion Sgt. Major's private hootch which was located right in front of us on our little, dirt, parade ground road.

Our Captain Colgrove threw the NCO out into the road and thoroughly beat the living crapola out of the tipsy Sgt.

We were impressed...!

A Company drove through Phu Loc and past Fire Base Tomahawk, Los Banos, Hill 88, and the famous Rock Crusher. Dropping down the hill and into the village of Lang Co was like cruising into Honolulu in the early 1900s. Incredible! Bleached, golden sand beaches mixed with palm trees, a colorful maze of brick homes, churches and ancient castle ruins that sat on the end of a peninsula that choked the mouth of Cu Bai Bay. The north side of the mouth was the end of the strand which featured the village and surf break right in the ville. The south side shot straight up into triple canopy mountains, some with black, hundred-foot cliffs or north faces. Third platoon unloaded on the south side of the bridge near a little white tower that had to have been constructed by the French Foreign Legion.

My mission: find some place to sleep that was out of the rain. Our purpose: guard the bridge.

Inside the dank tower my plastic (ARVN) net hammock hung from one of the firing ports over to a steel ring near the entrance. I eased in to test it out.

TWANG!

The old rucksack strap broke and I did a bad Judo fall-flat on my back. Damn, I nearly broke my back on the cold, wet, stone floor. It was a close call. Everyone else thought it was funny.

Later the rain stopped and the platoon had lots to do. I sat up in the parapet of our outpost tower and shot pipe fish in the seawater below. Some of us dropped frags down around the footings for the bridge. Had to discourage enemy frogmen of course.

When truck convoys crossed the bridge the guards would throw us cans of beer and soda. All of us agreed we had never seen so much Fresca soda in our entire lives. That company was scoring big time in our little war. But Jack Henry and Rebel Odom wanted to treat everyone, really pile it on! They stopped the usual huge convoy and told them – to be careful crossing the bridge because of enemy frogmen! Slow, one at a time, on the bridge.

With Jack in the tower with M-60 pointed at the first trucks, Rebel – already in the back of one covered truck...began pitching cases upon cases of beer and soda overboard.

A driver saw this and climbed out with a grease gun threateningly. Jack leveled the M-60 at the surprised driver – while Rebel climbed out of the truck: not wishing to seem greedy or anything.

One of the newer guys, Jack Henry, got a Colt 45 from home. I borrowed the civilian weapon and with my .45 drew down on an imaginary foe like the original Two Gun Pete.

POW POW POW POWPOWPOWPOW POW

Water geysers erupted along the green bay surface. Hot lead and cold death spat from each hand.

Chapter 34

Sea Bee Camp

The 2/327th's new mission was to guard the bridges between Hue/Phu Bia and Da Nang. The railway bridges and tunnels were being rebuilt by the US. They were prime targets for destruction.

After several days of sitting on the Lang Co bridge, 3rd platoon packed up and split for parts unknown – without me! No reason was given, but I was to stay behind with a strange platoon. I was pissed! This was some sorry assed outfit. Nobody seemed to know what was going on. A bunch of career managers ran the unit. I asked what was up but was ignored. What the fiendish conspiracy to keep me from my platoon was about was never revealed to me. Later I found out 3rd platoon took up part of the perimeter at a Sea Bee camp. Damn, I knew something interesting had to be going on and I was missing out. The Navy was repairing a large railway bridge over the Race Hoi Dua river that emptied into Cu Bai Bay. The bridge was about a mile and a half away around a bend and north-west along the tracks. Bridge guard duty was considered in-country R&R. A kick back.

This particular camp was located in a spot that was Shangri la. The absolute best duty Company A ever pulled. Third 'herd' was delighted. Waterfalls tumbled out of the Bac Ma mountains and joined an ice-clear, slow moving river meandering through the middle of a lush valley. Bamboo stands and nipa palms grew along the banks. A beach and sandbar lay across the river from the Navy camp. But the best deal was that the platoon got to eat Navy chow! Hot meals every single day; pancakes, real meat and ice cream.

In a couple of days the Navy came up the tracks and took me back to my outfit. The first thing I did after settling in was to swim over to

150

the beach alone. I'd asked the lieutenant for permission and he'd replied with a cheery, "Be back for lunch," just like Mom. I was naked and about 200 yards from camp. Cicadas chirped and sang as I lay in the cool sand. Suddenly it dawned on me that I was in danger. I squinted over at the wire back on the bank at camp and asked myself, what the fuck was I doing over here? Propped up on one elbow the feeling of being watched pierced my soul like an AK slug. To make matters worse, the insects all stopped making noise. I got up and, with a falsely casual air, swam back to the perimeter. Christ, a one-legged gook could have run out of the bamboo and coup de graced me with a dull machete. I'd sensed something. Maybe it was the huge saltwater crocodiles I'd felt. The ones that probably considered the sandbar theirs. Like most visitors in the south seas, man-eating lizards were totally unexpected.

The Sea Bees used to haul ass up and down the railway tracks on their four wheeled mules. The tires were a perfect match for the narrow gauge rails. With nothing much to do but swim and eat ice cream, I volunteered to go cruise around on the mules and blow stuff up. We went looking for stray mortar rounds and dud bombs. I didn't know what I was doing and had no business doing it. Sometimes I picked up live shells and rockets before piling them in a heap for detonation. I wanted to blow the ordnance to make sure the enemy never got a chance to make booby traps out of it. In a pile of bombs I'd place a TNT explosive (about the size and shape of a ½ quart milk carton). I'd cut a couple of feet of powder fuse, jam it into a little silver blasting cap and push them into a pre-cut hole in the charge. One time a couple of Navy guys in white t-shirts and Marine style hats and I set up to blow a mortar round laying near the tracks. We lit the fuse and walked over behind the mule. Sometimes everything exploded and sometimes not. This time the TNT went off and launched the still unexploded and armed round up in the air, pin wheeling toward us. We dove to the ground to put the mule between us and the shell, and to keep from being killed. I closed my eyes and cringed, sweat dripped from my nose. Nothing happened. We stood up and saw the fucking bomb, now laying near the tracks right next to us! Sheepishly, we looked about. First up the tracks, then back towards camp, then up the tracks again. Regaining some composure and without a spoken word, we jumped on the Corvair powered mule and shagged ass for home. Yes, it was dirty, dangerous and very sloppy work, but by God someone had to do it. I must have been out of my fucking mind!

We tried to keep busy playing cards and such. We wrote letters home and once we were all treated to the thrill of Granny, back from R&R, and his class of Navy guys out on field maneuvers. Like an elementary class on a field trip, they followed their fearless leader off along the river to where the bushes started. Granny lined them all up behind the brush and on his command, everyone threw a hand grenade up and into the river. Great. Very spectacular. Like Navy Sea Bees didn't know how to lob grenades. But the fighting Sea Bees did have a name to live up to and maybe they were just bored like us.

Chapter 35

Surf City

Near Fire Base Tomahawk we humped down to a village on the sea shore. I sat on somebody's back stoop. A little boy about 10 years old with school books under his arm came over and sat down with me. He was your typical kid; short pants, flip flops and no hat. Right away I noticed his books were plastered with pages of *Surfer* magazine. I asked him if I could look at them. I couldn't believe it! He had pictures of Santa Cruz all over his books. My heart ached with home sickness as I tapped my chest and then the photos with an index finger, meaning that this was my village and these were us boys.

East and West met on those steps that morning. We really couldn't talk, yet we lived, played and went to school together on the Pacific Ocean. We were neighbors on opposite horizons.

Pointing at the lagoon and at the surf flicks and back at him, I asked if he wanted to be a surfer. I was trying to find out if waves broke into the lagoon. He looked up at me with startled eyes and then made a face. He thrashed his head back and forth, like a retarded child, stopped and began clapping his hands and arms together, arms straight out in front, ridged, like the jaws of a crocodile. He was telling me, I assumed, that no, he was afraid of the water. He used the common local expression: "Cock-O-Dial You" which meant: kill you – but sure sounded like crocodile! How the word 'cock-o-dial' came about was not clear but I had a good idea.

The company started moving again up into the dark section of the village where the bamboo and banana trees were thick. A low plateau made a tall backdrop behind the trees. A shot popped off up ahead. Another delay. Somebody had shot a villager we heard. Great.

Hours later we passed through the village and along the coast. Flooded rice paddies and the mountains were on our right flank.

More shots!

One of the tall, dark, platoon leaders was doing the Mexican two-step and 100 yard dash in front of a charging water buffalo. The Lieutenant had his 'commando' AR-15 almost up the monster's nose as they scuttled through the muck. He held the weapon like a machine gun pistol popping off rounds point plank. Finally the bull fell. Close call!

We didn't retreat. We maneuvered in the opposite direction setting up camp back above the village on top of the plateau. From the grassy bank we stared at odd sugar-loaf pinnacle formation mounts jutting up at the mouth of the lagoon like something out of a Japanese print. The rocks rose up off the beach like giant dorsal fins hundreds of feet high.

In the afternoon somebody sent one of the Kit Carson Scouts to scout up some cheap sex. Not long afterwards the scout returned with a stunning local girl dressed in pink and carrying a parasol. She strutted inside our perimeter and was immediately invited inside a hootch tied close to the ground. The hootch started flexing up and down in spasms. Soon, somebody hailed me and said, "Okay Doc … your turn. This was your idea remember?"

I was shy – I had changed my mind. I should have led her up the trail aways into the bamboo groves. How romantic that would be?!

What a day it had been. First we had shot somebody, then we killed some farming family's 'tractor', then we invited prostitutes and camp followers and paraded them through their village. What we would do for an encore I could not even imagine. No wonder they hated us. No wonder we were not winning the war. But we did have a plan for all this. In fact, we had two plans. But plan A seemed to be a bit of a failure so of course we had a backup. Plan B was we'd 'med cap' 'em and make 'everything' right.

By day's end the enemy probably knew exactly how many we were, what weapons we had and even our first names.

Chapter 36

Plan B

In November we went back to Thon Phuoc Tuong the ville on the lagoon we had terrorized. This time we went to help them.

Doc James and myself set up a table at the school. I laid down my aid bag and waited for some customers. The houses were in fruit trees right on the Dam Cau Hai Lagoon.

An hour later we were mobbed with people as an epidemic of scalp sores was running wild through town. Many of the baby-sans, the 1 to 2 year olds, had scars and scabs all over their heads. We started out washing the scalps with Phisohex soap but soon realized the hopelessness of the endeavor. Finally, James said to me, each of us with a baby in our laps,

"Screw this! Let's give 'em vitamins."

With that, we put away the soap and gave out pills which was a big hit right off. Everyone began trading the pills with their friends, trying to suck them like life savers or exchange them for cokes at the store.

An old man, looking exactly like Ho Chi Minh in a classic green silk shirt with black trim, sauntered up and wiggled a tooth at me. Our great uncle with his long grey whiskers and bad teeth made yanking motions with his fist so I grabbed a hemostat and clamped it on his loose tooth. I looked him in the eye to make sure and he nodded slightly and squinted up his eyes. I honked the sucker out by slapping down hard on the forearm holding the clamp and like a rotten apple off a tree, it just slid out. Wow, I was one happy medic. I actually did something good and entirely new with no real problems or effort.

Back on Tomahawk we could see paddy land – miles of it. We could see several mountain ranges and major ridge lines marching to the sea.

155

After dark we watched the entire battalion's AO from above on our mountain fort. This ancient land really had a unique attraction.

Several nights in a row Charlie Company blew ambushes close to Highway 1 and near the Song Bu Lu River. As A Company laid back to watch, tracers sprayed up and out like electric pin point water streams from a lawn sprinkler. Two miles below us red or blue green dots followed one another in slow motion. At first the night was silent. A minute later the 'knock, knock, knock' of a 60 would sound. Fire fights often mimicked a rifle range exercise. A solitary 'pop, pop, pop' would start, then a crescendo, and finally a few scattered bursts once again, then silence.

While we watched, Wolfgang and his platoon lit into a twenty-five-man NVA element. The NVA walked right into the platoon's kill zone.

Charlie Company had a butcher for a Kit Carson Scout. He gathered intelligence the old fashion way – at the point of a knife. Charlie Company was top dog in the battalion for body counts because of it.

The Screaming Eagles let them come within 30 meters before blowing off fifteen claymores all at once. Then they assaulted. Wolfgang stood and the entire platoon got on line. Like an American Civil War battle, the two groups merged. Wolf was sweating and firing from the hip. He felt invincible. The GIs crossed the road and then the railway tracks. Wolf picked up an AK and continued firing with an assault weapon in each hand. The owner of the AK another notch to Wolf's body count.

Wolfgang remembers the lowland ambushes: "It was a total obsession of killing gooks. I loved laying in complete anticipation, watching for a trip flare to ignite. I loved scanning with the starlight scope and turning the night into day. I loved a good turkey shoot, catching Charlie with his pants down over and over again. I lived for the high of adrenaline surging and pumping through my veins. My total intent was to make the other guy die for his country. They died like dogs. It was a slaughter with no remorse."

Wolf was a killer, no doubt about it. He was in at least twenty firefights of at least several minutes duration and in countless thirty-second type shoot outs. By the middle of 1969 it was rumored he had fifteen pairs of ears to prove that many kills, but probably more like thirty or forty was his score.

Later, on the night of January 16, 1969, we watched C Company follow up an ambush by walking artillery rounds through the running men. The enemy couldn't get away.

In the morning we drove over the Thu Luu bridge and watched the neat row of eighteen dead soldiers simmer in the heat. I waved at Wolfgang as we drove by and saw many in our truck were avoiding looking at the bodies. I wanted to stand up and fire a twenty-round burst I was so stoked. A couple of women walked among the dead.

Plato: "The only end of war is for the dead."

Chapter 37

Forced March

Once again we were up on Tomahawk and a bunch of the old timers left the unit. They DEROSed, and gladly.

One late afternoon we got the word to ruck-up and at dusk found ourselves trudging down Highway 1 south-east out of the base. It looked like the whole battalion was on the move.

We left the road at the bottom of the hills and struck out north for the Song Bu Lu River. I was tired just from walking down the road and by 21:00 was ready to set up for the night like usual. But no, we stood around and waited for the platoon leaders to orientate themselves among the maze of hamlets, sloughs and deep irrigation ditches we faced. By 02:30 we were still humping and word came back down the column we had to cross a one-man bridge. When my turn came, I knew I was going to fall off the thing ... I just knew it. I got ready to chuck my gear, for damn if I was going to drown. It all depended on getting the equipment off; the ruck and pistol belt and keeping them from snagging on something under water.

The bridge was a tied bundle of three or four bamboo poles for walking and another single pole, almost waist high, as a hand rail. These were supported by crossed tripod poles planted in the ditch. That was it! At night the footing was about as sure as walking down a banister with a cane, blindfolded. About half-way across (it was so dark everything was by feel) the bridge started shaking. Something or somebody was either on the bridge or in the water. Vertigo grabbed me by the senses and threatened to spin me off into the dark. No landmarks were visible. Nothing to key on to avoid disorientation, I kept feeling like I was leaning too far into the single rail, and it would give way at some point, by bending or breaking and forcing me to fall over into the sky-black water. Wasn't a thing to hold onto except the one pole. You could smell the water. Something slapped the surface underneath me. The footbridge shook and something big seemed to be rubbing against the supports. Sweat ran into my eyes and down my collar. I could smell my own fear and it smelled dead.

Once safely on shore we waited for Wolfgang's company to cross. Men filed past us, not knowing we were resting next to the trail. John Wolfgang had just crossed over when suddenly he heard a muffled cry, "HELP!"

I heard a Godforsaken splash that could be only one thing. The slow current gurgled for a second then was silent. No one knew where he fell, and whoever it was, was gone in an instant. I couldn't understand why a guy couldn't at least have a good chance, pull the quick release on the ruck's straps, undo the web gear and at least be able to call out again. Unless ... unless a crocodile, a native of the brackish water in the lowlands and one of the largest and deadliest animals alive, a kind of mean-spirited killer whale with arms and legs, had been waiting all this time underwater with his jaws open for one of us to fall off. I'd seen alligators in Florida just waiting, open mouthed, underwater, staring barking dogs down just wishing the doggie would come a little bit closer. But crocs were way meaner!

Their company commander was pissed off; seemed at the moment the most important factor was the lost M-16. Nevermind the never-to-be-found soldier.

At first light we were slogging up the ankle-deep Song Bu Lu towards Hill 184. All day we humped; past the graveyards, rice paddies and in the late afternoon, cut trail through the boulder strewn and thick brush of the saddle between Hill 184 and the Loc Thuy mountains. We were beat, disgusted and filthy.

As we dropped down over the saddle into the low lands and beach, we crossed paddies and fresh water, clear streams with deep holes in, under and through fresh grass waving with the current. I wanted desperately to jump in but realized that this was finally the end of the line. Our platoon was the last element to set up a massive cordon (human trap) that wrapped the foot hills for miles. But we didn't give a flying douche bag. All we wanted to do was drop rucks. We'd just humped, with full gear, twenty-four stinking hours non-stop and were 'bushed', literally.

The night passed quietly and we bagged nothing in our extended net. I knew I wanted out of this line company, if for no other reason than a change. We couldn't win a war humping around like we were doing.

Chapter 38

Vanishing Point

Another time, another day the shadow of the Bac Ma spread over Phu Loc and the flats around Highway 1 and the paddies where we were operating. We got a call. A LRP team or somebody had spotted an enemy camp up in the hills. However, instead of flying, we were to walk. The element of surprise, you know. We crossed over the highway and after an hour or so started to climb. The word came back down our file to look out for booby traps; we were going right up a damn trail and without any kind of blocking force to help or make the move worthwhile. Some surprise this would be, I cursed! Anybody could see where we were headed. The terrain turned to tall trees and jungle smothering a massive ravine. We were strung out in column as usual and finally stopped. I guessed the point element was checking something out. Standing in the hot sun had me pissed off. Most of my tour had been spent waiting on some stinking trail. The days were usually a series of hump and wait, hump and wait. I hardly ever knew what the object of our blundering over the countryside was. Usually, I just prayed the next rest stop would be the last and we could set up for the night. This constant stop or go agony never stopped. It was always a gamble as to how long we would stop. It was taking a chance to plop on my butt and relieve the dead weight cutting into both shoulders. The bitch of it was that it took so much effort to get back on your feet again. It was often better to endure the full load kicking your ass and just stand in the trail. The game was to guess if the stop would be long or short. If you had to crawl to your feet as soon as you touched down, you lost miserably. If you relaxed in the dirt and maybe even got a bit to eat, you won a major victory.

I'd just located a place to crash when the column started back up the trail. I hadn't sat down or rested, but hadn't had to get up. I stood like an idiot. Call it a draw.

We walked into an NVA base camp. The move reminded me of a Zoro movie with Mexicans (us) chasing the 'fox'. By the time we pulled in it was deserted of course.

What a hideout it was! Gargantuan boulders four stories high, wedged into a narrow creek forcing the water to form deep pools and waterfalls around the rocks. The camp was a semi-exposed cave system with dark miniature lakes tucked under the boulders. A small army could have hidden out and survived a point-blank naval bombardment from the *New Jersey*'s 16-inch guns. Left behind were bamboo sleeping platforms, some wedged in the crevices above the creek while others lay next to the water. Tall trees grew thickly over the whole ravine, hiding the place from the air. I imagined the soldiers lying in bed and reaching out to dip water. In the gravel stream swollen rice grains could be seen.

We humped up the ravine leaving the complex behind, up and over the ridge top and down the other side into the paddies and flat land. It was miserable going as we'd already been on the move since early morning. The men's feet were a mess. On the way up the mountain, right on our trail, I started finding M-79 rounds. One of the grenadiers was throwing out grenades to lighten his load. I was disgusted with this line company attitude; the shithead might as well have left the rounds in a neat row back at the boulders. I picked some up and handed them to one of the squad leaders. The enemy would love to get those rounds, as surely as they were … following us.

Walking down to the flats and the ocean I started to notice familiar landmarks. I was sure we were near the village by the sea where I had extracted the old man's tooth. The beautiful village with the banana plants and sampans pulled up on the shore.

At the water's edge A Company barely managed a staggered death march around a brush covered point. On the other side was the village, I was pretty sure. I could make out the boulders and plateau where we camped before. We broke from the brush and at first I thought my mental navigation was off. I thought we had missed the village until we started walking over fresh bulldozer tracks. My equilibrium reeled as it took me several minutes to realize the horror of it all. The banana trees, huts, boats, people, general vegetation and any sign of life was scorched and Rhome plowed under. They'd buried the damn place! I was in shock. How must the people who'd lived here feel? Where were they? Where was the little surfer boy? We'd shot and killed them before – no reason not to believe they were all three feet under right now. Jesus Christ … we'd really fucked them up this time. Baked bare earth was the answer. Was that still part of Plan A or now Plan C, the final 'solution'.

Slumped over, I stared at the ground and just put one foot in front of another. I tried to make myself believe the NVA had burned the village and our engineers had leveled the wreckage. But that didn't make sense. Fuck it … didn't mean nothing!

We dragged our sorry asses up Route 1 and back onto Fire Base Tomahawk. The medics from A Company herded into formation to get our CMBs (Combat Medic Bagdes) from our new battalion commander LTC Dyke, self-named Ramrod.

About this time Wolfgang, elsewhere on the base, got his Article 15 for his fishing expedition, lost a stripe and was fined $101.

Photographers snapped our pictures and Ramrod passed out the medals. When he got to me and as he shook my hand he started into me about something on my upper lip. He expected us to shave for the shindig.

"What's this?" he asked.

Instead of telling the man I didn't shave yet, I told him I was too busy treating the men's feet for rot and trench foot, which a lot of us had. I took the easy way out not wanting to argue with this jerk.

I was glad to get the CMB; it meant something. But this colonel sapped what glamour I associated with the event. The photographers recorded the dismal spectacle and my 'mustache' looking about as slick as a snail's tail and my helmet cocked back at a rakish angle like some Greek hero.

Chapter 39

The Hawks

The last I saw of the 3rd platoon was up on Los Banos. I told the medical platoon sergeant I wanted in the recon platoon and he agreed. The aid station on Los Banos was built into and among a slew of two-storey boulders. I'd helped lay flooring inside for Dr. Paisley, our new battalion doctor. I had even gone so far as to suggest that work around the aid station probably wouldn't kill me. The aid station would be the safe place to be but I knew it wouldn't work out. Boonie rat medics were out of place in the rear, and I felt better in the field. I considered the fire bases the rear but that didn't mean they were safe by any means.

Over at my platoon, 3rd Herd's CP bunker, I left some of my line doggie junk. I got rid of one set of rain gear that LTC Dyke had ceremoniously given me in the middle of a rain storm after I was already soaked completely. He made a big deal in front of everyone, taking off his gear and handing them over. An extra waterproof bag went and the air mattress as well. I wanted to lighten up like a real commando. Somebody from the platoon asked me, "Who's going to look after us, Doc?"

I didn't know and frankly I was glad to get away from Alpha Company. So far we hadn't fought anybody and managed to get plenty of us killed or wounded doing it. Stewart, Rebel Odom, Havorka, Sergeant Clark, Granny, Sergeant Rock from San Jose, White Boy and the rest would be but fond memories now. But many of the 3rd Herd boys were long ago transferred into the Hawk Recon so we would meet again.

A few days later I walked into the recon platoon's CP. They were out in the open, exposed and in the middle of paddy land. They were not hiding at all – possibly waiting for me. It had to be 100 degrees out.

When their short, white medic, whom I'd never seen before, left, he was so happy he kept looking over his shoulder to make sure I was still in the CP, and hadn't changed my mind or bolted! I was staying and he was leaving. The platoon had about twenty people, maybe twenty-five then. We were on our own most of the time. When I joined up we were below Los Banos, about half a mile south of the road.

I introduced myself to Lieutenant Good, the recon leader, again to Fellows and Richard Lappin, the RTOs. I'd seen them around somewhere before. Lieutenant Good not only had a name like mine, he looked like me; tall, skinny, short hair and glasses. Fellows immediately engaged me with questions about who was where and what was up with A Company. Fellows was tall, big and almost good looking – the typical Southern Californian. He was a surfer and had a wise ass but pleasant personality and was fun to be around. John Wolfgang, who must have been in every company in the battalion at one point, was back in the unit. I'd heard stories about him and knew we'd get along. A lot of my buddies from 3rd platoon who'd come over to recon with Viney were still here. Present were: Bollinger, Joe Mann, Nelson Ramos, JJ Smith, Danny Shaw, Dennis 'The Eskimo' Sinka (actually an Indian from Holy Cross on the Yukon River), Bob Crouch the FO Sergeant, Hass, Chico Guiterrez, TJ Wersman, Stearns, Triplet, Dan Hickman, Murphy, Robert Culver and Ron Hutchins also known as 'Cowboy,' and others. Long gone were the old time Hawks like Richard Knight and Pee Wee Dobbs, Skip Peppie, Walter Jackson, 'Lurch' Hickman, Sergeant Brown, Doc Brown, Doc White and Spanky. I was the only medic. I was the medical commander of the unit.

Over the years the Hawk Recon saw a bevy of famous and really tough men. The likes of Alan Lloyd, George Fallon, Bob Martin, and medic Jay Molyneaux. These men found themselves in the Hawks and in an all night battle! Surrounded Alan Loyd lost an eye and a leg from tossing grenades back and forth, but continued fighting, all night, while bleeding to death! At some point George Fallon was able to get to Lloyd, stop the bleeding, and save Alan's life. Both were awarded Silver Stars years later!

However, one of the most famous all-around Ranger, LRP and Hawk was Lester 'Super Spade' Hite. Lester was notorious as a team leader in the 101st Airborne Ranger company!

The first thing we did was to get the hell out of the sun and try to hide. We cut into the wood line and an area that was a mixture of lush bamboo groves, scattered huts and creeks, and awesome 40 ft high bridges with steps spanning wide emerald waterways. In short, a wonderland; a Japanese tea garden gone wild.

This was it. I had arrived about as far down the line as I would get. The Hawk Recon was as bad a crowd as the 2/327th had. They wore boonie hats, knives of all descriptions, camo fatigues and humped commando M-16s or rifles with wicked, long, black Sionics sound suppressors looking like big silencers.

We camped out in the backyard and inside of someone's house next to a bamboo grove and bank above a still stream. As soon as I could I snuck off by myself and dropped into the coolness behind the house. Naked, I soaked in the clear yellow-tinted water.

In a few minutes the wildlife settled down and started to move around me. Mud skippers walked out of the water on tiny legs. Eyes popped up and watched me. I stared back and suddenly realized the water under the brush on the opposite bank was crawling with crocodiles. Holy shit! These were small ones, but I'd had enough. Small ones meant big ones somewhere. These were not caimans. I crawled up the bank and put my clothes on.

Chapter 40

Fix Bayonets … the Ballad of Hawk Hill

Back around May 1968, the Hawks were out near FSB Bastogne, near the A Shau and Delta Junction area. I heard the story when I first tried to get into Hawk Recon. Later Rick Knight told me all about it.

It was deadly ass country, full of enemy, storage areas and NVA base camps. The battalion had finally cleared Highway 547 all the way into the A Shau. But sometime in May an NVA team had ambushed one of our tanks on Heart Break Curve. The Hawks hit the boonies!

Afterwards, the handsome head RTO Rick Knight, who had picked up the hilarious nick-name 'Gook', perhaps to show nobody was at all prejudiced, spent the night in heavy terrain and jungle with the Hawks as usual. Rick usually packed a case and a half of Lurp rations.

The heavy recon killer team was spooked, but after forty days straight of hunting NVA they were highly pissed, too. And it was getting spookier and spookier. They had been out too long already – getting resupplied every six days. They were mad but finally found what they were looking for. It was kind of hard to miss. This was Beckwith's style: long range roving and recon hunting, patterned after Merril's Marauders of Burma. The Hawks simply stayed in the boonies longer than any other unit in the war. Way longer than any LRP or SOG team. Of the three recon platoons of 1st Brigade 101st, the Hawks were said to be the only one never wiped out. Tiger Force was and the Reconds of the 2/502 were rumored to have all been shot through the nifty black berets they wore.

Anyway, the problem of 'camping out' where they were was that it was next to, and almost in, a seventy-man, occupied, and bunkered enemy base camp!

The Hawks had found, and been following, heavy telephone commo wire with porcelain insulators for five days and I guess didn't realize they had found the terminus. The old Hawks had highly developed 'jungle smarts' and noise discipline. They knew the enemy were near and Charger knew they were near. They could actually 'feel' them. They just didn't know how close they were. However, they cooked two meals and, even as quiet as they were, it was clearly suicidal – but they did it anyway. Dinner and breakfast. Screw the consequences. The Hawks attitude was: attack and kill anything then back-off if necessary ... if possible.

Long before sunrise the team was packed up, site cleared, and ready to go.

Squawk ... hiss ... Rick whispered into his handset: "Romeo element is floating at this time."

Rick, his buddy Tony Chavez and J. Gaurin rucked up. Rick felt the familiar weight of the ruck and reassured himself the SOI code book and his ever-present Dr Grabow pipe were still all aboard ... in his jungle jacket. The 2/327th's 'Foreign Legion' slipped through the bush in characteristically filthy 'iron red' mud-stained 'striker' or tiger fatigues often mixed with US woodland pattern or French/Korean 'duck hunter' cammo. Included were customized boonie hats and assorted exotic weapons.

At that instant an NVA AA crew was changing shifts on a 12.7 RPD heavy machine gun on their perimeter.

With Gaurin on point, the Hawks slithered out a mere 25 yards when the head RTO suddenly saw two NVA getting down in position to pull guard behind a tripod mounted AA gun. Rick couldn't fire because point and the column was directly between him and the NVA regulars. Point was almost stepping on them. The US and NVA groups had bivouacked right next to one another all night.

The NVA had no clue a Canadian ex-British Royal Marine Commando, Lieutenant Anthony Harbord and his dirty two dozen were penetrating their base camp.

Rick immediately sat down behind a tree. He flinched, dreading the 1st shot. Gaurin was 5ft away from the NVA troops and still nothing happened. Rick couldn't believe it. He knew the proverbial shit was going to destroy the fan.

Suddenly Gaurin stiffened and moved like Frankenstein – he tromped forward and shot both North Vietnamese dead ... point blank, like a good point man should!

Rick was ready, he screamed: "One four, one four Romeo element in contact! I'll keep you informed ... OUT!"

Rick later explained:

"I wanted to let the TOC commandos know we were in the shit BIG TIME – so by violating my normal excellent radio procedure ... they'd get the message.

You could hear the firing and deep thump of a heavy machine gun ... behind my somewhat strained voice over the open mic back in the headquarters TOC bunker."

Beckwith was listening! He grabbed the horn, "Niner Stubbs ... this is Cross Palms-one four. Did you roger Romeos X-ray?"

"Most affirm ... one four ... he said heez en contact!"

"Okay ... Niner Stubbs ... go help him out. Get in the ballpark ... FAST!"

Beckwith was calling somebody ... probably one of our company elements not too far away. LTC Beckwith – an ex-college football player who was drafted by Green Bay would more than once refer to firefight strategy, on the radio, in sport jargon ... an effective code.

A cacophony of US weapons and enemy AKs reverberated through the tall and ancient forest and blasted the smell of flashed gunpowder – strong enough to taste. Enemy projectiles eventually started ripping up the greenery around the advancing Hawk Recon. Grass right alongside the face or chest of the Hawks just snipped off and toppled to the ground. The FO took a bad hit in the shoulder and dropped his handset. For a second the officer's RTO panicked and Rick the command RTO screamed at him to pick up the horn. In seconds, however, the Hawks warmed up to the battle while their RTOs called in artillery.

Rick remembers feeling, after ten months in the field, the least scared of any firefight he'd been in. He calmly narrated the events to Charger – like a major league radio announcer during the fight.

The Hawks quickly overran the camp and regrouped back to let air strikes and 8-inch shells work out on the still entrenched NVA. The 'red legs' said to pull back 100 meters but of course that was out of the question. The recondos might have pulled back 100ft, but most likely it was 20ft.

During the airstrike the Hawks took their only KIA ... their aggressiveness cost them, but probably saved the day, protecting them in the long run. John W. Bowden was killed by a 500lb USAF bomb.

Rick reported the WIA and the KIA back to Charger.

"We got one Dogwood 8 and one Dogwood 6!"

After a quick artillery and air support shut-off the entire recon platoon saddled up, got on line and assaulted the newly claimed 'Hawk Hill'. Lieutenant Harbord gave the order, "fix bayonets!" Just like the British facing a wall of spear-chucking, charging Africans!

Bayonets snapped into place below and around flash suppressors (even 12-gauge shotguns took on bayonets) and the Hawks ran the survivors clean out of their bunkers leaving weapons, cooked rice, tables and chairs behind. I don't know if Charger ordered 'Fix Bayonets' this time, but that was his style as per his call sign. Tony Chavez and Rick Knight carried Bowden's body in the charge up the hill and past a mess hall, rec. area and sleeping positions.

The Hawks dropped rucks and settled into their hill. Cameras came out and Rick posed with a new SKS carbine – shiny bayonet extended and Dr Grabow proudly displayed it. Pee Wee Dobbs was photographed as was Pete Rossi. Doc Brown, the fighting medic, posed proudly. The men counted eleven bodies left behind and Rick got the word over the radio from Charger:

"Hey Tony," Rick announced so all could hear. "Charger says to hang our boonie hats on eleven dinks KIA."

But the mission wasn't quite over yet. Charger ordered them back to FSB Bastogne the hard way. On foot!

On the sixty-second day of the mission Lieutenant Harbord, always with a touch for the dramatic, ordered his men to smear on a heavy coat of green and black war paint. They were going to breach and enter Bastogne's perimeter wire for the first time in a very long time.

With jungle jackets rotting and falling apart off their backs they waded the vodka clear creek at the water point road. The stream eroded the ground below the hilly FSB. As they strode into the base, standing proud and feeling victorious, all the REMFs stood up and gawked.

That evening as the dust settled around the Hawks and their beat up gear – out came the bowls and fresh dew. Miller time for the juicers and weed washed down with beer for the heads and freaks.

That night the boys watched an odd trail of fire leading into the fire base, the one they created after Beckwith ordered them to "Burn the God Damn jungle down!" on the way into the base.

Orders were orders, so out came the thermite grenades, fuel tabs, Zippos and green C-rat match books.

That concluded a sixty-two-day mission that had to be a record for the war. Nobody did that except possibly the original Green Beret Project Delta commanded by no other than Charlie 'Charger' Beckwith!

Chapter 41

Phantoms and Wolves

My first mission with the Hawks was up the Bac Ma, above the Lang Co bridge. We saddled up in a tiny valley inland from the highway. I was glad to get off the road, as it was hazardous to your health.

When we had humped up Highway 1 to the trailhead, we were headed up the north side of the notorious Hai Van Pass. The road was loaded with everything from tanks on flatbed trucks to Honda 50s.

I noticed one large Army truck parked and its driver thrashing away underneath his shut-down diesel. I wandered over to see what was wrong and got a glimpse of a young girl underneath him with her eyes closed. For a second, I thought the worst, then backed away finally remembering we had camp followers around here.

Across the road from the start of the trail we rested in the grass, grateful to leave the mad rush. A nice salt breeze dried the sweat in our hair. We looked straight down into Lang Co village and a fine view of the beach, all the way to Hue. We made a point of ignoring the group of 'jar-heads' standing around below us about 40ft away. Just when we thought it was safe, I noticed, almost too late, that they were armed. Marines with guns – always a dangerous sign. Suddenly the one with the 12-gauge pump shotgun tensed and his buddy threw a foam cup into the wind. As the cup left the dude's hand the wind caught it and it flew back and directly over Fellows, Wolfgang and me. As the trap-shooter spun around and drew a bead on my head, his eyes locked on the cup, I tried to open my mouth and scream. No time to duck. No time to think. No time to scream … it was time to die.

Blammo! Double 'O' man-killing buckshot followed the foam cup past our ears.

Holy Cow!

A squad of droopy jawed Marines watched us quickly but methodically haul ass and scamper back to the road. At the side of the highway Wolf slowly turned towards the sportsters. As Wolf turned, his M-16 swung around pointing down at the Marines. We left them looking like a gang of hillbillies who'd just found Granny face down in the cement pond.

The Kit Carsons didn't want to go. Minh and Di were usually pretty good soldiers. Today they rolled around on the ground holding their stomachs. I could not believe Lieutenant Good called for me to check them out. I ignored the idea. Everyone knew nothing was wrong with them. It was pathetic. If Lieutenant Good had offered a three-day pass to the first one to get rid of these gooks the whole platoon would have opened up and wasted them right on the spot.

We started up the trail on a ridge line. The terrain behind us dropped away into the South China Sea. To our front were the rock cliffs showing throughout the jungle, the upper Bac Ma, our destination. Some of the peaks were 8,000ft plus and once we even saw the tops through the branches along the trail. Clouds hovered over most of the summit. This was the sanctuary of the NVA. We entered the rain forest. Minh and Di dragged ass at the very rear.

The Hawks climbed all morning, ate lunch, then climbed some more. At mid-afternoon, almost on top of the ridge we were climbing, we came to a hole ripped through the trees. Debris littered the whole scene, it covered the ground, it hung in the trees, it was everywhere. At first it looked like pieces of paper. It looked like we were standing in the parking lot of K-mart on a windy Saturday near the Mexican border. Trash was piled high everywhere in odd-sized shapes. A lot of the garbage was thin metal. What the hell happened here, I wondered. Then I saw one. The mutilated body lay at the bottom of a shallow draw 300ft down from us. I could see through the trees that its wings were ripped off. Two F-4s had clipped the top of the peak and together, flown into the mountain with one of the Phantoms still upright.

Wolf was the team leader of the point element and remembers:

"The mountains were extremely high, with little sign that defoliant had been used. The weather was near the 100-degree mark with humidity so heavy it was hard to breathe. My 90lb rucksack kicked my ass every step of the way. Shortly upon leaving the small valley by the road we received information over the PRC-25 that an Air Force jet was down somewhere in our area. The information was vague. All we knew was that the jet was an F-4C or D model. The men were pissed off because everyone wanted a piece of Charlie's ass. We made contact with trail watchers and this indicated that Charlie was attempting to change our course. The gook smell was strong, very strong. It had the habit of making the hair on a man's neck stand straight up. We were making our way up the ridge, usual stuff, one foot in front of the other in mud or clouds of dust.

"I first noticed an unusual opening in the canopy and instantly observed a large part of an American jet fuselage which seemed to contain and spread miles of electrical wiring. The crash site was largely scattered. A single parachute had been deployed high in the canopy. Upon the squad's dispersion we moved in for a closer look. We didn't know what to expect. There were no signs of life, emergency equipment and no signal devices activated.

"Up near the chute there appeared to be an orange tape textured substance with a lot of flies being attracted to it. I then recognized it to be the intestines of a human due to past combat experience. The mood of my squad became fairly intense. As the radio operator notified the lieutenant, we began our search for the remains of possibly one or more persons.

"My first finding was that of a human leg severed from below the knee, partially clothed with the boot intact and a knife still in place. My next find was that of a human hand; the left hand was severed midway from the elbow. This hand had a gold wedding band on the ring finger. The flesh and bone was intact. There were other body parts found by other members of the platoon as they advanced to the site. As others secured a defensive position another squad cleared an LZ for extraction of the remains. We were all very mad due to the fact that we were unable to locate any of the officers' heads or any form of ID. The enemy had most likely deprived us of the complete recovery of the remains.

"A squad went down to probe around the fuselage and wreckage. I didn't want any part of it. I didn't want to see any dead people or mess with any unexploded bombs. I had quite enough bombs, exploded and unexploded. The squad returned and I heard somebody found a boot with a foot in it. Terrific!

"What we had was a mountain range that sucked A/C in like fly paper all during the war. Navy pilots used to finding a carrier in bad weather would sometimes emergency divert into Da Nang. The fact that the air base was on the coast belied the big picture, which was: Da Dang was surrounded with sierra 'stratagranitus'. More than one airman had flown into the tree tops, at first thinking the pitter-patter on his nose to be rain or hail before discovering he was flying through a forest without his wings. Once, a Crusader landed in Da Nang with its rockets ripped off, covered with green stains and the radome gone. Also gone was the pilot's wingman who had been right under him. The wingman had ejected after finding himself in the classic pilot's nightmare: flying through, but not seeing the forest for the trees."

Chapter 42

Malaria Madness

We waited at the F-4 crash site for the resupply chopper. B Company had already joined us after humping up the mountain. It looked as though we were in a hot area. Well used trails, footprints and an eerie feeling that hung over the place like a plague convinced me.

Stearns, the tall, slow-eyed youngster came over to me and complained of a high temperature. I broke out a thermometer and found that indeed he had a temperature of over 103 degrees.

"Jesus Christ! What's wrong with you, Stearns?"

"Well, I think it's malaria, Doc. I've had it before," he said.

"You got malaria and you're out here humping a ruck? That's crazy! What did they do to ya last time?" I asked.

"Sent me to Japan then right back to Nam. Said I might get it again once in a while."

"Well, sona-va-bitch, you're not humping the bush no more, I can tell ya that! Not with a 103-degree temp."

"But Doc, the battalion doctor sent me out himself."

"Well, no shit. But get this – I'm in charge out here. I'm the fucking battalion doctor out here in this unit and you are going in on this bird. That guy is an asshole. You've got to hold your ground on this shit. You tell him, if I see you out here ever again, first I'll shoot you between the eyes then I'm gonna kill that dipshit in the rear. Fucking REMF anyway."

Stearns was a nice guy. The kind of person that tends to take a lot of pushing around before he flips out. Doc Smitty, one of the old Hawk medics now with Bravo, came over and said, "Just give him some aspirin. He's okay."

"Bullshit! That grunt's goin' in," I replied. End of conversation.

176

Meanwhile, one of Bravo's platoons was humping up a trail on patrol. They ran dead assed into a NVA force. The point elements of the two groups shot it out. I was sitting in the shade relaxing when they opened up. Just a few short bursts at first.

POP, POP, POP … POPOPOPOPOPOPOPOPOPOP went the AKs. BLAMBLAMBLAMBLAMBLAM the 16s answered. They were close to us.

"Must be Bravo," I said, checking to see my weapon was near.

"Yeah, wake me up when the chopper comes in, will ya Doc?" Stearns was laid out underneath a huge log, in the shade, up against his ruck with his grenade launcher propped up against a limb. The guy acted like he was in his bedroom back in the world.

The sound of the chopper, faint at first, got louder. Later its steady WOP, WOP, WOP, WOP indicated it was in a hover up the ridge aways. The aircrew were pulling bodies out of the canopy! It wasn't the resupply ship but a medivac for Bravo. Bravo's Kit Carson had taken a round through the head and they had some other wounded. When the air ambulance pulled off, the silence closed in around us, save for the clicking and chirping of insects in the hot afternoon sun. Minh and little Di were right, this was a bad place. I scanned the wall of green around us for movement.

Chapter 43

Monsoon Come!

The Huey swung in and landed on the LZ made by the crashed jets. It was a squeeze. I made damn sure Stearns got on along with all the fliers' body parts we could find. The crew threw out a few boxes of C-rats and some radio batteries and no one questioned Stearns or asked for a boarding pass ... as if such a thing existed. We rucked up and made ready to push up the mountain some more.

"If ya fuck up, ya ruck up," Fellows hissed out the REMF phrase to no one in particular. We entered the forbidden forest. It was cooler and darker immediately, in the unscarred jungle. It started to rain. After fifteen minutes of walking, we passed where Bravo had its shoot out. We kept going. It got even darker and the rain came down harder. We were soaked to the skin, half rain, half sweat. Just before dark the lieutenant called a halt and we set up on NDP right on the trail. Cowboy, one of the squad leaders, stood next to me in the gloom and bitched.

"Just fucking great! Sir Charles will come diddy bopping down this tango and before I know what's happening, he'll be in my position telling me to move over."

Cowboy was from Utah and a tall, lanky, real cowboy.

Some of us rolled up inside our poncho and poncho liner. I found this worked if you placed the snapped together seam underneath you and tucked the foot end under like a burrito. I lay in the dirt of the trail and slept dry as a cockroach with the rain gently tattooing my back all night.

During the darkness a full-blown tropical typhoon smashed into I Corps and I didn't even know it.

The next day we wisely moved off the trail and I put up a hootch between two small trees and hung my hammock and poncho liner under the outstretched poncho. After dragging my ruck and aid bag under cover I quickly tore off the soaking jungle jacket and hurriedly pulled the jungle sweater on. The sweater was part wool and I was freezing. After that I changed into my spare pair of socks and felt almost comfortable.

It rained for three days and nights straight. I either lay or sat in my hammock the whole time, getting up occasionally to piss. On the third day we all ran out of food. Guys crawled from position-to-position begging for food: anything, even peanut butter tins. Everyone had camouflaged their hootch with fan palms, leaves or branches. Lieutenant Good couldn't get a chopper in for resupply, so we sat it out.

Finally, I had to take a crap. It was pouring rain and around 02:00. What to do? Looking around my hootch I could make out the silhouette of my machete stuck in the mud. Still slung in the hammock, I clamped my hand around the handle and started digging underneath me. The waterlogged soil yielded easily and soon I had a deep if narrow hole. I turned sideways in the netting, hung my butt over the side and tried to relax. Finally … bombs away! Direct hit, dead center. Simply scraping a bit of earth to fill in the latrine tidied up the whole mess. Like shitting down a gopher hole. Underneath me lay an entombed turd, sealed and sanitary, US government inspected and medically approved. A new boonie rat trick was invented that morning. What a life! One didn't even have to get out of bed to take a dump. Life was a bowl of cherries. Or was that a body bag of cherries?

The sun came out! When a log ship finally got to us Wolfgang left; the battalion rover was off to another company.

North-east of the Bac Ma was our new course, all downhill. We treated ourselves to a glimpse of heaven through the trees. Far down below a rainbow straddled a gorgeous little river valley. Suddenly it dawned on me. I knew this place! We were going back to the Sea Bee Camp.

The camp was about the same and after we dug in and redid some of the bunkers the Hawks posed for a group photo sitting on a pile of sand bags.

Chapter 44

A Buck Knife Christmas

Christmas 1968

Christmas Day we spent with the Navy. I tried to make it seem special since the next day would be my 21st birthday. I would turn 21 in a foreign land and be able to drink beer while I smoked weed and killed people. Great! I couldn't wait.

Lappin passed out mail as usual and I got a couple of packages from home. In one, from Dad, was the longest, biggest, meanest knife that the Buck knife company made. This honey was called 'The General'. We couldn't believe they delivered our packages and mail in time for Christmas. My knife was the greatest gift. Later, on the black handle I carved the words: Airborne, Hawk Recon, 101st, 2/327th, and then the name of a young lady I would meet in Japan. Mieko was her name and showing soldiers a good time was her game. Her nickname was 'Dynamite Pussy'. Like the saying of the time, she was dynamite and outta sight. I also got a can of homemade cookies from Mom and a red yo-yo which everyone had to try out.

My knife came in a black holster – like the one for the .45 I carried ... only narrower. I used the blade every day. It was heavy enough to cut down small trees like a miniature machete.

All Hawks carried knives including the Gerber MkII, Puma, Randall and the famous K-Bar, the Marine's official fighting knife made by Camillus. Of course, we also had the Army's M-6 and M-7 bayonet series which fit on the M-14 and M-16. Another interesting weapon was the Sykes Fairborne commando dagger. The Fairborne, being perhaps

180

the most evil looking stiletto ever made, was a favorite of the British. Just eyeballing one revealed its only possible function: killing human beings.

The Buck Company made a Bowie knife which is our famous American fighting blade, but my 'General' was a badass looker and a little longer than the Buck Bowie, but still a Bowie design. For years, Buck ran ads showing a hammer pounding one of its products through a steel bolt. It is a good, inexpensive knife.

One of the Hawks carried a Gurkha Kukri, the oblong, dog-legged, sinister boomerang-looking giant razor. With it came a neat collection of baby Kukris, tiny all-around tools, holstered on the sheath. The Kukri, chopper, was turned out by craftsmen from Nepal. The hilt was animal horn from India and the edged blade was forged on ancient bellows and foot-powered grinding wheels. The hilt and blade were not secured with a guard, while the wood scabbard was covered tightly in stretched black leather. 200 Kukris a month was about an average yield from the workshops.

The Randall was an especially nice tool. All were hand made and developed for survival, fighting or hunting. Randall's leather handled standard was a wolf in sheep's clothing; long and wicked, it was very popular. Randalls made in Florida had a special astronaut model and an air crew survival model plus a diver's knife. The classic survival knife is easily recognized by its saw top edge for trying to cut through Plexiglass aircraft canopies and windshields. The sharpening stone and snap pouch on the sheath are also well known. This style was issued to all flight crews in the Air Force, but was manufactured by someone other than Randall who was the original designer I believe. The cheap AF knives were poor substitutes, brittle and small. They looked real pretty on a survival vest, however.

Puma knives were exotic looking and the double-edged daggers the Green Berets favored, the Gerber MkII combat knife was a fine machine.

Another Bowie, carried by the Hawk's platoon sergeant was the elephantine Western W-49, a wooden-handled, brass-guarded sucker with a thick blade that looked good for chopping fish heads.

The most famous blade of the war was the legendary SOG 'sterile' Bowie – custom forged in Japan. It was awarded to the top graduate of Recondo school and some times found its way into the clutches of the 101st's LRPs. An evil, bad luck curse some said followed the weapon so it was rarely seen in the field.

Chapter 45

Air Cav Cowboys

A day or so after departing the Sea Bee Camp the men got up as usual, before even the faintest hint of a dawn. I rolled over and slept on.

A Bird Dog (0-2-A) twin Cessna pilot made his preflight and taxied, already in possession of a take-off clearance. He knew he'd soon have his own private sunrise. The tanks were topped off, his M-16 was in the rack behind his seat and he had a full load of smoke rockets. The Zoomie captain cursed his luck for providing him with a 337 Cessna Skymaster for his first combat ride. The things were unlovingly called a 'suck and blow', and sometimes worse.

The recon soldiers moved out and I was still grabbing my shit so I wouldn't be left behind. I became tail-end Charlie out in the flats, a good target for snipers.

Good and Lappin paused up ahead, not waiting for their medic, but talking on the radio. The 'bug smasher' Bird Dog was overhead in the sunlight. The pilot informed Lieutenant Good, whose codename was Peepers 46, that gooks were all over the place right in front of us. The enemy activity was west of the village Thon Phu Hai, between the gap in the hills and up against the eastern base of Nui Da Kep mountain. They were a couple of miles north of Los Banos and Hill 88 – a state side National Guard fire base. Both artillery bases with 105s or larger. But the guns were useless because the Niu Da Kep ridge was in the way. The queen of battle, us, would have to go in and do the job. But unlike artillery or even an airstrike, we would eyeball the results instantly!

The pilot told Good he had a couple of Hueys inbound, five miles out. Good yelled for Cowboy to put out security and standby with smoke. He told Cowboy to get a fire team ready and drop rucks. They'd go in light.

183

"We got gooks in the open!" another squad leader barked.

Shit, I'd heard that before. Bob Crouch, our debonair and handsome Buck Sergeant FO who called everyone 'buddy', dropped his pack in the dirt. All around the perimeter rucks bit the dust. It was great shedding all the dead weight.

I slung my M-5 bag and prepared for another dry run on some civilians. The birds came in and skidded across the dry paddy. Good, Lappin, Crouch, Dany Shaw, Bob Culver, Cowboy and half the platoon tried to get on the lead ship. I walked over to the second bird and jumped on, alone, before the others realized we had plenty of room. Our new cherries, Billiter, Tick and some others quickly joined me. I pulled back the bolt on my 16 and checked for brass and shining death. Locked and cocked, lets go get 'em, I mused.

The Hueys climbed out in formation but hugged the trees for a quick hop over to the enemy. Lieutenant Good's bird peeled off immediately and dove for the foot of the mountains facing the beach. As we turned into a low holding pattern I looked out the right door and directly into the eyes of a young man ... a man running for his life. He turned and looked over his shoulder at me. We were going to catch them by surprise because the ridgeline was between us and their group when we took off! The Bird Dog, however, was so high up he could see the whole countryside plainly like a chess board.

The lead assault craft came in for a landing. They slammed into a patch of grassy dry ground next to flooded rice paddies. Lappin saw enemy soldiers on both sides of the chopper. One soldier was running across the paddies and others swarmed around a collection of boulders in front of the nearby tree line. Chiaramonte was RTO for Redick as they unassed the helicopter. The new RTO was so shocked at all the firepower and the tracers from the door gunners flying through the air that he tripped and fell into chest-deep water. The VC out in the paddy hightailed it around the tail of the Huey as Lappin and the rest of the CP group hit the ground running. Lappin felt free and light and like he could probably out run the gooners even with the radio kicking his butt. As Bob Culver noticed the chopper blast off, he clicked the safety off and walked a burst across the paddy water and into a running figure. He was startled to see the enemy disappear directly in front of him. He'd shot from the hip, dead on. Culver didn't know if he had hit his target or if, more likely, the crafty fucker had gotten away in a tunnel somehow. Typical, the point man fumed. Why was it so hard to make a clean kill? While Culver was shooting, Cowboy was pumping bursts into the running desperado also.

Cowboy approached the last known position of the man he'd just shot. The rancher was as puzzled as Culver. When the chopper pulled out Lappin noticed Crouch running towards the tree line and the boulders. Lappin yelled, "Wait! Bob, gooks all over the rocks!"

Lappin realizing Crouch was going it alone and with his radio on his back, took off after the fearless FO. When the chief RTO got up into the rocks he saw a nest of enemy in groups of twos and threes melting into the high brush. He leaped up on the nearest boulder and wasted one of the last VC as the rest of the fire team caught up. Meanwhile, Crouch had another VC cornered behind a rock. Cowering back the enemy troop dropped his weapon and was yanked off his feet as Crouch collared him. Somebody was screaming through Lappin's handset so he dutifully answered and reported to higher that the Hawks had made a prisoner snatch!

Crouch flattened the rearguard VC and had him on his back shrieking, "Chui Hoi, Chui Hoi!" at the top of his lungs.

At the same instant I realized that nobody else had seen the terrorized runner on the beach, even though our pilot had practically run him over. I wedged myself up in between the chopper jocks and yelled, "There's VC right on the beach!"

We circled around once and I held my breath waiting for one of the door gunners to open up. I sat on the radio console jamming myself up in the cockpit, looking out the front windshield.

Back on the ground the CP group was standing over the live body. My pilots turned short final to get us on the ground, the guy on the beach forgotten by everyone except me. The guy had out run a million dollar techno-miracle. Damn, I cursed and thought: "Why is it so fucking hard to gun these dicks down."

We unloaded just in time to see Bob Culver reach down in the paddy water and pull an arm out. He and Cowboy had not missed.

Unexpectedly Lieutenant Good suddenly pulled his bayonet and went at the VC PoW laying in the grass. The poor dipshit's eyes looked like golf balls and he tripled his efforts at announcing his immediate intentions to defect to the US forces. Good reached out and grabbed a tangle of ripped t-shirt that had twisted around the Vietnamese's neck and elbow. Peepers 46 inserted the needle sharp assault knife and cut the cloth from around the PoW's neck.

As the two Hueys orbited to the east, we all watched Culver drag the dead VC out of the water and across the grass by the hair. The dead man's clothes were twisted and ripped as well; they were full of jellied black globs of blood which oozed out like diarrhea. Cowboy summed up the affair: "Finally!"

Chapter 46

Walk the Plank

The platoon was catching its breath. We took a break in the shade of some reeds and brush along a swampy stream. The area was flat with dry rice paddies and miles of 12ft bushes and reeds. We were approximately a mile north of where we made the last CA and prisoner snatch. The platoon sergeant was jawing away like a loud buffoon and I made a 'shut up' motion with a finger. The fool had no idea that people could be following us. We were in the flats with no hills so the enemy could not watch us from afar. So … if they were following us it would be closely and they could hear our jack-ass head NCO a mile away!

Part of the sniper team had been cutting brush and walking point. The unit started to move out. I crawled and strained until I was standing.

The snipers, Richard 'Jeff' Jeffries and Mike Cline had recently graduated from Marine sniper school. They sported new camouflage fatigues and M-14s with scopes. But what pissed us off was that Lieutenant Good never unleashed the deadly duo. He never let them go out by themselves and set up like they had trained to do.

If only I had known that plank bridge was up ahead, I could have shouted a warning.

When troops first got to Vietnam everyone was handed a card with a list of lessons learned way back in the French and Indian Wars. The lessons were from Roger's Rangers. One of the more important and obvious rules was: never ford a stream at a regular crossing.

During the break we changed up the point element and had a pretty good team going: Cowboy was the slack man and he was letting a new guy walk in front of him on point. Jeff, one of the snipers, was behind Cowboy. They HAD seen somebody following them on the left flank, all day, peeking out of the tall reeds. The point man wanted to fire 'em up a couple of times but Cowboy said to wait for a better shot.

The point man was Bob 'Kav' Kavaney. When they came to the simple one plank bridge, they apparently held a brief discussion whether to cross the stream on the bridge or get their feet wet. Kav had actually looked to see if anything appeared to be out of the ordinary and it didn't. When he stepped on the wood, however, he knew something was wrong as the board gave way and he heard a metallic 'click'.

Jeff, who was almost ready to cross, was a big, blonde-haired, blue-eyed surfer who should have been a movie star. A boyish enthusiasm and constant up-beat mood belied the deadly sharpshooter's new goal in life.

WHAAAPP!

The blast was set behind Kavaney and the three Hawks behind him got it! The concussion knocked Kav forward off the bridge and put shrapnel through his ruck and the back of his jacket was torn up. Either 'Kav's' boot caught on a tripwire or the mortar round the enemy soldiers placed beneath the wooden 2x12 detonated by pressure, exploding and splintering the bridge. The expanding gases dug a crater and flattened all the surrounding brush. The crushed vegetation was burned and plastered with grey mud. Two Hawks were down. Jeff lay in the crater, scarlet billows spurted from both legs; his face was the color of the mud. Cowboy was hit in the legs also and another dude was nicked in the hand.

Breaking into a run, I headed up the column. I knew it was a booby trap. I'd seen the bits of earth fly up. I stumbled onto the scene and my first thought was, how could they do this? It was such an obvious danger area.

Lieutenant Good put out the squads for security as I slid alongside Jeff. He was conscious but his legs were wrecked. They were torn, ripped and looked as though somebody had stabbed them with a dagger about 100 times. I shrugged out of my ruck and unstrapped my aid-bag. Our new junior medic, Red, arrived and I told him to attend the other wounded. Cowboy was moaning and cussing, flat on his butt.

"Check him out, Red," I barked, totally serious for once. I tore open field dressings as fast as I could. This is simple. Stop the bleeding, I thought. Lucky for me. I whipped out my surgical scissors and cut off both pant legs. Tying on the dressings, the thick part over the bleeders, was crucial here. The battlefield dressings were the single most important item medics carried. My bag was half full of them.

"Jeff! Jeff! You okay?" I pleaded.

"Yummy, yea man," he answered quietly and slurred.

I was afraid he'd been hit above the waist somewhere.

"Is my ... you know what okay?" he whispered.

Jesus H Christ, what a time for modesty. I was going crazy, both hands flying back and forth trying to stop the massive hemorrhaging from twenty of the bigger holes, and he was worried about the family jewels. His pecker and scrotum were intact but the guy was in deep shit.

"You're okay in the parts department," I tried to joke. I then realized I had to roll him over a little, back and forth, to peek under and see if he was bleeding on the undersides. He could have bled to death from a missed exit wound and I would have just sat in the mud like a fool. He moaned, "God Damn that hurts ... Doc!?"

Red reported back that he was finished with Cowboy and the other guy had taken a piece of steel in his hand.

"Shoot this guy up with morphine," I instructed Red with a nod to Jeff. I couldn't stop the blood. Jeff would be dead in no time. I'd used up all but one dressing and still he bled.

"Look, Jeff, you're going to be alright. Everything's in one piece. You just got a few holes in you." I tried to reassure him by telling him the *basic* truth. He looked terrible. I knew he was in shock. His face was ashen grey.

"Jeff, Jeff, talk to me buddy!" I pleaded.

"What do you want to talk about?" he replied like we were waiting for the dentist.

"I don't know, just talk to me," I almost screamed. I knew he could die on me just from the shock.

I was out of dressings and some of the bandages were saturated with blood. A couple of wounds were still oozing. I honestly thought he'd die on me.

"Red, give me all your dressings and get some more from the squads," I implored.

Most of the grunts carried at least one, usually over the heart in a rectangular pouch. I wrapped dressings over dressings and tied them off tight. Panic started to grab me but finally the leaks stopped. I sat back in a pile of discarded plastic and paper, the wrappers from the dressings. I must have used thirty or forty easy.

With the bleeding under control, Red and I set up an IV to replace the fluid lost. It took me at least ten minutes to get it going. At first I couldn't even find a vein to begin. I switched needles; I used a tiny 26-gauge and slipped it into a collapsed and shocked blood system. The process could probably best be described as hiding a tiny salmon egg fish hook deep inside a small earth worm.

"Bird'll be here in five," Lappin screamed.

"Jeff, how do you feel?" I asked.

"Good, Doc, good," he babbled dreamily. The morphine had worked.

"The Dustoff'll be here in a few minutes. Just relax. You're on your way home," I told him.

The IV was barely draining, I noticed, so I told Red, "Blow into the air hole on the neck of the bottle. Need to force the blood expander out." Is the fucking needle too small, I wondered?

Before he could act, two Hueys shot in fast and landed. The battalion commander in his C&C ship followed the ambulance. Ramrod tried to help us lug Jeff up the bank and into the ship. I was forced to watch my friend clench his teeth in pain with every bump. Stupidly I had forgotten to splint his legs which would have eased the pain. I should have splinted automatically in case the leg was broken, but only if I was sure the bleeding had stopped. But really, I was still worried about the blood flow. I should have had a couple of months in an emergency room hospital before ever coming out to the field. Hands-on experience with doctors and nurses around would have been a huge help. I just wasn't getting enough exposure hiking around looking for gooks.

I realized I was a lousy medic. I should have been a sniper. I had trained for that job all my life. I should have been a door gunner. Anything but a medic.

The smell of blood, cordite and sweat poured over me and stuck in my hair as the Bell Hueys blasted off.

Later I watched Lieutenant Good talk on the radio and he informed us the boys were okay and that Jeff was on the way to Japan. Talk about relieved! Cowboy had received a characteristically painful shrapnel wound and would be back. Jeff's leg had been broken.

What next, I wondered?

Chapter 47

Bee-Ware

Our team lay hidden in thick foliage. Trembling and wet with the dew, I listened to the radio. The constant hiss kept me company. The hissing stopped for a second.

"Gooooo-ood morning Vietnam," a voice whispered from the handset.

At the first sign of light we were fed and on the move. What next, will I survive another day? I wondered to myself, shouldering my 60lb 'home' and checking for a shiny 'gold' chambered round and a clear flash suppressor. We were soon cutting trail, slipping and grabbing vines, humping up another ridge.

Tick was walking slack behind Culver, on point, and Billiter was right behind Tick. Culver turned to look back down the trail and Tick was suddenly looking at a VC squad coming down the rocky trail-at us. They were only 50ft away and right in the middle of the trail. Tick pulled out his shotgun round, inserted a HE, and bent over to whisper in Culver's ear, "ARVNs."

Culver spun around like he'd been kicked in the ass. Tick, realizing his mistake, snapped his weapon shut and fired at the now gawking, enemy soldiers, over Culver's shoulder. The VC point man never saw the grenade coming; it was dead on and going to hit him in his front teeth! Somehow, some way, the round sailed by and off towards the lowlands. Billiter was shocked, it couldn't have missed by more than a 10th of an inch! Before anyone else could gather their wits, the VC reacted and hauled ass back the way they came, to the top of the hill.

In the middle of the column, we stood around in a dry creek that cut across the trail. Each man cursed the delay; as usual we had no idea what was going on.

Suddenly, sharp objects zapped my face. I was hit in the hands, the mouth and the eyes. Stinging pain racked my body.

"Damn!" I cried.

What was happening … my clothes were crawling with … with insects!?

Tiny poisonous bees were stinging me to death! I screamed, "Don't move," and spat live bugs as beefy SSG Oliver and his lanky RTO – T.J. Wersman collapsed in front of me covering their faces and beating the air. It was one wild scene as troopers broke ranks and ran!

The sarge bellowed, "Don't move. Doc says to stay down!"

Releasing my rifle and laying on top of it, I pulled my jungle jacket collar up with both hands protecting my head. I gritted my teeth and thought, *when is this going to end?*

The little bastards stung again and again striking my fists and crawling past my lips and into my nose while others shrieked past my ears like a load of rock salt from a 12-gauge. They were in my mouth biting my tongue and gums!

Finally, they let us go!

Regrouping at the top of the hill and after having Culver the professional point man carry my ruck, Chiaramonte remarked, "Hey Doc, you don't look so good."

That was the first time somebody had to carry my ruck. I don't remember much of what happened after the bees hit and it was only much later I heard about Tick shooting at the enemy squad. All I remember was stumbling up the hill behind Culver. I carried my rifle at least. My head swelled up and started to look more like a basketball, according to Mike Chiaramonte. You know: no nose, no lips etc. I had to laugh because all the guys who had run had not been stung at all, and all of us who had made like the Boy Scouts, playing dead, had been bitten unmercifully.

A little later, sitting on my ruck, I suddenly went totally blind. My eyes were wide open but it was as dark as the inside of a dead water buffalo. Near panic, I hollered for the junior medic and handed him a disposable syringe loaded with epinephrine (my special emergency kit).

"Shoot that sonofabitch into my heart when I tell ya," I instructed.

After a while I began to see a little gray and realized, hoped, my sight was returning on its own. I hadn't really felt like trying to jump-start whatever was wrong with my eyes with needles and drugs!

Standing up, drained and weak, the color vision flooded back. Thank God!

"What a way to make a living," I said.

"Yeah, ain't it a bitch," Chiaramonte sighed, "got allll fucked up … ambushed by bugs!"

Later we figured somebody had hit a bee hive accidentally or … the VC had thrown a bag with a bees' nest inside … down the trail at us.

Chapter 48

Death This Way Comes

We were slogging through hell, as usual, just like in the movies. The Hawks were back in action after the bee ambush! The Hawk Recon (2/327, 101bn) platoon was spread out and approaching a long sea strand. The flat sand formed a narrow 200ft wide, two-mile long, peninsula. The South China Sea bordered on the northwest and a shallow inland slough, like a gentle river, ran for miles on the southeast. Everything ran parallel: the slough, then the strand, then the beach and finally the ocean. The end of the strand almost touched the base of the nearby hills, but the two were separated by the mouth of the slough where its foul waters picked up a little speed and flushed into the sea.

Totally exposed in open paddy fields and sand, a slight sea breeze tried to dry the sweat running down from behind my ears. Fuck it was hot! We were south of the slough and a few miles off Highway 1, getting precious little relief from the nearly cool sea air. It seemed like I'd been here before and I had the eerie feeling that Mr Death himself watched our every move. Just waiting to say, hello boys! Point hit the slough and plunged in targeting the sand spit and beach. Dwarf pine trees, about 12ft high and clumps of brush were our destination for the crossing.

Once established on dry ground, I plopped down next to one of the pine trees while SSG Oliver went off by himself to look for his wallet that had floated out of his pocket. We all kept our wallets in plastic bags and his floated up, out and away during his wading across. Lieutenant Good, our four-eyed leader, told us to fan out in a hasty perimeter to await Oliver and his billfold. I took my M-16 completely apart to clean it while one of the guys maneuvered around in the weeds taking pictures with an instamatic camera. I'd just put my weapon back together and was considering taking all the clips apart to clean the ammo and springs when suddenly a bullet screamed right by my face! More rounds followed. A sniper unloaded slugs in our direction. He was in the hills about a half mile away. Right then a flashbulb exploded in my brain as I remembered the time we were up in those very same hills and the enemy was down here on the beach.

Months before, in November of '68, we woke up overlooking the spit of sand and miles of tropical beach. This was back when some of the Hawks and myself humped with Captain Leslie Colegrove's Alpha Company. That morning I was the only one out of over a hundred (a whole company) to notice an NVA weapons' platoon just calmly walking along the waters' edge after swimming or wading across the mouth of the slough. They were right in front of us. A group of ten, armed with automatic weapons, RPGs and wearing helmets. They were, for a moment, trapped out on the sand, surrounded by water on three sides. I jumped up and grabbed our young squad leader, Sergeant Clark by the sleeve, pointing at the enemy infantry. I believe they were about half a mile away more or less. The sarge quickly told the 'old man'. The 'old man' ordered the M-60 gunners to open up in an effort to pin the NVA down.

"Keep their heads down!" he bellowed.

Wrong move! Tracers and slugs spat out and arced to the body of live targets – for a while. It was a long shot, even for the machine guns I guess.

The guns both jammed!

Sergeant 'Rebel' Odom was cussing and throwing his M-60 around like his hair was on fire and his ass was a-catching. Both weapons were worthless. I couldn't believe it. The NVA started to run and because the FO, if one existed, and the captain, had probably not initiated a fire mission from nearby Los Banos fire base or Hill 88 before we opened up with small arms, they escaped. Ran like a bunch of stripe-assed apes, as my daddy would say. Finally, as 105mm rounds began ripping the shit out of the spit with their ghastly loud explosions, some landing in the water, and later when a couple of Hueys showed up with troops, we all knew the 'gook-a-sans' were long gone.

What should have been an easy body count simply disappeared along the strand to the north where it blended in with the mainland and main beach.

What a disgrace that had been. We had them trapped! All that was needed was to call 'arty' ... say Gooks in the open ... fire for effect along beach line in front of their only real route of escape. Pre-arranged plots sighted in the day before on the obvious highspeed trail along the spit, would have done it. We could have sent a fire team hauling ass toward the mouth of the slough, to box them in. To me the feeling was like losing a record size rainbow trout because somebody else had put on rotten line.

Now it was us who crouched in the weeds next to the slough, the very same exact place the NVA troops had made their getaway. Now we were the targets. Funny really. I slapped my 16 on 'rock and roll' and sent a wild stream of tracers up into the high terrain. A whole clip emptied in seconds. Lieutenant Good and Lappin fired off a few rounds as well. Then for some reason the sniper stopped firing. Probably he was out of ammo or didn't want to waste more on unlikely kills. Probably he was just late for supper and had to go. At least we had fired back.

We'd been spotted, of course, but Lieutenant Good put us into an NDP right where we were anyway. We set up in a tight circle that afforded us a ringside seat view of the sea to our front and the slough to our rear. It was getting dark and after the sun went down someone deployed a claymore mine pointed at the ocean. I helped bury the wire from the mine and took unusual interest in the location and killing zone of the deadly device. We made little effort in covering our tracks and telltale GI jungle boot prints in the sand.

The CP was on its own as the squads went out on ambush to kill something over by the hills. Maybe catch our sniper going home.

I lay back for the night knowing the beach was a natural highway for the Viet Cong and the NVA units fighting in the vicinity. No one bothered, or even knew or mentioned the fact to us grunts of course, but I knew it from that sunny morning with A Company. I should have told Lieutenant Good ... but I didn't. But it was possible higher command

197

had noted my observations long ago and that's why we were sitting right on the spit. I had grave doubts however.

The hissing radio was once again my only companion. Around 0100, after I'd been roused for my watch, I scanned the beach and guarded the guys wrapped in camouflage poncho liners. I was irritated in always getting the middle watch; it meant I had to go to sleep and wake up twice. I knew now why John Wayne always said "I'll take the first watch."

It was the year of the monkey; it was the hour of the mouse.

I gazed at my little collection of weapons and fingered the claymore clacker-type detonator. M-26 hand grenades, Colt .45, Buck fighting knife, and M-16 lay in the sand or rested on my aid bag. The Kit Carson Scouts, Di and Nung, on either side of me, dreamed about women in long white dresses, or boats on the beach or whatever little lean ex-NVA soldiers dreamed about. Suddenly, something moved over on the left. I caught it out of the corner of my eye. Instantly, I was wide awake, heart pounding. This was it! I held my breath as I considered waking one of the scouts. But I did not want any goofy GI or otherwise sleepy asshole to fuck this up this time. Instead, I kept my eyes latched on the movement knowing we were in a free-fire zone. Anything was fair game – even civilians. On it came. It looked like a bent-over little old man. He was carrying a sack over his shoulder like some terrible wizard. Exposed in the moonlight, this dark figure of death jogged up the beach towards us. I held my breath again and unlatched the safety on the claymore's trigger. This one would not run and get away! Now the specter was right in front of me, only 30ft away. Clouds drifted near the moon. He was very, very close to where the mine waited on its little folding legs. In a split second the man trotted into the killing zone while the Hawks slept on. Probably they dreamed about blondes in pink Cadillacs and home; the CP slept like dead rocks.

I watched the silhouette grow even larger. It started into pitch black shadow. I strained forward, hair wet with sweat, trying to see, when quickly the clouds moved across the moon. I couldn't see a thing! It was like he had simply vanished. Easing down behind my aid bag to duck the back blast I knew was coming, I squeezed the trigger … Kaaaaablamm!

Hell might as well have risen up out of a hole in the ground and come upon the land as hundreds of steel pellets shrieked out and ripped the night. Supersonic stainless-steel hornets preceded a surprisingly large sand cloud. The rest of the team jumped out of their skins! They rolled around searching for weapons, eyes wild and looking in my direction.

I saw something dart to the left. Was this guy still alive, did he turn back, I wondered? Quickly, I grabbed a grenade and heaved it down the beach.

I was afraid of giving away our position. My grenade could have come from anywhere. Any gooks down on the beach had no real fix on us. No firearms discharged, no muzzle flashes in the dark gave us away. It could have been the whole NVA Army behind a lone point man for all I knew. Lieutenant Good crawled over to me and croaked, "Doc ... what the hell is going on!?"

"I just blew away a gook coming down the beach ... left to right," I stammered.

"What ... you're shittin' me ... sonofabitch ... no shit, Doc?" He asked in a hoarse whisper.

The word went out that I had blown a claymore on a gook and the entire platoon went to 100 per cent alert. Everybody stayed awake trying to spot movement, bodies, body parts, anything.

Mike Chiaramonte, Jim Billiter and 'Tick' Braley huddled at their ambush site half a mile away. Some had tried to sleep, on ambush, while others stayed awake. Like the CP, Billiter was watching a sandy trail that appeared gray in the moonlight. When the claymore went off, his ambush team immediately roused. Reddick, the Hawk's goof-ball (leg) team leader, tucked a forearm under his chest, lifted up and stuck his face directly into Billiter's.

"Someone threw a grenade, I think," Billiter ventured.

"That wasn't no grenade, cherry, that was a claymore," the lanky junior NCO sneered. The sound of a second explosion carried across the water and cut Reddick off.

"That, young cherry, was a grenade. Somebody got a gook," another veteran Hawk hissed.

199

The ambush party's radio broke squelch and Lappin whispered,
"Doc got a gook, and we got movement!"

The clouds cleared the moon and I tried to follow the claymore wire
out to the blast area. We could see the beach somewhat better but no
body or anything was visible. I'd either vaporized him, winged him and
he had run, or missed him entirely. I suspected it was a miss because the
target had suddenly vanished in the dark and I was forced to estimate
his speed and distance, detonating on a wild-assed guess. I knew it ...
got away AGAIN – just like fishing for steelhead trout. Damn it, killing
humans was hard work ... and tricky.

Our platoon leader pulled an aluminum tube out of his rucksack, took
the firing pin cap off one end and slid it on the opposite end. He now had
a miniature and loaded flare launcher, a tiny mortar. Good slapped the
closed end with the butt of his palm, and fired the missile out the open
end. Seconds later the rocket deployed its parachute and dangling pop-
flare, spilling an intense light that broadcast to the entire world what we
had done and where we were located! Lappin cursed, "Fuck it!", and
probed out towards ground zero, M-16 at port arms and safety off. Before
the flare hit the ground we were all out on the beach looking around, like
idiot cherries, exposing ourselves to anyone that was watching. And they
were watching.

After poking around for a while, I went back to the CP and went to
sleep ... watch over! I wanted just to forget about the situation; it was
fucked up beyond all recognition.

The next morning, I sat up, looked down the beach to where the
grenade had exploded and was greeted with the sight of Lieutenant
Good standing over a body. Grabbing my weapon, I was on my feet in
half a second, sleeping fully clothed as usual. I started towards them. The
beach was covered in tracks. The morning was cool and fresh. The body
lay on the sand, belly up, with legs crossed at the ankles. In a death grip
he clutched an AK-47 assault rifle. I had killed him.

The young man, a courier with a bag of money and some documents
was dead! Someone had already gone through his stuff and discovered a
picture of a cute teenage girl. After a cursory glance, I avoided the photo

and the letters from Haiphong, North Vietnam. I really didn't want to see any of his gear but realized it was a little late to worry about it now. I was still alive and only glad it was him lying in the sand and not me. The man had made the ultimate sacrifice for his country and was now nothing but crab bait. Too bad. What amazed me was nothing appeared to be wrong with him, no blood or disfigurement, just a few holes in his shirt and bag. I was so glad he wasn't all mangled up like I'd expected.

The cameras came out and while groups formed up and posed behind the grunt NVA, I took possession of his weapon. The stock and butt were missing so it looked like some kind of outer-space machine gun pistol. It also looked like a folding paratrooper model AK. Someone mentioned 'ears' and I saw one of the boys draw an obsidian sharp Puma knife. He squatted next to our new stranger and looked up at me, I shook my head, no, I for one didn't want anybody's ear. As far as I knew the soldier left us in one piece.

Well, it was done, and I had done it – the thing soldiers are supposed to do, kill. I was scared, awed, sad, and yet at the same time I felt the power ... the power Indian legends speak of. I went with that – it was very heavy.

Later that morning, a chopper landed on the beach after Lappin tossed a smoke and we were treated to a visit from some colonel and his aides. The reps from headquarters grabbed the cadaver and threw it on the bird. As the body hit the cabin floor, I was still in shock. I'd actually managed to impress the shit out of myself to the point of scaring myself. I wondered if I would be forever haunted by the NVA's departed spirit. I thought about revenge for the A Shau ambush that killed Bulmer and very nearly myself. The two incidents didn't seem related ... similar, but not related. Certainly nothing was gained, nothing settled, justice had not been accomplished.

As the Huey banked over the South China Sea taking the brave young soldier towards his home, his limp figure tumbled out to slam onto the surface of the ocean.

Far off on a distant beach a small group of recon men went back to work.

Chapter 49

Viet Cong Princess

I had become bloodthirsty. I had just made my first personal kill and I wanted more. I started carrying extra grenades and extra clips of M-16 ammunition. I took to staying awake at night and pulling extra shifts of guard duty. Instead of going to sleep after my shift with the radio, I would lay awake, staring off into the gloom, next to my pile of clips, grenades and the usual stuff. After several days in this condition, I returned to a state of more normal behavior. That is to say, I stopped pulling extra guard duty.

The day after the CP ambush we were still on the same beach area. The country side was flat with scattered hedge rows and deserted buildings.

Lieutenant Good was on the horn. He handed the handset back to Lappin and informed us all, "They spotted a bunch of dinks in the open! Chopper will be here in a minute to pick up a team!"

"Hey Lieutenant Good ... let me go with 'em," I asked. Later I would regret it.

"Sure thing, Doc, go ahead."

Five of us strolled out onto the beach to wait for the pickup. One of the 11Bs had thrown me a 'thump gun' and a bag of M-79 rounds. We were in the open and had walked down to where the beach became a muddy tidal basin, a mile or so wide.

"Hey ... looks like a flight of geese," Billiter, the cherry, red-cheeked lad pointed. "How'd you guys like goose for dinner?"

I locked and loaded one 40mm round of high explosive by snapping the barrel down on the stock, like the large bore shotgun it was.

"Wouldn't mind a bit," I replied leading the flight of birds Billiter was pointing at. I squeezed off a round. THUMMPHT!

We watched as the projectile spun and shot at the lead birds. The grenade vanished, the birds held formation and the bomb exploded after falling back off its trajectory. I tried again and again, but the shells fell and slammed into the water.

"Hey Doc, ya want to knock it off … here comes our ride," Tick, our RTO for the event sneered. A Huey grew larger coming right for us.

Like a big fool, I sat in the right door, legs hanging out, between Di and Tick. If the bird had at any time lurched over to starboard I would have made my first and last chopper jump. Like some country bumpkin, sliding off a tail gate, I would have slipped away. But it was combat, no time for common sense precaution. We had gooks in the open!

Over the water the pilots spotted the enemy. They were in a giant dug-out canoe, South Vietnamese flags crackling the breeze on the bow and stern. Unfortunately, they were in a free fire zone. That is, they were in an area (well known to us of course, we made it) that was open season on any living thing that happened to get in it. All civilians were of course notified by US government authorities – of course. Why every Vietnamese in the whole country had to know 'exactly' where the boundaries of these particular FFZs were. If you asked any 10-year-old on the streets of Hue, he would not hesitate to say,

"Yeah, GI, big free fire zone north of Lang Co, beau coup numba ten thou, we never go there, just VC there. 101 chicken men, sky soldiers there."

Why, I was positive they must have taught all the first graders, in all the schools, in every province and hamlet the whereabouts of every single zone in the whole country. I was sure of it, positively, we were trying to win their hearts and minds. We wouldn't let them down now … would we?

We circled the boat. The door gunner on the left side stood up and poked his head into the cabin.

"Hold your fire," he screamed.

We circled in a left-hand pattern waiting for the pilots to check. We waited for someone to make the decision to what was already established policy. I guess some un-seeing REMF in the rear made the final decision.

I doubt any of the Hawks will ever forget the look on that gunner's face when he snarled, "Shoot to kill ... shoot to kill!"

I wanted a boat of NVA. This was great! I wanted booty, pistols, US green backs, anything. I strained to get a shot at the boat. I wanted to kill more soldiers. Later, thinking back, I would have loved to have shot and killed that gunner.

Inside the chopper mayhem ruled. The left door gunner was blasting away with his gun. We could see nothing on our side ... until finally I saw the target. It was surrounded with thin geyser jets. Bullets. Now the assistant A/C was pumping rounds out his window like some mad speed freak. He had a M-79 too. Extra, golden-tipped rounds for his thump gun rolled around the floor in the cockpit. The H&E shells rolled out from under his seat and up into the rudder pedals. The right gunner was screaming at me and pointing out the door,

"Don't hit the rotor ... watch what the fuck yer dooen!"

You could see the main rotor outside the door, a blur normally overhead. Suddenly the A/C banked even further around in an orbit to the right. I got a clear shot.

I fired a round making sure the kickback traveled under my armpit through the butt and stock. My round detonated in a white splash, way wide of the mark. The starboard gunner was going berserk behind us – firing and shouting. Di, sitting forward of me, waved his arm in my face ... to stop. I noticed our scout was wisely holding onto the pilot's seat with his other hand. I wished to God for something to hang onto, but sitting between the two Hawks put me out of reach of any hand hold. We banked hard and I stared straight down through the rotor disk. I almost dropped the 'blooper' and grabbed Di. Chiaramonte fired his M-60 and hot shells flew everywhere!

The boaters flashed into view again and they sure didn't look like combatants. They looked like civilians. I still wanted to fire but didn't.

By then the boat beached. It was full of old people and kids. My heart sank! They had to be soldiers, they just had to be.

We'd all stopped firing and the pilots landed next to the boat. The hunters became the rescuers. It was a catch-22, literally a vicious circle.

Save them so we could kill them; kill them so we could save them. How miserably pathetic.

Miraculously no one was hit in the canoe except a little 16-year-old girl. All that firepower and we only wounded one person. Thank God! Maybe no one was really aiming, I couldn't say. I had only gotten off one quick shot.

Someone from the Hawks got out and then walked back from the boat, to the bird, with the girl. I took her in my arms. Here was a living, breathing, beautiful, warm, human being. Her thigh was split open from knee to pelvis joint. The wound was deep and ugly, exposing every muscle, bone and nerve. It didn't bleed. We were all lucky that the femoral artery was intact as she probably would have bled to death in seconds.

I carefully and gently wrapped her wound with GI field dressings. She went into shock. She watched me with dull, fearless gorgeous eyes. As the chopper lifted off I squeezed up between the fly boys and yelled for all I was worth, "Get us to a doctor ... now!"

We flew back to the highway and I handed her over to one of our battalion medics on bridge guard duty. Her mother was still with her ... and watched helpless.

When I had first looked at the wound, the massive damage had fucked *me* up. It put *me* in shock just looking at it, knowing we had done that. I had to do something I thought. I had pulled off my tourniquet and tied it around her upper thigh. It was a mistake. One of the other medics told me later that I fucked up with the tourniquet. He was correct.

No need to stop the blood flow that was doing its job okay ... at a time when blood was helping heal the wound already. She wasn't bleeding at all. She could have gotten a horrible infection and lost the leg with my tourniquet hindering the femoral flow. I was mortified!

Chapter 50

Loach Attack

The aero scout ship hovered in at low level looking and probing for the enemy under the trees. The pilot felt his bird lift and float in ground effect coming over the ridge. The skids of the 'loach' batted the leaves.

The Hawks were on guard duty and as for me, healing flesh around my skull indicated that I would survive the killer bee attack. I was still a little weak but I could see.

Fellows was fucking around inside my aid bag, going through it, taking inventory of my stock. I didn't mind at first but his attitude was giving me a case of the ass. This guy had to be the grandson of Dick Fellows, our famous California outlaw. His pot pipe rode its ever present position, stem anchored down in right breast pocket while he started through his pockets looking for matches. We were all guarding a bridge on one of the southern forks of the Song Bu Lu. The span supported a section of Highway 1 that crossed the river. Different villages hid behind palm trees up and down the road. We were near the spot I dropped the girl off after shooting up her family.

I was explaining to my best friend that I never let anyone poke around in my bag and that if he did it again I'd do something silly. I considered pulling my .45 to show I was serious.

SFC Solivan clawed the air in a dead run and screamed at me, all out of breath, "Doc, get down to the chopper pad with your bag ASAP!" I grabbed my rifle, claymore bag of M-16 clips and my medical pack. Giving Fellows a dirty look I said, "Excuse me … if you don't mind."

As the pad was nearby I trotted on over. What the fuck, over…I wondered. Something must have hit the fan, shit, I guessed. Fellows had split with our platoon Sergeant and I was alone until some stranger showed up carrying a radio. He heaved a pink smoke grenade out onto the pad and yelled at me, "Birds coming in!"

The smoke looked like fluffs of cotton candy. Two minutes later a Hughes 500 'loach' roared in overhead. Despite the warning, he'd caught us by surprise; we didn't hear him until the last second. The pilot banked sharply, circled, slowed abruptly and settled in on our steel plank heliport. As the turbine whined down I walked over to the cockpit. That's when I noticed the holes. The whole lower half of the bubble windshield was shot away. The seat and the cockpit was smeared and splattered with blood. Holy shit ... Luke the Gook had unloaded on this guy. Probably from close range.

The aviator unstrapped himself and fell out of the doorless machine. I caught him as he fell.

"Where are you hit ... Sir?" I asked.

"In the Goddamn legs," he moaned.

A crowd was around us then and we laid him out on a stretcher. Slicing off his pant legs with my chrome surgical scissors revealed several bullet holes piercing all the way out the back of his legs. Sometimes with serious wounds pain doesn't set in if at all, but I still felt kind of dumb because I had to ask, "Hurt much, Sir?"

"Hell yes it hurts much!" he answered back as I cringed.

Liquid opiate surged into his blood from my syrette needle. I'd already covered the bullet holes and was satisfied, for the moment, with my handy work. I'd splinted his legs together also. The bleeding had stopped. Another below-the-waist shot up GI, I could deal with those.

"Another bird is coming in, gonna land on the road!" the radio man called.

I grabbed one handle of the litter and yelled, "Let's get him up on the road then." I paused to let the others grab hold.

We gently set the young warrant officer down in the middle of Highway 1. I watched my patient for signs of shock. He seemed okay, but just to make sure and maybe stimulate him a little I asked, "Hey, Sir, are you jump qualified?"

I'd already noticed he was wearing jump wings below his flight wings.

"Fucking A," was his reply as he showed signs of raising up and grabbing my throat for emphasis.

"Well, airborne all the way, Sir," I returned. I chuckled and thought, you'll be okay Ace.

A big CH-47 'shit hook' came lumbering down the road. Its mighty twin set of props scooping the air and launching drying laundry from the back yards facing the road. The patient had only been waiting a couple of minutes. The rear cargo door was already down as the Boeing rolled to a stop. We fought the rotor wash and road dirt to set our WIA pilot down inside the dark fuselage. Inside, the jet engines made a pitched whine that was most deafening and had it not been for a few tiny colored lights, we'd of been blind as well.

Watching the green monster depart, after a record 'pit stop', reassured me the scout jock would probably be in surgery within fifteen minutes, up in the Hue/Phu Bia area somewhere. The 'shit hook' had probably been nearby and simply diverted off another mission. Ah … Army aviation, the camaraderie, the gallantry, the free ambulance rides. That was nothing to sneeze at.

The helicopter was most likely from the 159th Assault Battalion with its three companies of CH-47s. The companies were colorfully named: Alpha – the Pachyderms, Bravo – the Varsity, and Charlie – the Playtex. Personally, I favored the 'Playtex' cowboys. With a name like that, they had to be some bad studs or at least … different.

The next day I saw a crowd of civilians around one of the bunkers near the bridge. Up on the road a little girl was sitting on top of a wall of sand bags. A couple of Mama-Sans were fussing over her. These people looked familiar for some reason. They looked like they were waiting for a bus or something. Working my way through the crowd a lump formed in my throat; could this be her? I couldn't see her legs, Mama-San was in the way. I eased in next to them and stared at the girl's long shapely legs. Guess not, I thought, she sure looked like her. Then I did a double take, the inside of her left thigh was a total mass of scar tissue. It looked like a large skin graft was cut out. The raw area was green tinted but the wound in general was not infected. It had healed about as much as it was going to. At least she hadn't lost her left leg from the tourniquet. It was dangerous and useless using a tourniquet for a wound with no bleeding. It was just that it had been such a large, open gash, I had expected it to gush out blood at any second. I had fucked up.

I wanted to talk with them, ask them how it was going. I wanted to say how sorry I was and especially how glad I was that she was alright. It was obvious she was very popular with everyone. Passerbys joked and called her name and she answered with a smile and a wave. I was an outsider here; I felt totally out of line. I walked away.

Chapter 51

Lions and Tigers and Tanks, Oh My!

March 22, 1969

By spring another invasion force was ready to go back into the A Shau Valley. The 3rd Squadron, 5th Cavalry pushed eighty tanks and APCs north of the valley and up against the Laotian border. The invasion was spearheaded by the 101st Airborne Division.

We staged out of FSB Birmingham again.

As Mike Chiaramonte, with his dimples, over-sized cheeks, sunny Mediterranean look and outlaw airborne Mohawk hair cut (WWII style) and I went through the out door mess line, we had to help ourselves. Nobody was around at the airstrip below Birmingham. When we got to the end of the chow line, Mike looked around and said, "Hey Doc, do you see what I see? It's ketchup!"

He cocked his eyebrows in the direction of some boxes and started humming in an exaggerated way as he edged over to the ketchup behind the serving line. His Abbot and Costello impersonation was famous in the Hawks and as he stuffed his jungle jacket with at least four bottles, he looked around at me and whined, "ABBO...TTT!"

God it was funny. So funny in fact, I had to go and steal a bottle too. It wasn't really stealing, it was Army appropriation. We needed the supplies and the REMF cooks had it. I could taste our C-rat meals already and realized we were scoring big time! Our meals would take on a flavor that only Mark Twain could explain. As I pocketed my bottle I noticed a brand new *Playboy* magazine just hiding inside one of the open ketchup cases. I stole that too. Or like Huck Finn might have said, I borrowed it.

The next day, Billiter thought that the sky looked choked with mosquitoes as the entire battalion choppered back into the valley. This time we targeted the old A Shau village airstrip for the LZ. This time we rode with slicks from the 158th aviation company, renamed the 'Lancers'. They had taken their name from the Huey gunships of the old 160th assault helicopter group. The Kingsmen were in the air and Frank Sloan a gunner crew chief with them and myself, both 'Knights' from Soquel High School, came close to meeting up. Frank spent a lot of time flying SOG missions half way to Burma, but today his crew flew grunts. Dick Detra was up ahead of us with the Spider gunships. Earlier he'd been shot down along Highway 547 but today they were protecting the slicks. The Spiders and Black Widows had the wildest A/C in Vietnam. Not enough just to be Huey gunships, Detra and crew painted huge, laughing, mean, spiders shooting rockets and cannons firing from the hip … like spider cowboys, on the entire front end of their bird in a red and white cartoon! 'LSD' in floor-to-roof black letters covered the whole of the pilot doors while white and black swastikas stuck out prominently on both gunners' brass catchers. Out-fucking-standing!

This trip was like touring a battleground of another war. In 1966 the A Shau strip and Green Beret camp was a major battleground. As the A camp was being over run, on March 10, Skyraider pilots strafed the NVA in the wire, point blank! Rescue choppers crashed in sickening intervals around the perimeter. 'Jump' Meyers was hit with small arms and crash landed on the litter fouled runway, right next to an army of gooners! His plane, when if finally jolted to a stop, was entirely covered in flames. Meyers calmly realized the situation, held his breath, opened the cockpit and jumped out. Major Bernie Fischer banked around and dove on the enemy infantry as they went for the pilot. Fischer attempted the impossible and landed on the runway to effect a pick up and rescue. He ran off the end, wheeled around and taxied back looking for his zoomie buddy. As bullets punched through the skin, Fischer was shocked to suddenly see a couple of beady little eyes flashing frantically as their owner tried to climb up on the wing. Just like Hollywood, as the yellow peril closed in for the kill, Meyers slithered into the one man fighter

211

bomber while Fischer jammed the throttle to the stop. The trusty SPAD rocketed them into the low overcast and into the medal of honor history books.

We had it a little easier this time. The only one hurt was Tick, as far as I knew. His chopper hovered over the 12ft saw grass and the door gunner kicked him out. Tick crashed through the elephant grass and busted his tail bone. He was extracted right back out to Fire Base Roy.

The Hawks formed up and instead of looking for cover we waited out in the open for some reason. LTC Dyke came diddy bopping along and ordered his black enlisted aid to dig a fox hole. We stood around trying to figure if we were here to defend the valley floor or what. Dyke looked odd in starched fatigues and all new gear – complete with shiny boots. It looked as if they were digging a shit hole out in the landing zone. Dyke was to fail this mission. As Charlie Beckwith told me later, "Dyke wasn't a recon man."

That night, as firefights raged around the valley, our platoon lay up in extremely thick brush and small trees. I lay in my hammock with my NVA boonie hat that I'd found on the trail, and listened to the chatter of assault rifles. I guess nobody wanted the so-called NVA 'water lily' boonie hat. The things did look like what Hanoi school girls might wear, maybe in blue or white. A fight broke out practically underneath my bed. Two of the Hawks duked it out, rolled around, and tried to choke one another. What a team!

Sometime during the next few days, after humping west, we crossed the border and invaded Laos, 'the land of a million elephants and a white parasol'. This was part of Operation Prairie Fire, and probably illegal. They called our part of the operation: Massachusetts Striker. We walked point for the battalion and climbed the steep side of the western A Shau. All day it sounded like a battle stormed around us. You could hear the small arms crack and pop, almost non-stop. The atmosphere took on an ominous feel as we started finding all kinds of enemy signs. Culver was up on point as usual and suddenly stumbled out of the jungle and onto a hard surfaced tank highway. When I got onto the road I noticed the tracks and large ruts. Good pulled us off the road and we set up to hide for the night. The weird sound of firing continued all night accentuated by the screams of Dowdy when he noticed a centipede had sunk its fangs into his face. The soldier shrieked out, probably scaring any tigers, cobras, Yeti half-breeds and centipedes deeper into Laos and clear into the Mekong River.

The next day Bob Culver, the only man to ever carry my rucksack, collapsed under the trees. Lieutenant Good told me to check him out. I knew some thought he was faking. I saddled in alongside his sweaty crumpled form that was propped up against a banyan tree.

"Doc, I got a temperature and I can't move my head. It's stuck!"

He had a temperature of around 103 degrees and did appear to have something wrong with his neck. I started a saline IV and told Good he'd have to go in. As we waited for the Dustoff, Bravo company made it to our position. When the medivac arrived on station Maurice helped sling Culver up and out through the tree tops, but first I reached for the seats coming down as Larry Wagoner, the crew chief, fed out cable.

"Oz, let it hit the ground first. Let it ground out."

"What?"

"Won't electrocute your ass," Maurice said.

We lost our best point team, first Fellows and now his buddy Culver. Fellows was a step ahead of me, in the LRPs.

Later we extracted and combat assaulted into another side valley of the A Shau. Cobras streaked by us, firing thick white 2.75 folding-fin rockets onto the LZ. A good size brush fire started up almost immediately and by the time we jumped out, smoke, sparks and bat-size black ashes whirled through the air. I suddenly realized what the sound was that had followed us for days. It was wildfire. The cracking and popping wasn't small arms, it was flames. By then the LZ was almost surrounded with a boiling wall of smoke as we waited to move off. I was towards the rear and watched the men jump into a small section of grass that wasn't burning. Almost too late, I scuttled off through the smoke and snapping flames.

We walked the old roads that ran in and out of Laos. We started finding more war junk laying around.

A group stood by a crater in the road; the thing was the size of a small open pit mine. One of the Hawks pointed to the bottom. An RPG rocket launcher, brand new, lay below. Somebody made to go down but stopped as J.J. Smith, the buffed out, giant, black M-60 gunner snarled, "Stay the fuck outta there. See those green balls. Them's cluster bombs."

Joe Mann walked over with his crooked smile and pushed some dirt around with the toe of his combat boot.

"These little OD things are armed and ready to go!" he said.

A steel orb the size of a tennis ball lay on the crater rim. Shit, I started another nervous fit.

Later on, point peered into a murky tight cluster of trees and brush and found a garage. Inside were ten trucks, tools and some kind of oil containers. I was not interested. I was upset from all the explosives laying around and was having flashbacks of booby traps. A truck park *was* interesting, but nothing new. It was too confining a spot for me to go poking around; a good place for booby traps.

The next day Joe Mann was humping behind me, leading his squad up a dirt road scraped across a 45-degree slope. A cliff is what it was. The contrast of the orange and yellow dirt and dead logs scattered around, to the surrounding lush, green, jungle, was incredible.

"Holy shit ... Doc! Look at this!"

I turned and looked where Joe was staring.

"It's a fucking tank." Half way down the bank, below the road sat a pair of tracks. "Damn, it's gotta be a tank, Doc It's upside down, but it looks like it's in good shape."

Sure enough, a tracked vehicle looking like it had just rolled off the road sat below us.

"It's kinda small," Joe went on, "could be a PT-76. That damn thing is either a bulldozer or a PT-76 Russian tank."

The wind blew like chimes through the trees. The south end of the A Shau Valley where the road takes off towards Da Nang gave us cover for fighting positions. The road cut through a hill. On both sides of the road, like kids' forts, we dug out fox holes high up the ridge and under the trees.

On this mission we missed big action and for about the third time, missed hitting into the area that would be Hamburger Hill.

I really didn't care what happened … I was going on R&R. A free trip with plenty of spending money to exotic ports … yes!

Chapter 52

Mieko, Sieko, and Sanyo

Winter 1969. R&R was in Japan so I could go skiing … righttt! At Bien Hoa they tempted us with free trips to Bangkok, Sydney, Hawaii, and all over the Pacific, but I would have none of that. I went from killing people in rice paddies in 100 degree heat one day, to skiing and sipping rice wine up in the alps of Japan in the dead of winter the next. It was hard on me.

At Camp Zama, Japan I inquired about Richard Jeffries. I wanted to see what exactly had been done and I suppose reassure myself that I didn't compound the leg wounds from that day at the plank bridge boobytrap. Jeff wasn't around; they told me he'd already been shipped back to the States, ending up in the hospital at Fort Ord, California. He was in my backyard. One of his pretty visitors became his future wife.

A lieutenant with a 101st combat patch who worked the R&R center from behind a desk, suggested Shiga Heights for skiing, so that's where I went of course. Off into a magic winter wonderland I flew on the bullet train, on another mystery tour of Asia. It was great! I got off somewhere east of the Nagaio Prefecture and 200 miles southwest of Tokyo.

Man was I surprised, the people up in the mountains were real down home folks. They liked to party. Shiga Heights was spectacular and huge – a world class resort. The World Pro Championships had just ended in Febuary but the place was still jumping.

One of the Australian skiers was still in town and he and I went out. First stop for this Greek-god looking daddy-o and myself was a stripper club. After the show Lawence and I accepted the invitation from *all* the girls, for a night on the town. We all climbed on a bus and ended up back at the hotel – in the hot tub! Hot spring water gushed in from magma heated pools out in the snow. Inside was a scene from a Samurai orgy. Girls washed us, fed us, and served up little jars of Saki wine. I noticed a phone next to me, by the tub, and called Mom and Dad direct. Boy were they surprised!

"Bill, you sound so happy. Is everything okay? Are they treating you alright?"

"Mom, I'm 'skiing' now in Japan. Eating prime steak and drinking vine ... I mean fine vine ... ah wine!"

Our hostesses giggled and I gagged and inhaled some wine making it hard to talk.

"Gotta run ... Dad, call yah from Tokyo," I hacked.

The snow and ski runs were super but it sure was cold! They had plenty of steep-assed cliffs to try ... just like home.

Back in Godzillaville I took up a life of sin, again. It suited me. And again I took up the acquaintance of disreputable characters out of the boiling night mists in back alleys.

John just appeared, it must have been at some bar Lumpy told me about. Lumpy had let the medics see polaroids of gorgeous, young, naked, women swarming over him. He was responsible for me being in Tokyo.

John told me he was a combat soldier from Nam but it was hard to tell. I didn't question him, like asking him what unit he was in ... how blasé ... I did not give a rat's ass! John was a mystery man, however. He was smooth, cool, and a half-assed intellect ... another handsome businessman of adventure. We got along super. He knew the city well. He wore nice clothes that obviously hadn't come from any PX. The slicked-back hair and pleasant face could have belonged to a deserter or some general's kid.

John took me under his wing and grabbed my arm to show me the town. We traveled the back streets and alleys. We ate terrible looking plant life-forms, cooked in tin cans on open fires and served in the gutter side of very dark alleyways. I tried most of it and everything tasted great. We drank beer in nice bars with distinguished friendly businessmen. We had a blast. John was well known. People would crowd around us when he pulled out his Japanese/English dictionary. The night was filled with Saki toasts to our fine new Asian friends.

Around midnight, I became hungry again. John said, "Listen, I know where we can get the best American hamburger in all of Japan!"

"Sounds good to me," I slurred.

We walked into a small burger-shack type joint, right out of 'Archie' comics, you know, with a long counter and high stools. It was a fucking 'theme' bar from the American 1950s. They had a soda fountain 'manned' by some young guy all in white with a goofy white hat that looked more like a chef's hat than a 'soda jerk's' paper cap. Through a side door was some sort of disco full of noise, darkness, dayglow posters and rock & roll. I munched out on one of the juiciest, grade triple A burgers known to man!

"Hey John, this is gud stump!" I managed.

Just then a couple of extremely foxy little girls walked in and started conversing with old John. Hell, he knew them! They were like high school cheerleaders and even dressed the part. I was in lust. They sat with us. I was stunned!

"Mieko, Suzy, this is Bill a great Samurai from across the sea." John explained.

I shot him a pained looking grin. Out of the blue heavens Mieko, sitting next to me on one of the stools, slid her little hand under the counter and placed it daintily on my pecker area. Something told me right then that we had scored somehow. I almost choked, but turned to Johnny and coughed out, "Hey, John, this is gud stumppp."

John and Suzy with the blonde hair vanished and I was left all alone with Mieko. I later found myself at Mieko's place. I moved right in. I was in lust or love; I didn't care which or even know the difference. She really liked me … I could tell. Those girls didn't just go with anybody.

Like any good marriage we established ground rules right off. Only two rules here: first rule: obey all rules; second rule: I paid her up front, a very fair amount, and she spent it! She paid for everything we did for the next few days. I'll never ever forget the first night with my stunning young call-girl. In heaven I was. Her apartment had one room stuffed full of stereos, stuffed toys, baby pianos, and drum sets. The house looked like a combination toy store and discotheque. She dimmed the lights, turned on a large reel to reel stereo and plugged in the light show. Thousands of tiny spot lights flew around the room like snowflakes chasing themselves. A beam of light aimed at a revolving ball hanging from the ceiling, reflected off glass sectioned squares. Points of light swirled over our faces. Mieko took my clothes off, then stripped. As Nancy Sinatra and *These Boots are Made for Walking* blasted out, just right, Mieko dragged her hard, large, breasts down my face and found my stiff as hell cock with her wet, little, crimson mouth! She was extremely well proportioned and had the smoothest skin I could remember touching. Hell, for sure it was the smoothest skin I ever touched! With my nose in her crotch, I had to admit the sexy clit was a bit intimidating; so much the better.

This was all like dating a new girlfriend. Never mind I was paying for it: isn't that how it goes anyway?

The next day she showed me all over the wilds of Tokyo. We went to see the new film just out, *2001: A Space Odyssey*, and ate steak cooked on large stainless steel grills built into the tables. I thought the fancy place was the original 'Benihana' as the chefs danced around with knives and silly grins and chopped the local chop-chop! Too good! Those guys could flip shrimp 4ft off the table, up in the air, and rim a bowl of ice and lettuce with tiny juicy animals.

That evening as I soaked in a deep tiled tub right in Mieko's living room; I actually found myself missing the Hawks. They were right then out in the A Shau, hot, cold, and miserable, swatting bugs and shit. Couldn't help reminding myself about the war, a poster from the 82nd Airborne and the 173 Airborne hung above the tub. Mieko was a real airborne girl … all the way. So, I drew my own 101st Airborne design in the wet condensation formed on the glass wall of the tub.

Man, it was hard to go when the time came. A phony, macho, ego tried to tell me I should just split – no looking back. It was hard to fool myself however. This was the best time I had ever had. I told Mieko I would be back ... and I did too! I loved her. Just like the movie, *World of Susie Wong.*

At the R&R center I window shopped. This was another new experience for me: having money at the end of a trip! But for some reason the shops were all closed. Suddenly a little Japanese man emerged from one shop, turned and fumbled with his key. I asked him if I could buy a radio. He said politely,

"Impossible ... we are closed!"

I looked back into the display window and spied the biggest World-Wide Band Sanyo radio I believe they ever made.

"I want that radio," I pointed.

Inside the store I plunked down about 50 bucks for the radio and said, "Gimmie one of those watches too."

I grabbed a Sieko self-winding, alarm, stainless steel beauty; it too was 50 dollars. Damn, everything was 50 bucks around that place. The watch had a great luminous set of hands and numbers, perfect match for the jungle. It was to be my good luck jungle watch.

I did buy a small Minolta spy camera as well, 50 bucks. Big mistake!

Right in that store I made the biggest mistake of my life! I should have spent all my money on a professional 40mm movie camera and a case of film. I would have filmed the greatest spectacle of our age! I would have been famous. Nothing like that would ever be filmed, at least by a soldier.

Chapter 53

Hamburger Hell

The EM club REMF, back in the 2/327th area, sold me three cases of beer and three cases of soda. I tried for some ice but they were out.

On supply day for the Hawks I threw the cases on the log bird. The platoon was in the bottom of the A Shau. On the way I tried out my new Minolta spy camera, taking snaps out the door at the country side. The camera was to live a short but happy life.

For a while, all was peaches and cream. The whole of Vietnam seemed to be splash across the horizon before us. The next second the A Shau Valley trees towered all around and Cowboy was yelling at me against the chopper's wind storm, "Hey Doc, you take pictures of skiing? How about chicks? Come on Doc … lets see the naked chicks." Later he said, "Hey … thanks for the sodas, let's see, that's about two sodas and two beers for everyone. Trade my beer for your sodas?"

The next few days were another endless hump. I tried to keep up with Dennis Sinka mostly but I'd lose him in the 15ft elephant grass and fog. A couple of times I almost missed his trail of bent and broken grass. I liked walking behind Dennis generally; he seemed to be extra alert and know what he was doing as he was a native Alaskan and a natural hunter.. At the end of each day we'd pull into a NDP and our fatigues, black with sweat, clung and stuck onto our skin.

The Hawks had another medic now. Red was more or less permanent party. I worried about him. He was so skinny and white, he worried me sick. His real name was Doc Wallace.

On the next resupply day I left Red in charge. I was ordered back to headquarters. At Eagle SFC Bell told me I was going out on the line again. He wanted me to go out with one of the line companies. They were out on Fire Base Blaze and he wanted me to hump with a platoon. I was fucked! I told him, "Damn Sarge. Listen, I've been out ten months and now you want me to be a cherry-ass platoon medic? You gotta have some new medics. I know we got new medics out on the fire bases."

HHC was trying to get me out in the field again like a newbie, but I had a plan for all that bullshit. I made a deal with Bell that if I found one of the new medics out in the aid station at Blaze, the new guy would ruck up in my place. Fuck it, I thought. I'd been in-country for nearly eleven months, through all kinds of nasty crap, and had humped from one end of the stinking country to another. Let some cherry go out and hump some. Most of the time was just spent 'camping out' anyway. Bell gave me a name of a medic. Bell thought I was easy and I would just do what he said. It was an easy route for him to go. But I would buck all the way, after all … we had a vicious rumor that medics only stayed in the field for six months due to the dangerous nature of the job. A bad rumor I guess.

I was wandering around Blaze, feeling guilty about the medic. The guy and his new company had already split through the wire. He'd resigned himself to his lot, his new position as a real combat medic. We had all gone through it. He had simply turned around to get his gear.

BAPBAPBAPBAPBAPBAP … bapbapbap … bappabappa

A sound of machinery flew over the mountains and a helicopter closed in on us. He was in a hurry. They'd come in low, up one of ten or more narrow side valleys from the A Shau. The bird had stayed hidden behind a ridge until the last minute. Seconds later the sling-wing dusted off a pad nearby.

I walked over to the aircraft as GIs ran past me to unload; it was a medivac and it had wounded. The cargo bay was full of tree limbs with chop marks. Fresh leaves were scattered around or hung from the branches. Suspended from the roof the field-made stretchers hung in stacks of three, holding bodies laying on ponchos and liners stretched between raw poles.

Later, after the machine and everyone had wound down some, I chit-chatted with the medic. As he swept out the deck with a whisk broom he said, "Yeah, lotsa shit going on up there … fuckin' hill is bad news."

It's bad news I thought to myself. I was drawn to this chopper and this crew by some strange force; like a moth to flame. I wanted to go with them, wherever they went. I liked the looks of the Dustoff ship as it crouched on the pad. It was sexy looking and smelled good, like plastic, paint and jet fuel. It smelled like a new car … only better. Something told me to get on the bird.

"Listen," I said to the medic, "can I go with you? I'm a medic … been here eleven months, over eleven months," I lied. "I can help out … ask 'em."

He said he would and went over to hobnob with his A/C and the copilot. Suddenly the crew chief ran up to the airmen from wherever it was he had gotten to, stopped a second, then ran back to the tail and unhooked the main rotor tie down from the blade and around the stinger. The medic jumped in the back, ignoring me, as I tried to scream up at him.

"What'd they say … man? What'd they say?"

The flight medic calmly looked at me and said, "We might get loaded up pretty good. We could use you, but … we need the space more."

I didn't know it but I had just volunteered for a death ride on a greased pig, straight down the devils ass hole.

May 13, 1969

History records that James Margro, the medic with a sweet boyish smile, James Walters, the crew chief, 1st Lieutenant Jerry T. Lee, the co-pilot and 1st Lieutenant Gerald M. Torba honked up their bird SN67-17844. They knew what was what. The battle, the worst probably in the entire history of the 101st, at least politically, had been raging for three days. The 'Rakkasans' were jockeying for positions around the hill. The 1/506th 'Currahees' (always first) were soon to be closing in, finally attacking from the south over the same ground we had covered in our hike up Dong Ap Bia in '68. Delta, my old unit from III Corps, was trying to out flank in an RIF, and assault from the north. The problem was, Delta had to climb down a ravine, dropping northeast from the

223

battalion CP, and then attack back up the 'hill'. They never made it past the river at the bottom. They did start an assault up the 'hill' but before they got out of the riverbed, Pandora's box split wide open with a gush! The NVA ambushed them with a volley of RPGs and AK fire. When the dust had settled for a minute Captain Sanders called a medivac to get the wounded.

Staging out of the fire bases, Eagle Dustoff ships had only to cross the A Shau to support the battle. They were a few minutes away at the most. Dustoff 'Niner Two' (Torba) launched.

As the ambulance closed in on the western A Shau, Sanders waved the bird off telling Torba it was now too dangerous. The NVA had the high ground and it would be tough coming in until the point platoon took the high terrain. Torba started in above the canopy anyway. He knew Americans were wounded and dying down below among the boulders and in the trees along the bank. It was his job; he'd made it every time before. It was also Torba's job to keep his crew alive.

For a second the earth stood still. Horribly, a rocket launcher exploded and an RPG whooshed off the mountain, down and into the rotor disk! The missile struck the main rotor and dropped the whirly bird. Torba and the crew chief were working the basket when the rocket hit and showered the crew with hot metal. Torba was hit hard, peppered and torn below his left knee. As the aircraft picked up speed, straight down, PFC Pickel rode the basket and was promptly crushed under the wreck. The main rotors flew off and Torba's survival knife cracked him in the teeth as the decking rushed up and broke the crew's backs. The Rakkasans surrounded the ship and pulled Torba out. The other crew were tangled in the wreckage and before they could be extracted, the twisted hull exploded in a ghastly conflagration of vapor and still moving parts. Torba was out but the rest burned to death.

Had I known what was happening to Delta I probably would have done something stupid like take an in-country 'R&R' and snuck out on the next chopper. Maybe that was why I had felt attracted to the Dustoff; I don't know.

At the time Maurice and I had no idea what, if anything, had happened to any medivac. We were concerned about what fate had in mind for us. Somehow I had gotten the idea that we would be working in the rear at Camp Eagle. Well, we were informed that we would in fact be working in an aid-station in the rear, the one out on Berchtesgaden.

Back on the east face of Dong Ap Bai, Delta Company hauled the Eagle pilot back up the ravine. Sanders suggested a call for another Dustoff, but LTC Honeycutt (Blackjack) the 187th Co. vetoed the idea. Company D endured snipers, mud, rain, cold and wind, humping out their wounded while seven dead waited back at the river. They spent what seemed like days fighting the elements and tugging the delirious pilot hand over hand up vertical banks and around trees. He rode the Stokes litter salvaged from the crash. They took Torba and threw him in a pile of dead back at the CP. Later, after almost fifteen hours of abandonment, somebody noticed the resurrection of one blonde-haired Army pilot with a mangled leg. Luckily Torba survived the ordeal and like some famous pilots, continued flying, minus a foot.

Berchtesgaden was a disaster. Maurice ended up back in Bravo Company and left me all alone up on the fire base. I arrived in a haze of dust and confusion. The days themselves blended together in one big bewildering haze. GIs darted in between the trees and flopped down hollering,

"Fire in the hole ... fire in the hole ... fire in the fucking HOLE!"

They placed shaped charges on clumps of trees, jumped back a couple of yards and blew C-4 in ear-destroying sonic blasts. Shards and splinters showered out in clouds of beige dust and gravel. I hated it!

I was a loose cannon. No one knew what to do with me it seemed. The job in the aid-station wasn't really happening. I was short and a man without a unit. I could have just left the whole spasmodic effort behind. Word came to me to report to C Company as a medic. I actually reported to the CO but he ignored me. Okay, I turned and walked away. Nothing ever came of it and it was the last time I ever reported to anybody other than the Hawk platoon.

Wolfgang watched one of the teams walk in. He sat on a firing position with shaving cream soaking into his facial pores. His knees were bare, threw blown out, ripped and filthy fatigue pants. Wolf's life was ripped and worn out like his pants. He was torn between his love for his men and the adventure and magnetic horror of combat, and a lousy gutless longing for his movie-star girlfriend down in Australia. When his eyes spied me walking down the fire base road he almost fell off his sandbag chair. I was home, the Hawks were here.

Wolf and I hung out together. We understood one another. Wolf told me SFC Solivan had been shot through the neck on May 5 walking down a creek while I had been in Tokyo again. Wolf seemed kind of shocked, hurt. I'd never seen him like that before, he seemed to try and throw up a wall to hide all emotions. He tried to trick himself, reasoning that it was war, people (friends) got killed. You couldn't flip out about it. What had he expected? he asked himself.

None of the Hawks realized what was really happening across the valley, over on Hamburger Hill, at the time. You couldn't hear the firing unless the wind was right, and even then it sounded like a distant jet.

At night, the mountains jumped out in silhouette. The sky exploded with light as if someone had soaked the clouds with jet fuel and thrown in a torch. Some of the fireworks was heat lightning, some of it was thunderstorms and some of it was artillery duels. The gooners could out shoot us with their long-range guns. Like the Hindenburg Line on the Western front they hid their big cannons in caves and on mountain sides.

During the day a lot of aircraft bored holes in the airspace over the western A Shau rim. The Hawks sensed something was going on. Daily, artillery jacked rounds directly into Hamburger Hill. We supposedly had the honor and responsibility of backup to the Rakkassans. Supposedly we were next! The 3rd Brigade had taken over Berchtesgaden for their forward command point, Colonel Conmy and his staff in person. In the daylight we watched the air strikes through the trees. Only later, after the fight, were B-52s allowed to cream the top.

Billiter remembers a rather lax attitude around the base around Berchtesgaden. Trees were left standing, right up next to the wire and near some of the bunkers.

'Jo Jo' Billiter went through his AIT school with a bunch of 'shake and bakes'. One of the new NCOs earned the name Georgia Peach from Billiter and another named Hughes got something less poetic. Hughes rode Billiter and told him he'd never make it back from the war.

The 3rd Brigade shuffled a lot of personnel and gear across the valley. One day, as Billiter watched, a lone Huey shut down on the pad. Out staggered old Georgia Peach! On board the bird was a batch of wounded right out of the bloody cauldron on the 'Hill'. Billiter rushed over to his old friend, "Well hello there Georgia Peach! How are ya bro?"

The young NCO was upset, filthy, dirty and tired. He gasped, "It's a fucking massacre up there!" and swung his arm drunkenly towards the way they had come. Georgia Peach wanted to go back up the hill, but before he left he told Billiter, "Remember Hughes? I remember the way he used to tell you you'd never make it back. Well, Hughes is the one who won't be making it back."

One night near the end of the epic battle I heard the story of SFC Solivan. As beautiful parabolas of green, red and white tracers roped off, up and down hill 937, Lappin and Wolf told me what happened. As flares spotlighted the ongoing assault and served as a beacon for the NVA coming down the trail, in case any doubt existed about the location of the latest A Shau engagement, Lappin explained:

"We were in column going down a stream bed. Everybody was all bitching about being in the creek, but were told LTC Dyke was in a hurry for us to move up. Solivan was towards the rear, next to me. The word went through the line that a bunker was up ahead. I saw a bunker opening, up a dry side creek, heard a shot and saw him go down, right behind me. God, his eyes were open. Sarge got it in the neck with one shot and ya know, he shouldn't have been out in the field."

Wolf cut in, "He loved us, ya know that. Doc, you know what? I ... we loved his boonie humping ass too."

Lappin went on, "He was too old, well not too old to do the job, just ... too old to die I guess. After they flew the body out, Dyke ordered us up on the ridge line, outta the blue, where we should have fuckin' been in the first fuckin' place! Fuck, what a waste of a damn fine man!"

Well, the Hawks missed Hamburger Hill. General Stilwell, the XXIV Corps Commander and son of 'Vinegar Joe' called in the ARVNs toward the last, probably so they could say they participated.

Some called the actions in and around the Valley of Death, one humongous battle. If so, it lasted for years. The region was never US controlled and was the NVA's largest camp in South Vietnam. The place was infested with artillery and tank parks. Fire bases were assaulted, enemy battalions made stands and famous battles and firefights on Fire Base Ripcord, Airborne, O'Rielly, Hill 937, Berchtesgaden, Bastogne, Veghle, Eagle's nest and Bloody Ridge were the worst days ever for the Screaming Eagles. The Division lost twice as many casualties in Vietnam than all of WWII. As for the Hawks on Berchtesgaden, their worst nightmare, their rendezvous with destiny was on its way.

On May 20, 1969, the butchering on the hill was over. Ho Chi Minh's last birthday, May 19, saw the clash coming to a close and one day later, a solid defeat for the people's army. Uncle Ho died four months later.

How Maurice and myself missed our death call was a mystery to me. By rights we should have been with our original unit on Hill 937. The reports of the casualties vary like a goddamn fishing story. But, at a cost of at least ninety-two GIs killed and hundreds wounded, Ho lost a major part of the 29th NVA Regiment. To the medics that were in the assault, it was a slaughter house. However, according to Colonel Conmy, a Green Beret recon team in Laos watched a macabre death march stream off the battle site and retreat back up the trail. The snake eaters counted over 1,000 dead and wounded!

Chapter 54

Uncle Ho's Birthday

May 19, 1969

Wolf and I were on guard duty during Uncle Ho's birthday. We had a radio and were sitting on the perimeter overlooking a 30ft cliff. The trees began below us on the other side of a black void. We were on full alert. We were only slightly nervous and talked about NVA regulars emerging from the tree line with ladders and flame throwers. Faint hissing on the radio was interrupted from time to time with light chatter. We called in negative 'set reps'.

Hamburger Hill was boiling to a head across the valley. Things were hopping. You could see enemy trucks down below in the mists and sometimes Soviet helicopters. One lumbering rotor-winged mammoth landed, at night, on one of our fire bases near us by mistake. Getting lost in the mountains in the dark is easy.

Company D 3/187th was more or less wiped out by now on the 'hill'.

Towards midnight things had quieted down. We figured the odds of a full scale attack were slim to none. We were wrong.

Wolf picked up a grenade. He pulled the pin and flipped it and the ring over the side. Wolf just looked at me and smiled. Then the crazy guy armed the thing, igniting the fuse by letting the spoon (thin piece of spring-loaded curved metal extending off the top) fly. It would explode in about six seconds. Wolf sat calmly holding it in his left hand. He stared at the bomb and turned to me, smiling again. Without breaking his macabre stare he slowly extended his arm. When the hand grenade was at arms length he casually released his grip and we both hit the deck. The damn thing dropped out of sight over the bank and exploded.

This was the manly art of 'cookin' them off', known and practised only by the few truly battle-hardened combat boonie rats, a technique used in close combat to discourage Charlie from throwing them back.

"What the hell is going on out there?" someone in the CP screamed over the radio. We giggled and smirked to ourselves. Some lieutenant in the command bunker was probably going nuts not knowing who did it, or what was happening out on the perimeter..

The defenders were nervous and who could blame them. A few days before, on May 12, the NVA hit Fire Base Airborne in what was called the most disastrous sapper attack in the history of the 101st. Of course us ground pounders knew nothing of that. The only thing Wolf and I knew was, we were ready. In fact we prayed for an attack; we dared them to bring on the ladders and flame throwers. We were two demons lurking in the dark, waiting and watching. In less than a month the NVA did, they came after us. They would accept our dare.

It was now my turn. I picked up a grenade from a box Wolf was sitting on.

"Hey Doc, can you believe how fucking hot it is tonight? There's no wind or nothin' … weird man."

Calmly I straightened the cotter pin with my fingers. I hope this thing doesn't malfunction or have a short fuse, I thought to myself. The pin extends through the top of the grenade and is pulled out by the wire ring. The pin holds the spoon in position. With the cotter pin straight, I pulled it out with my teeth just like in the movies. My fingers were now the only things keeping the spoon in place and the fuse from igniting. Smiling at Wolfgang, I spit the ring and pin out and over the cliff and eased my fingers back allowing the spoon to fling off. I stared at the smooth-sided, green killer. I lost track of time. Had a couple of seconds gone by already? Was this thing defective? Was I completely out of my mind? I remembered back to basic training where they had shown us the insides of these high explosive anti-personnel grenades. Inside was a coil of steel wire like a slinky toy, only this wire was partially cut through every half inch. The segments of wire would break off on detonation and spray out. I realized I must, in fact, be mad; I stood up and violently hurled the frag off into the void. Nothing happened. About three seconds later it went off with a muffled 'CRACK', far down in the trees. Just then someone on the other side of the perimeter let off a burst of small arms fire which was quickly joined by others.

"Knock it off, knock it off," the radio shrieked.

"Happy birthday, Uncle Ho," Wolfgang spit.

"Lovely bit of reconnaissance by fire, old man," I told Wolf as tracers arced out of the base.

"Gooks down there would shit and trigger an attack early."

"Yeah ... and I'd like to see some fucking dink throw one of those back up here!"

"Hey, Doc ... are we gonna drink this beer or what?"

Chapter 55

Arc Lightning

Malicious storm clouds boiled along the ridges and mountain peaks. Eagle's nest and some of the other fire bases were in solid overcast. We were vulnerable to ground attacks. The NVA were of course watching and knew the clouds protected them from our gunships and jets.

On some of the higher bases it was cold enough to wear field jackets and up on Berchtesgaden it was pleasantly cool for a change. Rain showers drenched the bare dirt and then moved on. Wolf and I tried to take showers in the sheets of rain. We soaped up okay but as hard as the rain pelted us it wasn't enough to rinse off. What a bitch. We had to settle with sloshing blood-warm water from our canteens over our naked hides. But it still wasn't enough! We had to go around, with our dorks handing down, 'borrowing' more water from our comrades!

While we finished douching off, I noticed Wolf peering into my helmet. Suddenly his eyes bugged out of his 'white walled' head and he started pointing.

"Hey Doc, is this yours?" he asked. I looked inside my pot and to my horror saw my new Minolta spy camera submerged in water. Rain drops made ripples on the clear surface. Wolf guffawed, "Nice underwater camera, Doc HAHAHAHA Haha. I wanted one of those, HEEHEEHEEEE WHOOOIE!" I picked it out and threw it as hard as I could off the fire base.

Yeah, Wolf was a funny guy. He was a stand-out in our battalion, a real wolfman. I hadn't seen him for a long time and asked him about it, "What's this I hear about you going AWOL or something?"

"Yea Doc, I spent a month or so in Australia. Gonna get married to a movie star."

The deadpan manner Wolf used to drop jewels of information was legend. Wolf had gone AWOL for his movie-star girlfriend. He was going to marry a movie star, a fact you could bet on it. We pulled our pants on after our extended bathing, suffering early stages of hypothermia.

"Hey Doc, you know, I got this new *Playboy*. I'll drop by your hootch later. But Doc ... now, no shit ... beating your meat doesn't ... you know ... make you weak or anything ... does it?"

I was flattered Wolf confided in me. It was obviously a touchy subject all the way around.

"Hell no, Wolf. Perfectly normal behavior, says so right in Playboy."

"Thanks Doc, catch you later. I'm gonna crash out."

After dressing I dug deep into my mildewed ruck and pulled out an old mud splashed can of beer. Hungrily I guzzled the warm contents, guessing that Wolf was probably asleep by now, out on the perimeter in a snug hootch.

I decided to take a walk and announced the decision with a loud belch of contentment. Lightning crackled in the distance, Mother Nature's artillery working out. Near the command bunker, on the highest part of the base, I walked along in the shallow mud. Suddenly a figure raced out from the dark guts of the reinforced TOC. He nearly slipped and fell, but nevertheless felt it was his duty to inform me,

"Bravo's got wounded ... lightning!"

The faceless bunker commando vanished around the corner on his urgent mission, all ass hole and elbows.

I walked over to the chopper pad and scanned the ridges; steam and mist rose from the streams and creeks behind each and every ridge top. A silent blinding flash, like a jagged laser beam, exited the cloud layer and smacked into sodden jungle.

CRRRAAACKK!

Holy shit, that was the biggest hunk of energy I'd ever seen! It was truly a frightening phenomenon.

I thought about Maurice out with his company. I visualized him out thrashing around in the rain forest, soaking wet amid the terror and confusion. They were human lightning rods, covered from head to toe in steel and iron. Their boots were steel soled and their headgear the same, not to mention the machetes, M-16s, grenades, radio antennas and so on.

A lone Huey came in from the west and settled on the pad. It looked like a return from a car wash. The rescue ship had picked up some of the casualties and meant to drop off some of the walking wounded with us. I stood and overlooked the pad. Two soaked grunts limped off the ship and the pilots instantly pulled up, nosed down and dove off the side of Berchtesgaden. The steel cargo deck was covered with bodies. I wondered about Maurice.

Chapter 56

Siege at Berchtesgaden

"Say a prayer for the common foot soldier,
Say a prayer for his back breaking chore ... .."

Mick Jagger/Keith Richards

June 14, 1969

About this time I screwed around Camp Eagle trying to weasel through and complete a flight physical. I was in poor shape for a 21-year-old Californian surf rat. I had blown out ear drums, a deformed back, bad eyes, drank too much and had been sprayed with agent orange. All from just being in the Nam. A perfect volunteer for Army aviation I was. I actually thought I was through with humping a ruck; I was wrong.

Meantime the Hawks were still on Berchtesgaden along with elements of the 1/506th. Ground radar had picked up enemy activity on hill 937 again. They were back! Enemy movement was also sneaking around Berchtesgaden which was only a few miles directly across from Hamburger Hill. The Hawks blew a new LZ extending the fire base some. They set up a listening post on a western knoll out from the base. The guys worked on the perimeter wire extending it as well. They worked their butts off digging two- and three-man fox holes. Rockets would zap the hill occasionally and at night it got worse. Every night incoming artillery would try for the trench line filled with pine boxes, the ammo dump.

Billiter remembers:

"It started to get serious after a while. One night Spooky came around. The NVA were probing the wire so we lit candles, put them in empty C-rat cans and set these at the bottom of our fox holes. Others turned on strobe lights. We outlined the fire base with dots of flame and flash lights. Spooky hosed the jungle down. We had mad minutes every hour – at night. The DC-3 gun ship's fire was terrifying to me. Everything alive was cowering away and at the mercy of the red rain! It was red rain from a black sky. The shit was so close … you could feel the heat of the burning tracers and hear the bullets pitter-patter punching holes through the leaves. It looked like fresh lava flows at night! Word was that 3,000 NVA were in the immediate area and intelligence said we'd get hit! We were on twenty-four hour alert and could only sleep from 11:00 to 13:00, the hottest part of the day.

"I tried some weed for the first time. After all these months I thought, Hell, we were all dead men anyway. Dewy got me to toke up a 'J' and I got my nickname 'Jo Jo' because the Beatles song was on the radio right then. Just like in the song, Jo Jo was a goner...left his home in Tucson, AZ, to get some Asian grass... That good weed knocked me out. I even slept through a mad minute 'fire em up'. We were so tired anyway."

Once during midday, Jo Jo opened a can of fruit cocktail (in heavy syrup), some crackers, peanut butter and a tropical candy bar. He had all his opened cans spread around him on top of the sandbags outside his fighting position. He reached for the fruit but before he could slake his munchies, a steam whistle caterwauling squeal drilled into his right ear canal informing him as to the close proximity of an incoming rocket. The sonofabitch impacted over 60ft away but blew him up in the air and into a tight summersault! The little picnic Billiter was trying to enjoy scattered and suddenly disappeared on a wave of heat, sand and dirt. Billiter was pelted with light shrapnel and then slammed down hard.

Berchtesgaden was one hellish eyesore contrasting with the green and black ridges. If a CH-47 'shit hook' dropped off a 105mm howitzer, the blowing, beige dust boiling through the mutilated and scattered tree parts and the running, ducking, figures was truly unworldly.

By 23:00 hours on the 13th, Richard Freeman was sound asleep in one of the 1/506th bunkers on the north slope near the top artillery positions.

It had been a hard day for the young troop. That evening he'd walked along towards the chow line behind Lieutenant Drypolcher, the latest Hawk platoon leader. Minding their own business the soldiers picked their way along the dirt road that ran the length of the place. Suddenly, out of the blue Asian sky a 122mm rocket, the size of a huge fence post, smashed into the bank above the road. As the smoke and dust settled, Bill Drypolcher stood. He was surprised to see his elbows and knees oozing blood. Freeman, unhurt, looked over at the officer and both cracked up … laughing.

Around 22:00 Lieutenant Drypolcher and his RTO 'Dynamite' Murphy, plus a couple of other RTOs got word to move off the hill.

Mike Chiaramonte remembers humping up to the artillery positions and then down the east side in the dark.

Jim Billiter remembers thinking it was a suicide mission. Only two nights before the third Brigade had made contact and hit people outside the fire base. Army Intelligence had confirmed enemy movement all around and suspected an attack straight up the ridges. The Hawks were ordered down the most likely approach – a ridge with the flattest and widest top. They were under strength as usual, with no more than eight or nine able-bodied recondos.

Colonel Comny, fresh from Hamburger Hill, walked the 'heavy' recon element to the wire and whispered to Drypolcher,

"I feel for you, son."

Outside the wire the slope was dark and treacherous and the path a tangle of dead trees and rocks. The pointman was a Chu Hoi – an ex-NVA. Billiter was seriously questioning the wisdom of being on a paratrooper recon team. In the gloom, as a moon rose over the A Shau, an artillery man watched the heavily armed file worm through the wire. His brain engaged and his tongue flew into gear,

"I wouldn't trade places with you for…" He clammed up, feeling a fool. Billiter stood up straight and smiled a wicked leer like he was really enjoying the show. He enjoyed the man's honest awe. Billiter just drummed

237

the pommel on his large Bowie knife and repeated over and over – "safety on … round in the chamber, safety on … round in the chamber."

The fire base was surrounded. Trail watchers and sappers nervously fingered their AK-47s, RPGs, satchel charges and signal whistles.

About 24:00 the moon was way too bright. The Hawks took it for a bad sign. A bad moon. They watched it glow behind black branches. Drypolcher dropped his men down the shadow side of the ridge East, away from the A Shau, and below the bulldozed rubble and trees. It was slow going.

It was June 14, 1969. Billiter remembers:

"Right off we spotted trail watchers and wanted to go after them. Drypolcher said no. They were right next to us letting us walk by. Somebody walked over to take a piss and takes one look down the hill. He sees gook soldiers and trail watchers standing around watching us!"

Typical of NVA/VC to obey orders and wait for a signal to attack the fire base … and that's all. No second-guessing superiors, no innovative, creative, brave actions. They hoped nobody knew they were just a few yards away, probably waiting for their sappers to cut paths through the wire. In fact, at that moment sappers were crawling into the wire with wire cutters and bamboo tie downs to foil the trip flares. Some of the NVA crawled naked to avoid getting snagged and giving themselves away. With pants and shirts outlining arms and legs they were easier to spot. A naked guy, with an earth-toned suntan, tended to blend into the ground, sans blue shorts.

Past midnight, a senior NCO from the 1/506th walked out of the TOC bunker towards his favorite piss tube. The pisser was on the north cliff face. Old Sarge was almost blind, trying to find his way while gaining some night vision. He knew the cliff was close by and was startled to see a head materialize from below ground level. A head with what looked like a steel helmet popped up. Sarge's mind jumped into fast forward, looking for possible explanations: GI or Kit Carson Scout or what? Sarge opened his mouth and his unit's password came out, "Currahee!"

The figure with the helmet immediately replied some choice Vietnamese … probably mistaking the password for Vietnamese.

By then the Hawks were 1,000 meters out and without commo. They sat in place to try and find their bearings. The NVA had let them go. Walter Jackson helped put out a whole shitload of claymore mines facing down the trail ready for anything.

Suddenly whistles blew and the North Vietnamse Army rushed the fortress. They hit all sides at once, *except* up the shadow ridge where the Hawks waited.

The stink of sweat, bug repellent, cammo grease, fear and mildewed nylon gear mingled in the 90 degree air among the Hawk team.

Mortars walked back and forth over the top of Berchtesgaden doing little damage but thoroughly stirring up mayhem!

The Currahee Sarge rolled a couple of grenades out his bunker and started killing NVA around his piss tube.

Mike Cline fingered the NVA knife he'd found on a water run. Mike was told to move forward and use his scope mounted on his M-14. Mike cursed the fire base REMFs for their beer-drinking and screw-checking the perimeter, ways. Mike cussed Drypolcher for putting him up front with a useless sniper rifle. All the months of walking point with the 14 and finally Mike got a sniper mission … in the dark! What a deal. Mike started to curse the staff officers and the TOC commandos, but up above he noticed a strange glow spread down the mountain. RPG rockets cascaded into the fiery blush. Something was burning on Berchtesgaden!

Voices and figures snapping off branches, seemed all around the Hawks. Gear and loose rounds in drawstring bags clattered as assault teams climbed a ridge not far from Tick's squad.

Mike Chiaramonte, now a new E-5 Sergeant-type, wanted to check in with the TOC but couldn't raise them. He figured nobody would answer anyway and if they did it would probably be some insane order to attack behind the invaders. An order he would disobey.

Sp/4 Richard Freeman, a veteran of Hamburger Hill with Bravo 1/506th and the one-time acting 1st sergeant during the May assault, remembers the night on Berchtesgaden.

"It was actually the morning of the 14th, around 3 am. I remember being asleep in our bunker when all hell started to break loose. Our guard on top of the bunker jumped down to the doorway and dove in, screaming, "We're being hit!"

"No shit! It didn't take his announcement to inform us of that. In retrospect, it is obvious that we hadn't mastered the fine points of engineering a fighting position. We had phu gas set out in front of our bunker with a blasting cap and wire leading back to the bunker. Well, not exactly back to the bunker. This is where you begin to think, 'WHOOPS!'

"Maybe this wasn't the way we should have set this up. As you recall, the bunkers had a chain link fence in front of them to act as a shield from rockets. We had attached our detonator to the fence maybe 3ft off the ground and to the front of the bunker. This was maybe 3–4ft from the entrance to our shelter. It might as well have been 1,000 yards!

"Calderon, a Puerto Rican, about 5ft 7in, husky, who could almost speak English and possessed a crazed look, fired his machine gun incessantly out the front and only gun port. I had no idea what he was firing at since he seemed to be shooting mainly at the sky. He was shooting, however. My damaged ears can testify to that. It is a wonder that anybody who has been through a heavy battle like that can still hear. Anyway, Calderon ordered someone to detonate the phu gas. I might have still been pretty new to Vietnam but I had learned that bravery didn't mean throwing away your life without weighing what could be gained. Yeah, I was one of those college dropouts who wanted to examine the pros and cons of an order before obeying. Well, no one moved for the detonator and Calderon stopped shooting long enough to mention something about 'pussies'. I guess he must have been horny or something because I know he wasn't talking about me. He sure didn't go do it himself so I realized that his reference to 'pussy' was purely some irrational sexual reaction to the battle.

"From our position in the draw below the main LZ, I had no idea what was going on around us. Plenty of firing and explosions but I couldn't see anything. We tried to establish communication with the company CP and eventually did. They wanted to make sure we were all alive and asked us to check on the bunker to our right. The wire to them was dead and it was still too dark to find our way to it or maybe it was too exposed. The bunker was about 50 yards or so away over very rough exposed terrain. As the fighting let up a little a couple of us crawled over to the neighbors and fortunately found them all alive. They were pretty shaken – just like the rest of us. We also found that the landline connecting our bunkers had been cut with something sharp and clean. The cut was right behind and to the right of our bunker. It looked like our guard had fallen asleep. We were lucky we weren't all gutted. War is a lot like life."

Calderon had looked out his gun port and when a flare went off saw a sight that made his skin crawl. The cliff under the TOC, on the north side, was a solid wall of NVA looking like flies and maggots climbing without ladders or any climbing gear. The gunner killed many.

That cliff was where John Wolfgang and I once begged the NVA to come up. Bodies fell back and crashed down into the trees making it easier for enemy medics and nurses to cart off the dead and dying.

A lot of sappers topped the hill and overran the base, blowing mortar pits and several 105 howitzers with satchel charges. One of the 2/327th's FOs was killed and two or three dudes in the bunkers. Old 'Rattle Snake' the 3rd Brigade commander was wounded. A 106 recoilless rifle crew from my Company (Company E: mortars and recon) was wiped out.

As for the Hawks, they spent the entire night outside the wire. Several of them had stayed behind for various reasons and ended up getting the worst of it for Recon. Platoon Sergeant Zamora was hit as were others. Zamora was pretty chunky and managed to get a deep nick from something flying through the air as well as severe burns over his arms and face.

After careful and repeated warning calls on the radio and shouts up through the trees to the trigger-happy defenders, the Hawks walked back in. Lieutenant Drypolcher put Vic Beard out front going back up into the wire because he was the only Hawk with a familiar American steel helmet(Hawks trench warfare gear used on the firebase). Bodies mostly clothed in a mixture of green and blue nylon shorts lay steaming in the humid morning air. It looked like Custer's Last Stand. Fires were still burning around the top of the base and some of the 105s had been spiked.

That morning, at about 06:00, Freeman saddled up with his platoon and went looking for more attackers. They found some bandages and blood trails, but that was it. Freeman estimates that thirty or so sappers were killed, most coming up over the south side through the tree tangles where the dozers had pushed a lot of dirt. He believed the human waves of NVA were stopped by point blank firing of the 155s and 106 rifles using fleshette shells.

The month before, Freeman had assaulted Hamburger Hill with Bravo 1/506th and had finally conquered the summit with the 3/187th after crawling through a sea of body parts, dead, wounded and tangled trees. Delta 3/187th by that time had lost around fifty men and suffered more than anyone in the ten-day battle.

On Berchesgaden lots of dead bad guys were policed up and thrown into a pile then slung off in a couple of cargo nets. A CH-47 flown by CWO Bob Patrick came in and the 'shit hook' ace granted a special request from the troops. Russell Balisok, with B Co. 158th, 101, call sign 'Lancer 16', was on short final into the hellhole and saw the whole thing. Paratroopers lined the crest of the prominence to watch the bodies leave. Rumor control went wild; something was 'up'.

The twin Boeing jacked the bodies up about 1,000ft and close enough so every swinging dick could see. Jim Billiter claims to have watched Patrick punch off the grizzly load and said he would take to the grave images of tumbling, draining, young bodies dumping out of those nets – on purpose. Bolisok thought he saw about fifteen corpses. Billiter says forty or more. As the bodies spilled out a guttural howl and cheer just spontaneously erupted from the over-stressed victors. Packs of wild animals would have understood. Fists raised to the heavens in uncontrolled salutes.

Only one little problem marred the operation. When Patrick took off up wind, as customary, he unloaded straight ahead instead of turning 'down wind'. The prevailing winds wafted rotting flesh smells over Berchtesgaden for weeks. I have no idea if the high-jinx was deliberate psychological warfare or what. However, any retreating NVA that may have been in the impact zone, probably turned white with horror as their old friends dropped in.

Chapter 57

The Land of Oz

"Hey Oz, what the fuck are you doing over there?" Chiaramonte hailed. The Hawks were back from Berchesgaden and I eased back in as head medic. We had walked into a pine forest. Could this possibly be Vietnam I wondered? This had to be a dream I thought to myself. The ground underfoot was a carpet of soft pine needles. This was a dream ... right ... I asked myself? This was like the Del Monte Forest in Carmel. My foot snagged a thin green wire. Too late. Even as I felt the tug, too late to stop forward momentum. The wire triggered the device.

The whole mission had been a dream. We'd started out in dugout canoes and motored up the River of Perfumes. I was still in the Hawks but was getting pretty short plus I was supposed to be flying. One of the Hawks grabbed the boatman's conical hat and grinned for the other boatmen to see his new cover. We unloaded on a dark swampy bank. We were near Camp Eagle and had trucked over to the river.

After humping up into the pine forest I had started daydreaming. You could see a long ways through the scattered trees.

The booby trap went off next to my foot! Goddamn! When the fucker blew I thought it was a grenade. Luckily, it was a trip flare. Luckily, it was the middle of the afternoon. I was rudely shaken from my dreams. The place was a nest of trip flares. Hundreds of the things were deployed throughout the woods. And they had no fuse it seemed ... hit the wire and it immediately ignited!

A flare sputtered and burned brightly a few feet away. White smoke poured from the fire. What an idiot I was. Had it been a high explosive booby trap I would have been all fucked up. Christ, hadn't I seen enough human meat pulverized into a wet mist to really try and watch for wires.

"Fucking trip flare," I yelled unnecessarily to Mike Chiaramonte. I had been playing commando again, walking the side of the trail like point was supposed to do. But as point had walked right up the path, I should have followed. Some large force had bivouacked here and just left all their trip wires and flares in place. Sounded like ARVNs ... something probably scared the shit out of them and they didi-maued most Rikki-Tik!

We walked out of the foot snares and up to the gates of the Emerald City. The lost Emerald City. I had never seen a sight like it before and knew I would never again. It was deserted, abandoned ... seemingly. The approach was paved with booby traps, possibly to protect the entrance. The place was simply gigantic! A 40ft wall with 40ft solid hard wood gates surrounded it. The roofs were red shingles. Cowboy and his point team cautiously entered and found the buildings gutted and scattered with debris. Somebody had left the gate ajar.

Inside the walls we saw lush, runaway, green gardens, humungous fish ponds and overgrown statues of elephants and soldiers. We were in an imperial palace, I thought. I was wrong.

We were in a tomb; it was a place for dead people.

Walking the stone cobbled grounds was like going back in time thousands of years to a land of splendor and ancient kingdoms. We stood on the terrace and overlooked acres and acres of fish ponds. Our mouths hung down. Lily pads choked the water. Large oversize statues of dragons and lions peeked out of bamboo clumps and from under Banyan tree root systems. The roots became Medusa hair and blended in perfectly around, in and over the top of some stone heads! I loved the place. It was like a science fiction movie. Hell, it was way better than when Mom took us to the Golden Gate Japanese Tea Garden.

We were in the tomb of Nguyen King: Tu Duc, the poet emperor. The name of the place was 'Where grief smiles and joy sighs'. Stone mandarins watched our every move from their hiding places back in the deep weeds.

The question in my mind was, if this was headquarters of the ancient Cham or Vietnamese civilization, then what happened to it and where were the people? These folks were obviously capable of building a civilization far greater than I thought possible. Some evil force, some invading nation had disrupted this special place. Barbarians from the north, just like the stone soldiers and elephants guarding our perimeter now, surrounding us out in the brush, were responsible. The NVA still used elephants. Of course, it was the NVA, they were the barbarians … or were they? The old courts of Hue had seen the future it seemed, they had built the tombs decorated with displays of military might. The people were still around, they were just in the cities and hamlets.

As for the civilization, I didn't know. Civilization seemed to have broken down even though some said we were in a civil war. Did they mean a 'nice' war? Nothing was nice or civil about this killing spree. We were spending month after month looking to kill invaders from the North. Maybe the tea leaves had forecast invaders from the East. But it wasn't us who were the invading barbarians, the hired mercenaries. Naw … not us. We had 'National Defense' ribbons to prove it. We were killing these royal people to defend our nation … shit.

I finally snapped out of my daydreams. Silly shit could get you killed. But I looked around at the Hawks and for a second, for a split second I saw walking, living, breathing, killing machines dressed in animal skins, bronze and copper and steel armor, but still clutching M-16s, M-60s, pistols, rockets, grenades and portable mines. We were walking point for Genghis Khan and his army and I had been the first to volunteer.

Chapter 58

The Paris of the Orient

Bravo was first in. They landed and secured the LZ. It was a giant mountain clearing in tall trees. This was my last major operation as the Hawks chief medic.

I sat in the door of the UH-IH Huey, legs hanging out, John Wayne style. I loved the flying – the combat assaults. I loved sitting behind the pilots, it was cool, comfortable and fun. We went in right behind Bravo. I was the one and only medic today and I felt like a flying superhero.

My ruck gave me a false sense of security plopped on the deck and strapped around my shoulders. It felt secure and anchored. However, I was realistic enough to know that if the ship suddenly banked over, the ruck and I would sail out into space like some kamikaze skydiver; falling like a greased anvil. A dead stupidhero. Rucksacks make poor anchors and even worse parachutes, being filled with 60lbs of tinned food and gear the way they are. We flew in low level formation. Treetops raced by outside. The choppers climbed and dropped slightly, in the heat waves, pulling up at the last second to clear the odd ball tree that had decided to grow higher than its neighbors.

The stick of Hueys dove into the hole that was our LZ. This was a five ship gaggle that slowed and flared for the touch down. We carried so much crap with us they would only let five grunts on board each aircraft. Other Divisions like the 1st Cavalry, carried eight to ten sky cavalry soldiers out on their day excursions. We, on the other hand, packed for a longer stay. I got out on the chopper's right skid for the last 100ft or so, holding on with my left hand. It was stupid, but I liked it. We were bad-assed air cavalry, right? We were expected to do things like that. The other trick was to see how high we could jump off without breaking

246

our dorks. This was some ridiculous point of honor, I suppose, because some of us were supposed to be paratroopers. Shock troops the Army called us. At that point in the war the 101st had a large percentage of non-jumpers … like 85 per cent or more. What *was* shocking to us was the fact that we were not even getting the extra $55 a month pay that was promised to all jump school graduates.

At 6ft, I released my grip and jumped off the skid. I hit the ground like a sack of burned shit. A Huey flashed by us really close pumping out a rather large smoke screen hiding our flight from some of the terrain above us. Meanwhile my ruck, with its four canteens flapping, bulging M-5 aid-bag and stuffed pouches and main compartment, slammed me into the grass and kept going, carried by its own momentum. Up and over my head the pack rolled; off into the weeds. Shocking! It just kept tumbling. The Hawks waddled off the crash zone, away from the birds with their whining mass of moving parts, arcing electricity and man-killing main blades. The main rotors ripped around trying to brain anyone stupid enough not to duck down. The blades changed pitch for lift off making a loud WOP, WOP, WOP while the tail rotor 'buzzed' along behind, looking to decapitate anyone missed by the mains. I looked around and saw we were surrounded by high ridges and trees; a perfect trap. I knew where my ruck was because it had left a trail.

It was a cold LZ. No one was trying to kill us … then. In Bravo's CP I stood around with all the RTOs and medics while Lieutenant Good shot the bull with their captain. Lieutenant Good looked down on Bravo's commander. He was a short little guy with crew cut and big ears; very collegiate looking. In fact their whole CP looked like some Ivy League sculling club. Doc Maurice was nearby, my buddy. He was their head pill. We shook hands, Vietnam style. We touched fists three times, my pinkie to his thumb then his pinkie to my thumb finishing with knuckles touching.

"What's happenin', Jim?" I asked.

"Same old bullshit," he replied.

"Bullshit … that's not very airborne is it…?"

Maurice, the ever good-natured medic.

"Hey man, check out my Seiko watch I bagged in Tokyo," I lifted my wrist so Jim could admire the timepiece.

"Bagged a good case of the clap too, I hope?"

"Fuck you ... they're ladies in Tokyo ... yes ... the Paris of the Orient."

"That's Saigon, Saigon's the ..."

"What ...?"

"Saigon's the Paris of the Orient. You know ... all the French."

"Right, right, look Jim, gotta run."

I noticed Lieutenant Good pulling his RTO along with the coiled radio handset cord connecting them, making for the perimeter Bravo was still setting up.

"Us recondos gotta go out and kill something, protect these sorry-ass little line companies," I added.

"Recondos ... you call yourself recondos? Dirty Dozen is more like it. Shit ..."

"Yeah ... right ... take care yah dumb fuck."

"Same to ya, take it easy ... buy ya a beer when we get to the rear."

What a generous offer ... a beer would set him back about 10 cents. We slipped through their perimeter and headed north-west down a dry stream bed. We'd gone about a 100 yards when suddenly I heard something odd. I thought I heard ... thump ... thump, phaffft, phaffft ... Pouahk, Pouahk! Incoming! I slipped and fell on the smooth rounded creek rock. Mortars, it had to be mortars. Karrumph, Karummph, Karrumph! Loud explosions ricocheted down the creek from B Company's position. My vision slipped into slow-motion mode. SFC Oliver tripped over my foot and sailed through the air. His large olive-skinned body seemingly floating, almost frozen in space. When he hit the ground, he hit hard, pushing a pile of rocks and gravel with his arms, shoulder and face. I almost laughed out loud. Karummph, Karummph! As the gooks laid a mortar barrage into the line company, Lieutenant Good yelled for the Hawks to form a perimeter. One of the new guys who I didn't know well, climbed the far bank. He peeked over a wall of brush, ducked back down and then lifted his '16 over the brush, firing away. He fired blindly with both arms overhead operating the weapon, but from a kneeling position.

Odd, but at least some rounds were spinning down range. It was all over in seconds. The gooks must have used up their ration of shells. They had Bravo trapped and nailed the CP with about twenty rounds. When it quieted we knew the NVA were waiting ... watching and re-arming.

We got up and humped out fast.

We walked till dark and then some. I felt eyes on me the whole time. Finally we stopped. I remember collapsing right on the trail, rolling up in my jungle blanket and cutting ZZZZZs. Around two in the morning I lurched up wide awake, soldiers were coming up the trail. It was Bravo filing past. I went back to sleep.

At first light I woke. Maurice was making coffee over a C-rat stove. It was still dark in the brush where we lay. My fatigues were covered with dirt, but were dry so I was content. The heat tabs in Jim's stove burned with bright blue flames through the triangle holes punched around the can with an old style beer can-opener. A canteen cup, full of water, sat on top.

"How was it yesterday?" I asked, referring to the attack.

"Fucked up!"

Jim continued, "You know those rounds hit right where we both stood yesterday ... with our thumbs up our ass. We just lay down and took it, hadn't dug in or anything. Got five wounded ... BAD."

"Damn."

How could our fearless leaders be so stupid to fly us into a tight jungle valley nobody had ever been to and then let us wander around near the LZ asking for trouble?

Suddenly the alarm went off. A faint dingdingdingdingding ...

"What the fuck is that, Oz?"

"It's the alarm on my Seiko ... time to kill something," I said merrily.

"All the comforts of home, huh ... ?"

"Yeah, ain't it great? This is my good luck, X-rated, jungle watch. See the hands glow?" I waved it up and down. The thick hour hand and the minute hand glowed green.

"How does it rate an X-rating?"

"It's a vibrator, of course. When the alarm goes off it vibrates like a scalded bumble bee. I just wind the alarm up all the way, strap it down on the head of my dick and when it goes off I get a reminder of R&R in Tokyo."

"Oz, you're not well ... you know that?" Jim said, shaking his head and choking on his coffee.

"Brother, you should have been there. Yeah, I can see it now, smell it ... taste it...feel it ... right here, right now ... Tokyo, the Paris of the Orient."

Chapter 59

Shooters

Lizard Man walked up the slope in full rucksack. He stopped and watched the rest of the grunts file past. We were back on fire base Berchtesgaden, going out on patrol on my very last hump, ever, I hoped. The grunts headed towards the wire. It was dark and Lizard Man turned to scan the faint outlines of the distant ridges. Lizard was the ugliest black man I'd ever seen. He was famous for his tattoo. The guy had a tattoo on his back depicting a man forcefully mating with a chicken. The artwork must have been designed by a 4-year-old. I think Lizard was from Dominica or Haiti.

Lizard surly felt the cool breeze and thought about humping the boonies yet again. He rested the muzzle of his M-16 on the front of his right boot and supported his torso with the butt and stock. Hand on pistol grip, he eased the rifle barrel directly over his big toe. He could feel a bump through the thin leather. He flicked the safety with his thumb, clockwise, to semi-auto and squeezed the trigger … BLAAMM!

The muffled report of a '16 exploded right in front of me! I wheeled towards the sound. Jeez…nothing like having the crap scared out of you at four in the morning. I checked my pants…good..seemed to be clean. I saw two guys shoot themselves over in the Nam. Lizard and some other yahoo. The incidents could have been accidents, but it's doubtful. Both times the bullet drilled through the big toe and both times by an M-16 at close range. Personally, I would have been afraid the weapon would have blown the toe off. I suppose that's why the big toe was selected as the smaller cousins might have come loose. But no, it simply blasted a clean little hole through the boot, through the sock, skin, bone and through the steel anti-spike sole. Later, back in the rear, I saw an X-ray of one toe shot. Very unimpressive – a dark spot in the center of the bone. I didn't bandage those wounds or give morphine but I would have given them a Band-Aid, if I'd been asked. After the shootings I never saw Lizard or the other guy again.

One day Nelson Ramos approached me out in the field. We'd dug in for some unknown reason.

"Doc, Doc, a rat bit me! Ya gotta send me in, I'm gonna die!"

Nelson shoved his hand in my face and pointed to a tiny nick on the back. The whole hand practically dripped some kind of red stain anti-septic which I figured was mostly for emphasis and authenticity – and of course a lot of sincerity. I'd been in the woods too long, my nerves were getting to me and I wasn't in the mood for any bullshit.

"I ain't gotta do jack diddley-squat," I said. "Go back to your position, Ramos; I don't believe you."

Ramos, a little Puerto Rican with short hair, persisted but his pleas lacked conviction. I was busy and had to order medical supplies over the radio. I didn't have time for the con game. .

About then, Ramos's squad leader, Mann slipped up to my fox hole.

Mann, the fair-skinned country boy from Pennsylvania. Mann, with his blue eyes, blond filthy hair and jungle rot. He was a jumper, handsome and a respected old timer.

"What's happenin', Doc?" he asked, peeking through a curtain of vines and brush.

"You are homie," I answered. "By the way Mann, I'm gonna order some medical shit … need anything?"

"No."

"Ya going to order some rabies serum for Nelson?" he asked. I hesitated. "Doc … you can't give that stuff out here … can you?" He pronounced 'Doc' in a whining tone used for the near stupid.

"Fuck … I don't know … but … I sure as hell don't *even* believe him … do you?"

I was fairly certain that rabies serum injections couldn't be administered in the field. But I wanted to call a bluff. I knew Mann was listening so I went ahead.

I stood in the CP area, next to one of the radios and grabbed the handset. Somebody was on the horn and ready to take my order.

"Give me two dozen throat lozenges, fifteen battle dressings, some Tinactin, a box of Band-Aids, six ace wraps, a large bottle of Darvon and some cotton tip applicators and … oh yah … better give me some rabies serum … over … and out."

"Roger that … will send out ASAP," an unquestioning voice hissed back at me from some distant outpost towards the rear.

Nelson never pushed his case or even returned for his 'medicine', or injections or any kind of treatment I might have come up with. He never again asked to go back to the rear. He stayed with us out in the field. He didn't die or even get sick. The funny thing was, I never received anything that even remotely resembled rabies serum; I probably wouldn't have recognized it if I had. Nelson knew I humped a wide assortment of needles. I had packs and packs of long syringes and he was positive I lived only for the day I got to slam 15 or 20 ccs of medicine deep into human flesh. He was right.

Nelson was a damn fine soldier, a typical Puerto Rican. He was in jump school with me. He was just sick and tired, like me.

I gave injections the airborne way. Guys wanted me to do it. They wanted to be shot up for VD. Usually prior to R&R or sometimes on return. They wanted liquid protection. I gave it to them. They dropped their pants and I broke out a whole pack of disposable syringes, already loaded. I had either penicillin or streptomycin – five to a pack. First, I marked the target with an alcohol swab. We learned to hit the upper right quadrant of the right butt. Then I grabbed the whole pack of six inch syringes in my sweaty little fist and fired away. Airborne! Injecting five hypos at once was no easy feat, no siree Bob. It took both thumbs to slowly push the fluid into reluctant flesh.

"You did say you wanted to get it over with … didn't you … ?" I'd ask with a grin.

The next day I flew out from Berchtesgaden for the very last time. I got dropped off at the 2/327th chopper pad and I made the 'Last Walk' down the hill to the barracks. I didn't realize it at the time, but this meant no more boonies; no more hunting humans – no more headhunting.

Chapter 60

DUST OFF!

I had a little problem. I had to make a couple of decisions. I had less than a month remaining of my combat tour and I didn't like the rear. I thought about extending for another tour, in-country. I was qualified for Army aviation and an air crewman position, as a medic, on medivac ships. The only other option, for me, was the LRPs. Well, I could have finally got back into the Green Berets like my buddy Mike Blecker from B company, and even on a MACV SOG team possibly, but I just didn't think about it. My ego wasn't out of control anymore. I probably just didn't give a flying fuck. The Army presented a pretty good deal, really. In order to get experienced troops to stay in Nam they would give early discharges for those who extended. I still had fourteen months to go, in service. A thirty-day stateside leave, the time cut, and another R&R was part of the 'agreement'. I would extend for about six months then leave Vietnam a free man ... or a dead one. A free ride home was available ... in a coffin!

SSG Bell had told me: "What ever ya do ... don't extend for the 2/327th."

I'd already opted to fly Dustoff. But first I had to finish a flight physical. I went down and flunked the hearing test. All the exposure to M-16s, LAWs and that old 30cal machine gun must have done some more damage. Plus I had had ear problems as a toddler.

The flight surgeon called me into his office.

"Hey troop, todays your lucky day. You just failed the hearing test."

"But I want to fly Dustoffs."

"What's the matter, you crazy or something? You know they use those red crosses for targets. Every time you go out somebody nearby wants to kill you. They got a medic just the other day, shot 'em through the head. And besides, if you go on flight status you'll lose even more hearing, you hear me," the colonel chuckled. He really tried to talk me out of it, it seemed, talking that shit. Of course, the bad hearing test was the perfect out but they needed fliers too.

"I don't care," I replied.

"You don't care, huh? Well, if you don't care I guess no one else does either. Go and try the hearing test again."

The second time around I must have 'passed' because the doctor signed me fit for flight duty. I would fly as third-man crew for Eagle Dustoff and if they accepted me, and if I still wanted to, I would extend.

Eagle Dustoff sat in a gully. The grounds were well oiled to keep the dust down, wouldn't you know. The dominate feature was the large chopper pad. The Hueys sat in sandbagged roofless bunkers (revetments) on the east side. The maintenance hanger squatted on the north and the headquarters and barracks overlooked the pad on the west side. Even had a control tower.

I was to sleep in one of the wooden barracks up on the hill. Still carrying my M-16, I checked out the sleeping area. Inside I walked onto the plywood floor. Army 38 revolvers hung in holsters above the cots. The place was huge and deserted.

Our SSG Bell was here too, part-time I guess: I couldn't shake the guy. He stuck his head inside the screen door of the barracks,

"Hey Osgood, let's get you some flight gear."

In the supply room a supply clerk held up his spread hand, palm first in front of my face.

"Hand size?" he asked. I pressed my spread fingers against his like some alien hand-shake.

"Number 9," he yelled over his shoulder. Another clerk appeared with a pair of flying gloves and a helmet. The gloves fit perfectly – skin tight. The gloves were the 'new' neat-looking soft grey leather and Nomex (pronounced nam-ex in Vietnam) flight gloves worn by all US pilots and crews. At the time these were made by a 'small Italian family company' out of New York I believe. What a contract that was. The palms were leather and the tops, 'flameproof' green Nomex. The helmet was flat black and sported a nifty, large, Confederate flag, on the back. The stars and bars were proudly displayed. Yea Haaaw ... the South is going to do it again.

My job was to get up early, walk down to the flight line and get the bird ready for the day. I was supposed to clean the plastic windshield and swamp out the cockpit.

The first morning found me trying to polish the Plexiglass with plastic cleaner. The sun was barley up and already I was sweating like a fat man. Damn the windows were big, I cussed. Once the cleaner got on the glass it took forever to wipe off. Inside the cockpit I brushed dirt off the radios with a hand brush. The inside was filthy. Small pebbles were stuck in between the radios and in all the hard-to-get nooks and crannys.

I sat on the steel cargo deck, in the shade, and waited for the crew chief and the other medic. Actually I dreaded their arrival, this was a new trip all together. All too soon the crew showed up. My M-16 lay on the bare steel next to my helmet and gloves. The medic walked up and said, "Okay, the first thing is, all flight crews wear their sleeves rolled down all the way ... all the time. Just the opposite the way ya did out in the boonies. Ya gotta wear your gloves all the time too. That's all cause of fire. Your face can burn off but the Army wants your body intact."

The pilots hadn't arrived yet but the crew chief went about untying the main rotors. A long, flat like a belt, red nylon webbed rope, weighted at the end and with a hook on the other, secured the blades. Hooked through a hole in one blade tip and with the heavy end flopped around the tail stinger (tail skid) a couple of times, the rope tied down the rotary wings. It kept the rotors from wind-milling free after shut down.

The medic walked around the cargo bay, hunched over.

"The left door is yours. Right is the chief's. He'll operate the winch."

I eyed the yellow winch attached from floor to roof behind the right seat. Steel wire cable ran up through an arm and slid over the side with either a 'jungle penetrator' or Stokes Basket at the end. The penetrator sat three wounded, with its narrow spring-loaded folding seats and safety straps.

The medic picked up my weapon and jammed it behind the seat and the engine compartment wall in the rearmost bay. We were conducting 'mercy flights', so we carried only personal weapons. No door gunners.

"You are responsible for maintaining traffic separation on our side of the aircraft along with the pilots," he continued.

"You know, so we don't run into anybody else and make Crispy Critters out of ourselves. Here's your chest protector, it's body armor … 'Chicken Skin'."

He slid a canvas vest over the deck to where I sat.

Hefting the vest I inspected the contents. "Pheewh this thing's heavy," I complained. "This ain't no ordinary flack vest."

Inside the canvas, front and back, were large, thick, concave, pieces of armor each in its own pouch. The stuff looked like naked chicken skin just before it hits the fire. This was a bulletproof vest, sort of.

"Just sit on the fucker, if ya want," I was told. I tried it on and it felt like 60lbs of dead weight, at least. Fuck that shit. I pulled it off over my head and dropped it onto the seat. It would stop rifle rounds coming up through the floor, I hoped.

The pilots showed up. The flight crews defined the word 'cool'. They wore dirty, tailored flight suits with thousands of wrinkles. Over the flight clothing were survival vests, pistol belts, sheath knives and one pilot wore love beads! Both rotor jocks had two-day-old beards and wore tired eyes that said 'fuck you' a dozen different ways.

The aircraft commander forced his hands into black and green oil-stained gloves before squeezing into his helmet. It was CWO Frank Hitchens (Dustoff niner 4) and his hard hat was painted glossy black with what looked like two buzzards mating in flight, on the left side. White letters proudly proclaimed: Fly United!

Chapter 61

Black Wolf Down

On almost my last mission the pilots kicked the fire after they had lit the tire ... or something. The jet engine lit up. I sat in back next to the bulletproof vest.

The tremendous force generated by the engine, instead of supplying direct thrust, turned the rotors and lift was had from the long skinny wings. The jet exhaust shot out the back like a pure jet, but these babies spent 99 per cent of the energy 'water-wheeling' the blades. It was a free-spinning turbine. Soon the rotor disk was a blur of black and yellow overhead. I was plugged into the ship's intercom system and static, in stereo, hissed in both ears. I listened to the crew's conversation for a quick mission brief. The medic and the crew chief called out,

"Tail clear left, tail clear right," as the bird became light on the skids and the power came up. The main blades' pitch changed as they dug into the air, thudding and slapping.

The Bell Aircraft 'Huey', officially named the IROQUOIS, and also known as the famous UH-1H, equipped with a 48ft rotor span, a gross weight of around 9,500lbs, a 1,100hp Lycoming T53-L-13 engine that produced a maximum speed of 120 mph and a crew of five, six litters, one Stokes basket and one jungle penetrator – came off the ground to a hover. God I loved it so!

We nosed over and gathered speed. The static was almost painful in my ears. It stopped,

"Got a Marine chopper on the ground north of Hue," one of the pilots broke squelch.

"Call sign ... Black Wolf."

The static returned. We climbed out of the gully and over small ridges and hills. We trucked along Highway 1, northward. Northbound traffic flew on the right side and south bound flew on the other side. How clever. Black Wolf was right next to the road, up to his cargo deck in water and mud. You could see his skid marks in the shallow part of the paddy were he slid in. He was painted flat black. The crew was out standing next to the machine up to their knees. They all waved us off and after a quick buzz job we did a 'one eighty' for home. For some reason they had skidded into the rice paddy after auto-rotating. They'd survived a forced landing and probably an engine failure. No biggie.

Over flying the fortress of Hue was interesting and I noticed the miles of outer walls looking very much like the Great Wall of China, only straighter. You could still see battle damage from the 68 Tet fighting.

Going back, south, along the road again, on the west side, we were very nearly all cremated. Suddenly the chopper keeled over to the right, HARD! We pulled big 'G's and I grabbed the seat with both hands.

"Goddamn it, keep your fucking eyes open back there," the A/C yelled to his crew. We had just missed another aircraft … in a near mid-air. I hadn't seen a thing but a lot of traffic abounded between Camp Eagle, Phu Bia airport and Hue. The pilots were all pissed off probably because they had missed an oncoming aircraft … invisible to us crew. In addition one of them told me to keep my head in the cargo bay as the slip stream was making too much noise whistling through my helmet mic. He was slightly irritated. Then, to make matters worse the stick jockeys started jabbering away about Migs, in a nervous high-pitched chatter. Migs, holy shit. Were Migs up here south of the DMZ? A minute later we took a sharp turn to the right to follow a fair-sized river. We dove to water level. We snaked wildly next to the trees, staying below the banks. Clearing a point of trees, put us almost on a collision course with a teenage girl taking a bath! Missed by 30ft she ducked down, a little, in the water naked as a new pig. She was gorgeous and as I waved, she grinned me a smile that made me forget all about N.V.A., Migs and exploding helicopters.

Back in the gully the crew chief and the first medic called out our elevation above the pad once we'd swung into the revetment.

"4 feet. 2 feet. 1 foot. 6 inches. Down!"

Chapter 62

If We Can't … .Nobody Can … !

An electronic cry for help wailed out of the jungle.

Near the main gate at Camp Eagle, a Huey UH-1H air ambulance hovered above the pad at Eagle Dustoff. The pilot nosed the bird over, pulled pitch, banked and swung west. We followed Route 547 toward Fire Base Bastogne. Palm trees flashed by as the pilots took us up the road, low level. 'Low level fun', we called it. Basically you had two choices when flying, you could go high or you could go low. Flying at altitude is like on the airliners with the earth slowly drifting beneath the wing. Flying low-level was like having sex with movie stars, better even. We booked right up the center of Route 547, 10ft off the ground! The trees towered overhead in groves of tattered black and green fronds and trunks with raw wounds of red tree meat. The pilots, Tom McCrawly and Frank Tiffany, grinned back and forth to one another. The road seemed deserted.

By the time we reached Birmingham, the main rotors were clawing for altitude. Ahead the Annamite Ranges stretched as far as Laos and towards the Mekong River. By the time we reached Bastogne, we had shot up to 3,000ft … still climbing.

The 101st combat engineers had blasted, bulldozed and chain-sawed some of the mountain tops around us free of trees for fire bases. I recognized Eagle's nest, Veghel, and Berchtesgaden, islands of safety in a sea of danger and death! Over a major ridge line, abeam of the highest fire base, we saw the valley for the first time that day. It looked like a shallow grave waiting for the dead.

The pilots talked to Division artillery, trying to get a clearance to cross the valley. They wanted to make bloody sure no 'cannon cockers' were slinging rounds our way. My ass was parked on top of the 'chicken-skin' bulletproof vest. I was in the seat where the door gunner would sit on a slick, in the 'hell-hole' all the way in the back. The 'chicken skin' wasn't the most comfortable seat in the world, but the ceramic chest and back plates stuffed into the OD canvas vest might turn small arms fire. Hopefully, it would prevent Sir Charles from providing me a new ass hole. Crockett, the first medic, spoke into his helmet mic, "Osgood ... try and remember this terrain. Don't ever want to get lost out here, especially after dark!"

We flew on. I reached behind my back and touched my M-16 that was wedged in between the seat and the transmission compartment wall. My '16 was the only rifle aboard this ship. The rest of the crew all sported .38 revolvers in leather holsters – western style. Eagle's choppers carried no M-60s in 1969. Seemed to me we should have the option to fire back if some asshole didn't believe we were on a mercy flight and did want to kill us. After all it wasn't unheard of to fly enemy troops to hospital.

To keep from falling out and playing superman, the crew in the cargo bay wore safety vests with umbilical cords or 'monkey straps'. Like astronauts, we attached ourselves to the mother ship. These vests were nylon net mesh with metal fasteners in front. A heavy nylon cord with a spring-loaded clamp at the far end ran off the back of the vest and this clamp could be hooked into various rings located around the cabin.

Once over the valley, I daydreamed about the choppers shot down here in August and the Skyraider rescue missions years ago. We flew over the abandoned air fields at A Shau, Ta Bat and A Loui as they baked in the sun. The air strips were still around, still part of the valley road system. The hidden AA sites were still around also waiting. It was a comfort to know that our ambulance was in range of half the enemy gunners from Laos to Bastogne! Also nice to know that, to see the red crosses we sported ... at any distance, was impossible. I felt like the guest of honor in a game of Russian roulette. Hamburger Hill, across the valley, was now back in enemy hands.

Suddenly, we started down. I suffered from a false sense of invincibility – I had much too great a confidence in the pilots and the bird. Somehow this whining, screeching machine that converted jet fuel into noise and exploding gases, this metallic mass of moving parts, comforted me. I felt as though we could fly through hell and back, as long as we kept moving. We dropped lower, aiming for the mountains on the far west side of the valley.

The A/C called the ground element, "Dustoff Niner Three to Delta 6, over …?"

"… Eagle Dustoff, this is Delta 6, go ahead."

"Roger, Delta 6, we're about ten klicks out to the east, standby with smoke."

"Okay, Eagle, we got one urgent WIA and no contact at this time, … over."

"Ah … roger that, no contact. What was the direction last incoming, sir … .?"

"Standby one … ah … last enemy contact was from 280 degrees … west … how copy Eagle?"

"Delta 6, we copy five by five … 280 degrees."

We had managed to cross the A Shau without drawing fire. We entered a steep, wide ravine on the west ridge. The terrain was truly awesome, the worst I'd ever seen in my life, all cliffs or tall trees. I mean gigantic cliffs, shear 90 degrees for maybe 1,000ft or more. It was great! It looked like we were going to cross the border into Laos.

On and on we came, smack up against the mountain. The pilot slowed us down and my earphones crackled to life, he said,

"Delta 6, this is Dust-off niner 3 with you here coming up on the high terrain, gimmie a smoke."

"Roger … Eagle, smokes out! Let me know when you see it."

The assistant A/C studied a map in his lap. From time to time his head popped up and swiveled around to study the surroundings. Below us was some of the thickest, toughest rainforest on the face of the earth. We flew into the place and it seemed to swallow us down. We closed on the tree tops and you could see that some of the area was dead from spray defoliant. This was Hamburger Hill country. The voice on the ground ripped through the static,

"Sssssssss Okay Eagle, we got ya now, we hear ya … .ah … I see you now! Keep on the way ya are."

"Roger Delta, we still don't see you, better throw another smoke."

"Smokes out, Eagle. We're near the defoliated area dead ahead."

Suddenly the co-pilot said, "I got 'em. Right there at 2 o'clock, low, purple." The A/C spoke with the ground element,

"We got ya … Delta … we got goofy grape at 2 o'clock now."

The goofy grape code was an attempt to prevent Sir Charles from overhearing us, popping purple smoke near an AA site, and blowing us out of the sky! The NVA had their own, captured smoke grenades of course and some of our radios (a few probably obtained for cash from US soldiers). Most probably from lifers who knew about those things.

"Roger Eagle, goofy grape … sssss … we got," the ground affirmed.

We circled in over Delta's position. They were down at the bottom of a skeleton forest, killed by agent orange. Most of the trees were leafless … courtesy of Monsanto Inc. To make matters worse, the grunts had managed to climb further down, into a ravine and creek bed. It was impossible to reach them with the hoist. It was also impossible to find a clearing to land in, most of the slope was at least 60 degrees and looked more like 90 anyway. We were, at least I was, shit out of luck and ideas. We had to somehow get under the trees. The ravine ran up the mountainside above us for thousands of feet.

They had big hairy 'eggs' our pilots. I was too ignorant to be afraid, I guess. I didn't know exactly how fragile the tail rotor was or what exactly would happen if it struck something or how much the main rotor could chop through before it shattered and dropped us like a new, grand piano from a skyscraper.

A quarter mile from Delta the A/C took us under the trees. We were actually going *into* the forest!

He had circled around looking for a hole. We entered between two tall trees and then inched along in a weird world of tangled dead vegetation. Some of the branches looked like arms reaching, trying to knock us down; it was like cave diving only much worse. Instead of air, we carried gas. Run out of gas and we'd crash. Get lost or hit a tree and we'd crash.

Get shot or take a rocket and we'd crash. We were surrounded. It was a tunnel with rooms. The old pilot golden rule, naturally, automatically, played somewhere in the pilot's subconscious: always leave yourself an out, even though the chopper could … 'back up!'

Snaking along, we dodged more trees, still almost 100ft above the ground. The pilot put the bird into a hover inside a clear area, an opening … a room. We had found Delta again. The crew chief, Barth Cutler, in the right door, already had the basket litter hooked up on the cable end and was lowering it over the side.

"Watch the tail rotor," the A/C commanded. I looked out and behind as the tail rotor blades cut and buzzed through the air a few feet from a snag of twigs and branches. I unhooked my cord and moved to the front of the cabin behind the pilot in the left seat. I hooked up on another cargo ring and stepped out onto the landing skid to balance the load when it came up. Flashing the OK sign at me and smiling slightly, the crew chief hung outside his door. He looked back and forth between the ground and the winch, located behind the A/C's seat. He watched the winch drop cable.

We were now sitting ducks, exposed and very vulnerable, especially with no chest armor on. Below my boots and the skid, smaller trees pointed straight up at us. My 'bullet-proof' vest lay on the seat in back. Shit! Real dumb!

The crew chief winched the basket back up and when it was level with the floor we grabbed it and slid it across the deck. Inside the wire basket liter was a 2nd lieutenant. He lay face up with a horribly swollen head and bulging eyeballs beneath closed eyelids. He was unconscious, thank God, so I grasped for the white tag fastened on the front of his jacket with copper wire … the overly complex, typical army form used by the field medics to identify ailments and injuries for the hospital and Dustoff people. Scrawled across this form were three words: 'gunshot-wounds-head'. Bending closer, I saw that several rounds had pierced his skull and the amazing thing was, he was still breathing and even had a weak pulse. The guy was still alive!

"Eagle Dustoff … Delta six, over … " the company called.

"Go ahead Delta."

"We got a TV news team wants permission to be extracted …?"

"… ah … roger that … ..standby … "

Tiffany and McCrawly glanced at each other and one of them said,

"Get 'em ready … "

Cutler monitored the radio conversation while unhooking the basket and attaching the jungle penetrator. Completing the hookup, he lowered the penetrator from beneath the arm which again stuck out the door from the winch. Hanging on with his left hand and straining out to watch the penetrator, the rotor wash whipped his clothing back and forth on his stout frame. He looked as though he was skydiving. The cable slipped down through his right hand.

The chief knew his stuff. He was like a ballet dancer and a natural for his job inside the cramped cargo bay. I'd known him but a short time but you could tell he loved his work. This guy also loved shocking anybody in sight by hovering a Huey around the company area all by himself … solo! Leering and grinning and nodding hello with a mischievous look from the command seat … he'd mastered the trickiest part of flying a chopper, the rest was easy.

But during an extraction his pixyish facial muscles focused on the task at hand.

"Jesus 'H' fucking Christ" we had a badly wounded GI aboard and some war lovers wanted to get their film on the 6 o'clock news. I was pissed! Maybe they had shit their britches and wanted to change them. Maybe they wanted their mothers. What ever it was, I was having my own problems coping with the situation. I wasn't used to the flying into the trees bit. If I hadn't been so busy, I'd have been a total wreck.

Our A/C continued fixing on a tree dead ahead to keep in exact position and worked at hovering in the confined space. Fighting off vertigo and claustrophobia he listened for Cutler's directions – directing him slightly left, right, up and down.

On the ground the head medic cocked his eyes skyward, watching the descending seats. The folding seats, in the upright position and narrow profile, were designed to slip through the thickest jungle. The head pill-pusher wisely let the yellow seat strike the ground before grabbing them. A healthy dose of static electricity generated by the chopper passed harmlessly to earth, instead of completing a circuit through his body. Next, other grunts pulled down two of the three spring-loaded seats and motioned for the newsmen to straddle them. After clinching the safety straps under the arms and around the upper torsos of the cameramen, the medic pumped his fist violently up and down signaling the chief to reel them up. The Hollywood camp followers gave me the ass!

Cutler began a running dialogue with the A/C. The idea, unknown to the medic on the ground, was to let the pilot ease into the load with the bird. The pilot used his controls as opposed to the crew chief yanking people off the ground. The rotor jock could get a gradual feel for the weight just before lift off. He waited for Cutler to yell. (A hoist or external sling load is one of the chopper's trickiest and most dangerous jobs). Slowly the A/C lifted the slack out of the cable and Cutler screamed,

"Breaking ground Sir!"

The ship took the load.

Instantly Cutler hit the switch to reel in the penetrator and we pulled up the two media saps while the young officer's life slowly drained away. When the news team broke ground we had drifted some and they were not directly under us anymore. They swung like a pendulum and crashed into leaves and branches. Like terrified chimpanzees in Hawaiian shirts, they clutched each other at the end of the wire. I was so fucking happy, I almost shit *my* pants!

The thought of the newsmen tangling up in the trees and snags made Cutler's skin crawl. The crew chief grasped the steel rope with his right hand trying to get it under control. He applied pressure on it as it fed into the winch arm and slipped through his clenched fist. The wire would twist and spin the upcoming loads at the best of times. If need be, the pilot and the chief could both trigger an explosive charge and cut the cable to free the ship, but dreaded the idea.

The lieutenant's head reminded me of the cartoon detective, Fosdick, that was always getting shot and always had bullet holes in his hat and a head that looked like paper punch holes. This guy's wounds were a little different. Each bullet hole had a droplet of moist, pink, flesh sticking out. A typical AK-47 wound. Had it been his own troops that fired him up, the M-16 rounds would have burst his skull like an overripe pumpkin.

After everyone was aboard, now eight people, the A/C eased the collective up and the cyclic slightly forward. We rose slowly and cautiously.

POPPOPPOPPOPPOP! … THWACK!THWACK!POP!THWACK!

Goddamn, what the hell was that? I was suddenly afraid we might not make it out. The main rotors were striking some branches and the blades impacting the limbs sounded like AA fire exploding. The whole bird shuddered and shook. Swinging around in a rudder pedal turn 180 degrees to the right, the aircraft cleared the nearby trees and the pilots looked for a way out. It didn't look the same going out as it did coming in of course. Glancing at hastily scribbled headings and directions on the windshield, our pilots attempted to backtrack. On the way in, the co-pilot had scrawled the magnetic compass headings and course changes for each leg through the maze, as best he could.

Straight 290, 200, R. Big tree, 320, left dead tree, 010 was scratched on the Plexiglass in grease pencil.

Cutler in the right door and Crockett in the left door, hung outside eyeing the delicate tail rotor. I worked on the patient. The news crew took pictures. I felt the bird make course changes while the crew sounded off with an occasional,

"Tail clear left," or "Tail clear right," informing the pilots going through a tight spot. We were still in the trees but I felt the ship accelerate and I watched the sunlight flood out and push the shadows around the cabin out of the corner of my eye. Dark shadows on glaring light and worn off paint, an ever-present characteristic of the interiors of all aircraft. Finally, we slipped out like a hummingbird fleeing a briar patch. Looking up, all I could see from my side was blue sky. Out the other side the mountain zoomed past.

On the way back we struggled to save the young lieutenant.

"Gotta get an IV going or he's gonna die," Crockett said to me. His voice was a desperate plea that implied, 'what are you waiting for?' Did he just say that this man is going to die? Gonna die ... no shit ... of course he was going to die! He'll die no matter what, I thought. Then I remembered the story about a mine worker who'd survived the impact of a dynamite tamping rod blown out of its hole and through his skull and brain. It was a miracle that the miner lived and it would be a bigger miracle if my patient survived.

It was a bitch trying to find a vein. On the first try the needle either missed or punched all the way out the back of the blood vessel. I could tell it was fucked up because the fluid bulged out the skin around the needle. It swelled, a growing bump, as the liquid pumped into the muscle like a large insect bite. The patient squirmed and thrashed, the tough, compact body fighting the trauma and shock, from side to side as I probed with the needle. Finally I got a goodly flow through the plastic hose and into his cardiovascular system. I was totally relieved. I was relieved partly because it seemed as though I was being tested. I hadn't been sure I would be allowed to work on the wounded. I was just a '3rd man' and had no right to interfere with this crew. However, it seemed that no one else relished the chore and seeing how I was supposed to be a battle-tested combat infantry medic, I got the honor. I guess.

"How's he doing ... Osgood?" One of the fly boy pilots asked.

"BAD ... !"

I spit into the helmet mic that was kissing into my lips. What could I have said? The guy was a dead man. Another 2nd Luey bites the dust.

Myself, I was way beyond sorrow. I was mad! I was mad, sick, tired and disgusted. I hated the war, I hated the Army, I hated the cameramen, I hated everything. Fuck this shit! Fuck the Army, FTA all the way. I quit, I give up. I would quit the war, I decided then and there. I was finished with it; should have done it sooner I suppose. I would not extend my tour for Division LRPs or Dustoff, or for Green Berets. I had grave doubts about surviving any more of this body rot – pun intended. Just get me on the double 'O' quick, the Freedom Bird, out of this stinking country, that was my plan.

Twenty minutes later we crossed the coast, headed out to sea. Four minutes after that we bounced onto the helicopter flightdeck of a Navy hospital ship, the USS *Sanctuary*!

Corpsmen in spotless white shoes and pants unloaded the infantry platoon leader before I could unhook myself. A sailor handed me five cold cans of Coke. Inside the cans, ice floated. I passed two cans through the left pilot door window. The Coke burned and stung my dry throat as I guzzled it whole.

Chapter 63

The Last Walk to a Court Martial

So I decided no more flying. No flying and no humping. I had moments to reflect on my tour of duty now that I was safely in the rear. I thought back a few weeks ago to the time I walked off the chopper pad for the last time … my 'Last Walk' with a rucksack. The last time with the Hawk Recon Platoon of our famous battalion. Our flight had landed above the battalion compound and dust saturated the air. We were in from Hamburger Hill country. We'd been on standby to hit 'the mountain', waiting on Berchtesgaden. Now we looked forward to sleeping past sun-up for a change and drinking cold beer for a change. So I wasn't prepared for what happened next. I was going to 'Walk the walk … and talk the talk!'

Loping down the road towards the battalion buildings I noticed him watching me. He was an officer and a gentleman, a captain in fact. He stood off to one side then approached. I looked down on him as I sauntered proudly by not bothering with a salute. The rather short but pleasant looking REMF officer spoke,

"Hey soldier, how's it going?" in welcome, it seemed. He looked like a nice guy but his tone of voice hinted trouble.

"Not bad, sir."

"What's that on your helmet, troop?" Before I could answer he said, "Those aren't jump wings are they?" I noticed he was a non-jumper, not airborne rated, didn't wear wings, hadn't been to jump school or hadn't made the grade. He was an officer in an airborne unit and was not a paratrooper. I knew the upper brass, who were all airborne qualified, mostly master jumpers, would favor others over this guy. Automatically, in my mind he was a pussy and a 'leg'.

"You can't wear those out in the field," he said, "too shiny."

"I always wear 'em," I countered, knowing that technically he was right. But I loved to flaunt my jump wings in the Division that couldn't make up its mind if it was airborne or not. I loved to show my wings to leg officers: to characters just like this! We'd been Air Cav, Airborne, Air Assault and Air Mobile.

"You address me as sir, you understand?" his voice rose in volume.

"Yes, sir," I replied in a mocking drawl. "You know we usually wear boonie hats."

"BOONIE HATS ... not authorized," was his answer. This creep knew all the details. Being a leg and a nitpicker must have gotten this mad dog sent out in the midday sun by the brass.

"Are you authorized jump wings, troop?" he persisted. I made up my mind to refuse if he tried to make me take them off. "Never mind," he snarled, "let's see that weapon!"

I started to hand the rifle over but he snatched it away. Right about then I wondered if this turd with legs could out run bullets. He wouldn't have tried that shit out in the field. Officers had been wasted for this sort of thing. I wondered how he would act if I pulled out my .45 and shot him between the eyes. I guess he would act dead.

"It's dirty ... you got a dirty weapon, troop."

"Sir, I just got off a chopper back there. Know what I mean? This place is a miniature dust storm, you can still see the ... "

"I'm going to bring you up on charges for this. What's your name and number?"

I told him after almost bursting out in laughter.

"You're in Echo company, correct?"

"No, I'm attached to Echo, but in headquarters company. I'm a medic."

"Oh ... yes, one of those," he sneered.

He thrust the rifle back at me and walked off, in a hurry, like he had a stick up his ass and needed someone to tell him how to remove it. I was dumbfounded. I guess he never figured on ever being sent out to the sticks or ever being hurt or wounded. Charges, he was going to bring me up on charges. What was that? They couldn't court martial me for that, could they? What were they going to do, send me to Vietnam? What were they going to do, send me to LBJ, for having a dirty weapon? Christ, we had just emerged from one of the dirtiest, dustiest, hottest, stinkiest, filthiest places on the planet. We'd been out for weeks without bathing. The clothes were rags on our backs. We'd just spent the whole day humping up a mountaintop, to a fire base, that was ankle deep in pulverized, powered dirt and vegetation from having all the trees blown off. We'd waited in the dust all afternoon and finally flew into Camp Eagle. Jumping out into a pounding rotor blast, dusting off the dry ground. Fuck that REMF motherfucker! I wasn't concerned.

A week later I happened to be occupying space in Echo Company's office for some strange reason. It was the clerk and me, alone. I must have been trying to get another leave.

"By the way, Doc, don't sweat that article 15. It'll never make it out of his office."

"Article 15 … what's that?"

"You don't know? Gee Doc … they don't give you a court martial for small shit anymore. They give out article 15s. Non-judicial punishment it's called. Fines, monetary deductions of pay. That's all there is to it. But don't sweat it, it won't even leave here." He pointed into a trash can alongside his desk in a sly manner.

Later, I realized just what the clerk was going to do. The clerks probably had a lot better things to do than process article 15s. He would simply shit-can the paper work. I loved it. That was what I called team work. The enlisted men stuck together. It was us against them. Team work, the best thing about the Army.

I walked outside and felt it necessary to give a little secret salute to our brother clerks, even if they were jerks or REMFs. A job well done lads!

Chapter 64

Porsches and Corvettes

I figured I'd buy a Porsche. A Land Rover would be nice, but I knew I'd get a Porsche when I got home.

Now I drove a jeep. It was an ambulance with canvas roof and sides. On the canvas were big red crosses with white backgrounds and the tops might as well have been gold. The medical platoon sergeant had me wash the red crosses off every day and back the jeeps up to the rear door of the aid-station. The first thing you saw when you entered the aid-station were the jeeps parked out back. The jeep rag tops were hard to replace. But the most important job was to clean the rear axle and differential as they stuck out parked up on a little grade.

I'd done my time in the boonies. I'd sweated blood and almost been killed several times. I wore silver jump wings and a CMB. I had made the rank of SP/5 (E-5), the same pay scale of a buck sergeant. I strutted around the unfamiliar compound. Some of the lifers said that I was enough of a hero, whatever that meant, after spotting my unauthorized Green Beret shoulder patch. Another had called me a murderer. I knew I hadn't done anything really unusual on my tour, but no one fucked with me much. I just tried to dodge work details. Life in the rear was Army life and life in the boonies was survival. Big difference. I'd always hated the rear, as I hated the Army. But now, with a month to go, I didn't want to hump the fucking bush anymore. I did not want to die.

My problems was how to amuse myself for a month. Life in the rear was such a bore. I already had taken my R&R and a leave. The leave had been a fluke, unheard of for boonie rats.

I had no friends. Jim Fellows had transferred to the Division LRP company. Jeff Jeffries had gone to Japan with his legs full of metal.

274

Maurice was still in the field and Mike Chiaramonte was out with the Hawks. Wolf was rumored dead in a chopper crash.

I'd never been into any city in Vietnam and now considered the unfamiliar prospect. I'd gotten laid on R&R enough and I didn't smoke weed or shoot heroine; I didn't have much reason to go. Anyway, it was off limits. Off limits ... now that *was* a reason to go.

One day I drove off the base, past the MPs and through the main gate. No one questioned an official US ambulance entering enemy territory. I did want some tiger fatigues. I took my trusty .45, so if I was ambushed and killed nobody could say I was stupid to go unarmed. Little did I know that GIs, most notably Bobby Garwood, were captured on little solo jeep drives near big cities like I was about to undertake.

Forcing myself to slow down I remembered how treacherous the jeeps were. The tires were for mud and sand and absolutely smooth in the centers. This thing that I was driving was a death trap on wet or oiled road.

The road out of Eagle wound from the dry hills and joined Highway one near Phu Bia. People were all about. People on bicycles or Lambrettas, people packed into ancient buses and people walking along the road or waiting for a ride. Young girls waved at me from behind the grave mounds, Lord knows why.

At the junction of Highway one I picked up a Vietnamese Ranger officer. I gunned the jeep out into the traffic, turning left northward into the imperial city of Hue, the former capital of all Vietnam.

My passenger was a handsome, tough-looking soldier wearing a set of tiger fatigues. He could have been a Viet Cong general. He was very polite and after I asked him if he knew where I could score some fatigues said, "Yes, I will buy them for you."

Outside the busy market place I waited in the jeep. I had just given the soldier a handful of money and he had split into the throng. I people watched and started to realize how vulnerable I was, especially with a Viet Cong general circling around behind me in the crowd. Ten minutes later he emerged from the madness and handed me a neat bundle tied with a string. A shirt and pants.

"Anything else you would like?" he asked.

"No, that's great. Thank you. Take care."

"Oh, thank you very much. You too be very careful around here." He vanished and I started the jeep.

Back inside Camp Eagle I hauled ass as fast as I could go. Clouds of dust pulsated out behind me. I dreamed of racing Porsches against Ferraris and Corvettes. I used to read a lot of Road and Track magazines and Dad was the original piston-head. He was a car salesman and had a couple of old Porsches and later a sleek XKE-type Jaguar with the smooth headlights.

The road changed from dirt to a dark shade. It was black from oil or Pentaprime, another chemical sure to cause cancer and make CEOs wealthy. By the time I noticed anything it was too late. The ambulance jumped from forward motion to a four wheel side-slip. The transition was ever so smooth. I knew the brakes were useless and I knew I was going to break something. The jeep was aiming itself directly for a ditch and some nice rolls of concertina wire. I knew what to do from driving in snow and racing in the rain, but it really was too late! Plunging into the ditch set the vehicle into a horrible wobbling bounce. I closed my eyes and hung on. My spine compacted in a jarring impact and the machine stalled. It came to rest upright, barely. Opening my eyes, as the dust cleared, I was amazed and shocked to find a nest of razor wire and steel fence stakes underneath my green chariot.

The battalion was right over the rise so I got out and started walking back. I hadn't covered one hundred yards when our other ambulance and a small gang of people crested the rise, balls to the wall. Ah ha, the air cavalry to the rescue. I'll be okay now. As the ambulance passed me I thought I saw the platoon sergeant in the right seat, his face a death mask. As the gang of strangers started by me, running, a new medic that I did recognize as fresh in-country and brand new to the no slackers, leered over at me and with a worried face shouted, "Ya didn't ruin the top, did yah?"

Life around the rear and aid station *was* boring most of the time. Such is the soldier's life. Once in a while odd or weird – or even spectacular things happened.

One of our truly motivated medics, Doc Ben Karan from Wisconsin, had been in the field only a couple of weeks but was now back at Eagle with a horrible infection on his ass. When he first flew out towards the A Shau he had grave doubts about what to do as a medic. Luckily, he was going to Bravo Company and ran into Maurice who was just leaving for home. Maurice being the chief pill jockey with Bravo kindly took the time to go over all Karan's medications and then discuss battle wounds. Doc Karan credits Maurice with turning himself into a real combat medic.

So Doc Karan was laying face down on a stretcher in our battalion aid shack while another medic cleaned out the sickening butt wound: cellulitis.

Doc Karan relates the story:

I was laying down being operated on when in bursts some wild-eyed, tall, slender dude. He was obviously a medic as he wore a CMB with a loop of surgical tubing sticking out of his breast pocket partially covering the badge. I think he had chrome surgical scissors protruding from the opposite pocket. This was a paratrooper medic with silver wings on his custom ball cap.

He walked in all nervous, jumpy and just plain freaking out somewhat. The man did seem to own the place and just looked our chief medic in the face and shoved a pair of dirty flight gloves at the aid station boss!

"Gray matter!"

No words … no hellos … just … gray matter. The specter of a soldier suddenly spun on his heels and thrust his gloves into my face!

"Gray matter!"

That was it, nobody said a word and he walked out, somewhat like a ghost.

"What was that?" I managed. Silence. Finally Sergeant Bell or somebody explained:

"Oh … that's Doc Osgood, he was with the Hawks, he's blown away NVA, humped an AK and a human skull! He's famous around here. Been flying Dust-off! You know Special Forces type … really crazy!"

Chapter 65

LRPs

Jim Fellows walked up to me at high noon. Jim had made the LRPs (Long-range reconnaissance patrol) and had even gone through Recondo school. He graduated number 2176. That school was the most prestigious school in Vietnam. It was run by Special Forces down in Na Trang and it was bad to the bone. Today Jim was looking good and dressed to kill, literally. The LRPs wore camouflage fatigues (woodland pattern) and black baseball caps in the rear. He had a Recondo patch on the front of his hat, nailed on with a set of jump wings. The Recondo patch was a white arrow head with the numbers 1-0-1 in black.

Today, Jim was honoring his old buddies from the 2/327th with a visit. He still had a great sense of humor and I liked him a lot. We extended our fists for the Nam hand shake, ritual and greeting.

"Hey, Jim. What's happenin' man?"

"Hey, Doc, it's cool, everything's cool. Just got back from Bangkok and didn't even want to leave. My third out of country R&R ya know."

"You got another R&R after extending for LRPs, huh?"

"*And* a couple of, in-country, to Da Nang and Quang Tri. You ought to extend and join us. Different world all together."

The battalion chaplain walked by and commented, "Looking good Fellows, looking good."

"Yeah man, what's shaken padre?" Jim replied. I continued,

"I think I will extend, Jim. Have to decide if it's Dustoff or LRPs," I lied.

"Listen, come on over to the compound and check it out. I'll show ya around," he offered.

LRPs

The LRP company area sat on a small hill overlooking their chopper pad aka the 'Acid Pad', and right next to the wire on the north perimeter of Camp Eagle. Above the LZ, up a steep bank, sat the operations bunker and some barracks. Stairs dove into the dark bowels of the top secret ops bunker and all sorts of antennas pointed skyward from the roof.

Jim and I hopped up the steps into his barracks. Inside, it reminded me of some college frat houses I'd seen. They'd constructed private rooms for themselves out of scrap plywood sheets and two by fours. Wild-looking but tidy sleeping units were available. They had solid box frame bunks and ladders leading up to lofts. They even had mattresses. Rangers in various costumes and dress smoked, joked and lounged around or crammed themselves into corners in the maze of cubicles and woodwork. Pinups and psychedelic posters were visible behind mosquito nets. Knives and commando M-16s hung from the walls. This was the home of the James Bonds of the boonie rats ... newly designated as RANGERS.

The super grunts had it good, but the job was kind of dangerous. The LRPs inserted into the mountains in six-man teams and diddy bopped up and down Ho Chi Minh's trail. They counted trucks and poked around NVA base camps. Sometimes they zapped out gooks with LRP killer teams instead of screwing around on pure intelligence sorties. Sometimes they got cornered by the NVA and sometimes they 'kicked back', called in artillery and peed all over Sir Charles. Sometimes they almost, but never quite, got wiped out completely.

Jumping off the front step, we almost plowed over the Company's 1st Sergeant, 'top', first shirt, head lifer, old asshole – they had many names. These senior NCOs had as much power as many officers, usually a lot more. They ran the Army.

"Okay Fellows, what are you doing? This ain't no open house."

"Ah ... yeah, TOP, just showing this guy ... hey, meet Doc, the no slack quack. He's okay. He's number one, beau coup gook killer."

The old NCO eyed my jump wings on my cap and maybe figured I just might be human. This was Sergeant Bob Gilbert.

"Okay Fellows, I guess you was just leaving."

We split.

"He just doesn't like strangers so close to the ops bunker. He's really okay," Jim said as we walked over to their club. A lot of the old Airborne lifers were pretty colorful. Some of the crusty paratroopers had gone in with the 101st, on night drops, in France and Holland. Our fire bases in Vietnam were named after some of these battles. You could tell these old dogs by the colorful and rare airborne combat patches that featured wings, fire, lightning bolts, skulls and, of course, parachutes. Some of these guys had liberated 'the rock' on Manilla Harbor, dropping low level onto Jap positions on top of a cliff called Corregidor. Others had fought in Korea in Airborne Ranger units or with the 187th RCT. Often the combat patches reflected these exploits. For example, the 503 Airborne 'the rock' patch showed a deployed parachute and an eagle descending onto an island. Another patch was called 'jump into hell', which General Westmoreland wore, and depicted the Rakkasans going down into flames. These NCO types didn't usually dish out or take too much Army bullshit. I knew the type, I'd had the honor of meeting one or two. They actually made the Army bearable, almost appealing. They tended to protect their boys like nasty old shepherds. They saved a lot of lives in Vietnam and I was proud to serve with them. You'd occasionally find an old geezer with silver hair and the vocabulary of a college professor. Some looked like Lee Marvin or Burt Lancaster and were capable of cussing out your ass anytime. Bob Gilbert was one of the good ones.

Jim and I sat in the shade inside a huge army tent with a colossal inflated parachute front door. We drank beer. This tent, Jim explained, belonged to the tank outfit outside, but the LRPs called it theirs.

"Yeah, TOP likes ya, I can tell. He'll probably make you an assistant team leader to start," Jim said. I gulped down a swallow of cold beer.

"Do you go out and actually see gooks walking around?" I asked.

"I hope the hell! All the time, man, all the fucking time. Some guys went out on a training mission the other day and the dinks chased them for ten miles, WITH DOGS! Another time the NVA got on our radio and told us to take a certain heading to an open LZ, safety guaranteed, or they would wipe us out! We were surrounded! We did…no questions asked."

We sat and relaxed, watching the flies scoot around on the table. We exchanged home addresses and drank beer until dusk.

"Ya know, Doc, you really ought to think twice about extending for LRPs," my friend finally admitted. "It's not what it's cracked up to be."

That day was the last time I talked to Jim. I never saw him again.

Chapter 66

No Stinking Badges

Our EM club had a tin roof now but was still dark with all the sandbags piled around and the cases of beer stacked to the roof behind the bar. A bunch of us lone-wolf types like myself and of course John Wolfgang – bigger than life as usual, sat at a table to the side. We'd heard Wolf was dead. I eyed the bar-tender showing off a human skull that looked suspiciously like the one I used to carry on my ruck and had been stolen when I returned to the bush. This one too, looked like a bad case of overbite.

Wilson, at the head of our table said,

"Doc, ain't that your skull over at the bar? I remember getting on our bird in the A Shau and here comes ole Doc with a bloody NVA skull perched up on his ruck ... kinda lookin' back the way they'd come. Well, Doc climbs into the Huey and the crew chief takes one look, his mouth opens and he slips and falls out of his seat! Only thing that saved him was ... he was tethered in. Funny as hell."

Somebody blew beer out his nose while we all choked and burst out laughing. Wilson, a black guy from Miami and the only E-6 with us in the EM club, had a way of telling a funny story even if it wasn't funny. I remembered that scene and it was twice as funny the way he told it.

The club was really crowded as the whole battalion was in the rear. We called it: the 'rear' with the sergeant major, the queer and the beer!

Presently in comes another lone figure. This guy was something else. A stranger. He was wickedly handsome, and wore a 173rd Airborne combat patch with the screaming eagle on the opposite shoulder. He was a lowly E-4 like most of us but wore a set of jump wings, CIB and on top: aviator wings! Holly shit, this guy was packing. He ignored us and saddled up to the bar. I made a note to seek him out sometime. I did later and he was the one who told me, slyly, I could get a R&R *and* a leave if I only asked for one.

I guess because when I was in the Boy Scouts I never got any merit badges, I wasn't interested, now I was obsessed with badges. Since sewing on cloth paratrooper wings, and especially the CMB, I wanted all the cool awards and badges you could get. You could wear 'em right on your everyday uniform and out-shine generals! You had the standard hardcore Vietnam 'old hand' CMB, CIB and jump wings, which was plenty, but so much more was available. I wanted a Jungle Expert badge, a Path Finder tab, maybe an Army Diver's award, I volunteered for HALO school and of course the 'leg' Ranger school. Lots of the brass had Vietnamese jump wings or some other foreign paratrooper badges. Even an enlisted guy could get real silver Army Aviator wings just likel a B-17 gunner or navigator. The fact was, medics just didn't get to do shit. I'd already been cheated out of a 'green beret' and some arrows and dagger crest because I was a medic.

Wolfgang, sitting at my elbow, looked pretty cool with his buck sergeant stripes under the Airborne Eagle combat patch *and* a unauthorized 'HAWK RECON' scroll topping everything. The Hawk patch was in gold and black and perfectly matched the Airborne tab it was riding. The local barber shop, tailor/spy made the patches for us right on base Camp Eagle.

Wolf was asking Wilson about the lone combat patch he wore on his jungle jacket: a 1st Cavalry yellow and black horse head affair which did have an airborne tab on top.

"Gee sarge, I know you did a tour with the 'Cav' and I know you were out with us … but really … it's good to let most of these fucking legs and REMFs know you're a 101st paratrooper. It fucks 'em up! You're Airborne ain't ya?"

"Troop, I went to jump school before my tour with the Cav and while I was back in the land of cotton, completed ranger school too!"

"Naww … come on sarge … I mean … well, if you're a Ranger were is your badge?"

Nobody spoke a word. The whole club seemed to drop dead. I heard that music from *The Good, the Bad and the Ugly* movie playing somewhere: Taaa Da, Daa, Da, … Daaa Da Daaa.

Wilson cocked his head sideways and sneered, "Badges? Badges … ? "We don't got no badges! I don't got to show you no stinkin' … badges!"

This time I blew a goodly yield of cheap beer out my nose and mouth! The table erupted in a fit of laughter, commotion and pounding fists! Wolfgang, however, stood up as he didn't want to drool on his shirt while laughing. The whole club laughed at something … I guess … 'cause we were laughing.

Chapter 67

Herron's Hooligans and
the Trojan War

At Camp Eagle I was a REMF and totally unashamed of it. Eleven months had passed and I found myself spending all my time in the rear. Officially, I'd always been in Headquarters Company but never lived or worked in the place. HHC had always forced me to hump the boonies. In my new role, I humped around the battalion area – the mess hall, motor pool, showers, and the aid-station. We also had our own bar and outdoor movie theatre. Sometimes, I hung around the aid-station when goofy Dr Paisley was away. All in all, it was a pretty boring life, dodging work details during the day and drinking beer at night.

It was a boring life, but a fairly safe one and as it looked like I might keep mine, it suited me.

One afternoon a whole shitload of us medics were sitting around the battalion medical facility. They used to call us 'Doc Herron's Happy Hooligans' when wonderful Doctor Herron was boss. Suddenly, a GI stuck his head inside and yelled at us,

"Anybody here seen Doc Stewart?"

Stewart had gone home for all I knew. Nobody had seen Doc Stewart for a long time, we told this guy at the door.

Then Beever, the aid-station 'ninety-one-charlie' (chief medic) and almost a nurse, walked in and turned to us,

"Okay, boys, what's it gonna be today?"

Nobody answered.

"Come on, come on, don't everybody jump at once. What do you guys usually do when I'm not here? Drink beer, smoke weed, no, no, I know, lets go out and frag some lifer."

"Oh yeah, Beever, that's a good idea and I do so want out of this chicken-shit battalion but, fraggings hard work and I hate hard work these days," I said, picking up on Beever's unusual black humor. He was usually so, so solid and, well, kinda straight. I think he secretly preferred we would wash the jeeps or fill sandbags.

I'd been watching Al Heart, or 'Lumpy' to us medics, who reminded me of Clarence Rutherford on *Leave it to Beaver*, examine a box of rubbers with his big fingers.

"I'll bet these things make good water balloons," Lumpy said with a yawn. I snatched a box of prophylactics, dug in deep, and walked over to the sink. Sure enough, the rubbers bloated out full of water just fine. In a flash everyone was elbowing their way towards the water, stuffing birth control devices into their jungle jackets or unwrapping the little packets. I had no idea what was on their minds: get water balloons and bomb visitors and brass outside in the road?

"You know, if I didn't know better I'd say, *this* looks like WAR!," Lumpy declared.

"The aid-station is off limits!" Beever shouted, sounding more like himself. Chunky Doc Ramsey, the old Hawk medic, bellowed,

"Far out ... it's every man for himself ... take no prisoners!"

It *was* war ... the GREAT TROJAN WAR.

I was first outside into the afternoon's white-hot blast furnace. Our jeeps stood parked in formation, ready to go. I quickly ducked down behind one. The first idiot that ran outside after me got it square in the chest. I hit him dead center with a pint or two of water surrounded in synthetic rubber.

"Aw gee, Lumpy, I'm sorry," I lied. I laughed till I cried. A minute later I was dodging, ducking and running between the bunkers in the headquarters compound with tears turning to mud as they ran down my cheeks. A pack of madmen snapped at my heels. A balloon sailed over my shoulder from behind.

The next hour saw a constant series of skirmishes, hasty ambushes, sniping attempts, charges in the opposite direction, nasty hand-to-hand combat and retreats. Fleshy, bulging, off-white orbs tumbled end over end through the air looking for likely targets. Everyone was soon soaked. Everyone but me.

Unbelievably, I hadn't been hit, not even once. Till then, I'd escaped my initial pursuers but soon found myself out of luck, ammo and breath. A gruesome twosome finally cornered me back up against the aid-station door. The door opened outward and I had nowhere to turn. It was two of them against one of me, with more on the way. One of them, taking his best shot, tossed a water bomb. It missed and splattered the ground at my feet. His partner, an ugly brute with murder in his eyes, lurched towards me. It was Doc Beever. He was hardly recognizable behind the snarling jowls and lips. He knew he had me. I tried to go around him but his skinny buddy with a walnut for an Adam's apple, cut me off. Beever came on like a rolling mountain of flesh, 3ft away he raised both hairy hands clutched around a 2lb aqua-grenade. I cowered down, closed my eyes and leaned forward. This was it! Done for, I surrendered to the inevitable. Smiling, he lunged at me, completely misjudging the range. The rubber exploded all over the aid-station door behind me. I opened my eyes and looked around ... bewildered. He had missed from point blank range. Beever's buddy, walnut neck, choked back a giggle. Beever glared at him and giggle-puss looked away.

By now all the other medics were watching and stood around dripping water. I was dry as a Gila Monster in summer. I jumped up, dancing around, leaping and bucking like a drunken Indian at Custer's last battle. Beever's jaw dropped.

"I won, I won, I won the fucking war!" I screamed.

Just then the aid-station door slowly opened and the head of our beloved platoon sergeant emerged. SSG Bell blinked his eyes, adjusting to the light. I stopped my wild cavorting. Bell was one of those grey-haired, distinguished looking, professional NCOs, but he was ugly. Still, when he spoke, people listened. Somehow he'd gotten a little water splattered on his shiny jungle boots. Oh my.

"If you gentlemen are through, would you be so kind as to police up all these ... these ... FUCKING US ARMY RUBBERS! It looks like the back door of some Goddamn whore house around here. Thank you."

The old sergeant paused and squinted at me like he had forgotten his glasses. The crows-feet at the corners of his eyes pulsated nervously.

"Osgood ... what the fuck is wrong with you? Oh yes, now I remember, you're supposed to go home soon, isn't that right?"

"That's right, Sarge," I replied weakly. Beever snickered.

"Well, Osgood ... just one final word of advice ... WATCH YOUR ASS!"

The door slammed shut.

My grandmother always said I had a guardian angel. Somebody or something who looked out for me. She was very religious. I'm not sure what she meant. I do know that someone was watching out for me in Vietnam – my grandmother. Her presence worked overtime to keep me alive, even during our harmless cluster-fuck games. She was working and watching twenty-four hours a day, seven days a week. That's how I won the Great 'fucking' Trojan War.

Chapter 68

Award Ceremony

I felt like a fool. I had forgotten the exact date I landed in Vietnam. It was time to get the hell out of Tombstone Territory and I couldn't remember if it was the 1st of July or the 4th when we could leave. How could anyone forget something like that? Screw it, call it the 4th I thought. Actually, it was more like the 7th. I guess I really hadn't expected to survive the year so I never bothered about the dates.

Maurice and I were ready to boogie. But where was he? He had probably left already on our correct DEROS date. Well, I was ready to 'sky up' and di di mau for the world on the double 'O' quick' (go home on the freedom bird jet).

Not wanting to abuse my luck I had canceled on flying the air ambulance or extending for LRPs. A year as a combat medic and then more time as a LRP or chopper crew seemed a bit much. Hell, I'd flown a lot of missions and had the experience ... about the same as a gunner on a B-17 albeit a gunner without a gun. Besides, a lot of our peers had good arguments for abandoning the whole sorry mess. I was shocked, at first, when I heard the saying: 'fighting for peace is like fucking for virginity', around Camp Eagle.

The last day in the battalion they called three of us outside. They took our picture. We formed a rank or file and stood at attention. This was our award ceremony. It was brief that was for sure. I got a bronze star, an ARCOM for heroism and an air medal. I had mixed emotions about the whole deal. At first, I was going to make a scene and refuse the decorations. Then I thought, well, I'll take them and send them back later. Plus the major that was doing the 'honors' was such a handsome movie-star looking fatherly type I didn't want to make trouble for him.

As I stood at attention I thought about the dead. I was definitely pissed off at somebody but couldn't quit figure out who.

289

The major pinned the hardware and ribbons on my chest and then, in an odd way, slipped something round into my hand when we shook. It was like a silver dollar. I was the only one of us three to get one. It was a challenge coin with jump wings, like the Green Beret coin, the two were the original and only at that time. If you pulled up to the bar with a bunch of soldiers you could challenge them all and they had to buy you drinks! A paratrooper thing. But I probably wouldn't be drinking with a pack of 'legs' to begin with!

The air medal was real pretty. It had a bright blue and orange ribbon with a bronze eagle diving with a clutch of arrows in its claws. It was for combat in aerial flight which was pretty cool. I think it was invented, in Army Aviation, for the gunners and navigators of bombers during WWII. It was a huge award in the Air Force and funny how we got multiple awards, one for each combat assault under fire. They had a saying: an air medal and a dollar bill will get you a cup of coffee anywhere, back in the States. I had enough for three cups with air medals alone. But like a lot of wise ass, 'no nothing' people and sayings, the truth was that years later air medals, real ones, were seen in pawn shops for $50 or more!

Back in the aid-station I sat down for the last time. In sashayed another distinguished-looking officer I'd never seen before. He started asking questions about Ed Stewart. Jeeze ... everyone was looking for Doc Stewart all the time. I always assumed he DEROSed long ago. Everyone looked over at me as it turned out I was the only medic present who knew Doc Stewart. The officer turned and asked me, "Do you think Stewart deserves the Silver Star?"

I was confused and didn't know what was going on, but automatically stuck up for our beloved brother medic.

"Hell yes ... he does ... at least, why?"

The officer looked at me kind of funny, swallowed, and added, "it's a ... posthumous award of course – you weren't with Delta during the air strike, were you?"

I couldn't move my mouth. I couldn't move period. But I had to get away from this! I didn't know Doc Stewart was killed with Delta.

Finally, I managed, "He was a damn fine troop,"

I choked. I was sick.

Chapter 69

Home

Don't crash, please don't crash, I prayed! We were flying the length of South Vietnam … again … from Phu Bai to basically Saigon. It was my 6th and last trip along that route, thank God. I sweated in the dark cargo hold of the C-130 turbo-prop 'Herk it don't Jerk it', we ain't got no parachutes here. I did notice a few flat-back ripcord-type chutes hanging up near the front.

The Air Force crew told us all to use the cargo straps for safety belts. Just how the hell we were supposed to secure ourselves with these things was beyond me. They stretched the width of the fuselage and were normally used for tying down jeeps and equipment. Now they were just laying around in loose heaps.

At Bien Hoa I tried to enjoy myself the last few days processing out. I shopped at the PX, drank at the NCO club and every day grabbed a sauna, massage and cigar. The 101st section of the air base hosted a big, full-on massage parlor, right on the compound.

I sauntered out the door one afternoon after a nice massage with the Vietnamese lovelies. Nothing like getting your penis checked with a pair of tight and pout little lips. Sucking a Hava-a-Tampa cigar I felt truly alive. Somehow the thin cigar was just right in the 110 degree July air. My body temperature was down after a cool shower, probably the best thing about the entire process. I said to myself: goodbye Vietnam … goodbye heat! On the runway a F-100 Super Saber hit its after-burner and cooked off the runway.

Waiting for the freedom bird was pure HELL! They shouted names continuously from the boarding rosters, twenty-four hours a day as thousands of GIs milled around. Barracks stood available but you

291

couldn't hear the callouts clearly from inside, at least I couldn't. As far as I knew no one had any idea when their name might be called. For two days I waited, standing up under the roofed overhead; we had no choice. Finally,

"Osgood, William," the professional shouter bleated. Damn, I was happy. The ordeal was over. I'd been worrying I'd missed my name – for the last twelve hours! I turned to go and caught the eye of Barth Cutler, the flying crew chief from Eagle Dustoff. He flashed the 'OK' sign. He was leaving too and right then I knew I was doing the correct thing, getting out of the madness. I beamed back at Barth and flipped him a left-handed salute.

A group of lunatics started into searching my duffle bag ... customs 'officials'. A pack of Specialist 4s. I outranked 'em. They were searching for contraband like explosives and drugs. Not good to have an airliner crash and burn on the way home – which did happen years later on the other side of the world to the 101st no less! I should have put my AK-47 inside, but the human skull lay in wait at the bottom instead. I wished it could bite any rough hands that touched it now. I'd just say, "Sorry bout that! I'm a head hunter don't ya know!" The lazy REMFs never found a thing.

Sipping a drink, I watched the California coast slide under a wing. As we melted rubber on the runway at Travis Air Force Base some cheers were had but no bands played, no crowds waved, no signs welcomed and no pretty girls met us on the ramp ... shit. But you know, funny thing... it wasn't hot! I almost cried.

Riding back to Oakland where this nightmare all started we smelled dead skunk. "Home sweet home!" some happy slickster cried out. He was right, when we smelled that beautiful, mashed varmint, we knew we were back. It was so sweet! Some little harmless animal gave us the best welcome.

In Oakland we processed out; 90 per cent of the guys were being cut loose onto the street who had, the day before, been playing Russian Roulette. Some of us had just been yanked out of the boonies and were now supposed to ease back into the weirdness of modern-day United

States of America. Then, I envied those who terminated their service careers. I myself was to go on leave and then report to Company A, 75th Airborne Rangers at Fort Benning. I was being made a real and original LRRP recon medic and would wear the original Merrill's Marauders crest! Back in Burma they were LRPs but it stood for Long Range Penetration! I assumed incorrectly I was going to Ranger school for some reason. But Company A, 75th Rangers was a secret outfit hidden at Fort Benning with a top secret mission. A suicide mission. Nothing really: just jumping into Russia with atomic bombs strapped to our ass! Just like "Dr. Strange Love"!

It took us all night to shed our combat jungle boots into a pile, dress out and do all the paperwork. I bloused my dress green pants into dull paratrooper boots as per regulation. Many of the 'leg' soldiers did the same thing ... against regulations. They were supposed to wear shiny 'disco' shoes. Finally, in the early morning, we were ready for our welcome home surprise. We got a steak dinner. Grill cooks slapped, stabbed, over-cooked, under-cooked and fried cow parts for the endless hordes twenty-four hours a day, seven days a week.

THANKS A LOT MEN, WELCOME HOME! a sign said in the kitchen. We got a sign as well. I knew we'd get a sign.

"So much for our welcome, lets get the fuck outta here," the stranger at my elbow hissed through his teeth.

A cabbie greeted me outside the front door.

"Need a cab soldier?"

"Sure do."

"Where to ... the airport?" he hoped. "Want to go downtown, bar, girls, over to 'the city' ... how about Mill Valley?"

Did I look like somebody from Mill Valley?

"No ... how much would it be to Santa Cruz?"

"Santa Cruz ... thats almost 100 miles. 50 bucks"

"Well ... what are we waiting for ... lets go!"

As we pulled off California Highway 17 the notorious 'over the hill' killer road from Los Gatos to Santa Cruz, I said, "Let me out over there will ya?"

293

"Don't ya want me to drop you at the door?"

"No, I want to walk the last little bit … thanks."

I tipped him about 40 bucks; military guys and gangsters were always over-tipping right? Just like in the movies, especially after pay-day and for going home.

In a daze I walked up the hill with my suitcase, like I had a million times before. My family was in the house on the hill, still asleep I guessed. It was pretty early. A couple of golfers nodded as we crossed paths. I'd been getting in the way of golfers around here since the age of 5. No "hello, glad to see ya, good job!" from them. I sensed fear perhaps, maybe hatred, and for sure: no interest. Well, so what, those two could well have been jumpers in the 101st and survived the Normandy jump for all I knew.

I walked around the house and quietly opened the front door. The sound of blood roared in my ears; my face was hot!

"GGGGGGGRRRRRRRRR … !"

A wad of pissed-off muscle and spiked hair got up and loped towards the door, growling from deep inside. What a welcome I was having. Unlike Argos, Ulysses's dog, Maverick my best friend didn't even recognize me. I'd changed. Or maybe it was the smell of death in my hair and on my hands.

Custer's Last Stand – An Historic Comparison

Nearly 100 years after the Battle of the Little Big Horn, on the Little Horn River, we nearly suffered the same fate as Custer's US 7th Cavalry. Sure, there were differences, but some things never change. On our hunt for the unknown position of our enemy's camps, on August 4, 1968, we flew into a large valley and were right off surrounded by the North Vietnamese and taking fire! We traveled with the Kiowas, Cayuse, Chinooks but mostly the Iroquois choppers. I rode in on an Iroquois. Several American Indian warriors rode with us 'troopers' just like the scouts with Custer. The fact is we were 'Cavalry'. The 101st Airborne had just been officially named the 101st Airborne Air Cavalry that summer. Crossed sabers, black 'cowboy' hats and red and white swallow tail flags were seen, mostly in our rear areas, hootches and bars.

Our high command didn't know where the enemy camps were and figured the N.V.A., when found, would run like they almost always did. Exactly the thoughts of Custer's leaders. We dismounted in the A Shau Valley and soon divided our forces. Col. Beckwith, a Custer clone, and General Zais sent two companies up the right side of the Rao Lao River and two companies along the left side like Reno and Benteen did by Custer's order. I was in Company A, on the right, and soon headed for the high terrain and probably a hornet's nest on Hill 800, 900 and 937. We turned north, again, just as Custer and his brothers did! It seemed nobody knew where the enemy was except possibly a couple of our Kit Carson Scouts.

Similar to Reno's attack and retreat, Company D on the left of the river was nearly wiped out. It was a massacre, with one major difference; a lot of the casualties were from friendly fire. We on the right, like 'yellow hair', persisted and headed to the high terrain and the most likely enemy camps. My platoon was attacked and a shoot out resulted with one KIA and bullets flying past our ears. We packed our new Colts, the famous name associated with the Wild West and the Indian wars, but just like Custer, we were out gunned. Custer's boys were armed with single shot Civil War carbines while his enemy had many Winchester and Henry lever action assault rifles originally designed to hold 16 bullets. In Nam, many considered the AK-47 to be far superior and fact is it pumped out 30 rounds to our usual load of 18. Oddly, some of our troops got a purple heart for you guessed, it-arrow wounds!

Our lieutenant followed a blood trail, but wisely stopped. I believe our officer had learned some lessons from Custer. Our higher ups wanted us to bust brush and attack, but had we continued we very possibly would have met with a vastly superior force and been wiped out to a man. The N.V.A. were all around us. Thousands of them, and close! At this point, half our battalion was either dead, wounded or miles away unable to offer assistance. Where we were headed was later found out to be a giant hilltop 'camp' with all kinds of structures that would soon be given the infamous name 'Hamburger Hill'. Our company ended up just a couple of 'clicks' away. Had we continued it was almost sure to be a battle larger than the Custer fight. I truly wish someone would tell me why we stopped. Perhaps General Zais had also studied Custer and wisely retreated.

A good comparison? This trooper thinks so.

Conclusion

I wanted to be a Marine. Then I saw the Green Berets. I wanted to be a soldier all my life until soon after becoming one. The Army was just plain lacking: boring, no imagination and no real interesting methods to ensure death and destruction to our enemies!

I just watched the ABC film called *The Hornets Nest*, filmed by a father and his son in Afghanistan with the 101st Airborne. As I watched another walk in the sun news cast, I realized this one was different. A battalion was getting cut to raw meat and bones. A patrol walked into an ambush while the rest of the battalion sat back inside a walled village and fired back at shadows. I listened as a medic was one of the first to die. Holy shit…others are hit; some are killed. Suddenly, the cameraman explains he is filming the 'No Slack' battalion. My God…a medic from my Vietnam company! The medevacs shuttle back and forth getting shot up as usual. Airstrikes are called in, but it's unclear if they do any damage. What the fuck…over!? They had learned nothing.

It was a horrible feeling of déjà vu. What the hell? Our future kids will do the same thing. 50 years from now the 2/327th will be in Mexico or somewhere getting the shit kicked out of them while the same wild-eyed battalion commander regrets writing the families after his 'going to the enemy's house' speech. After half a century, the story presented in living blood and color – a mirror of this book exactly. I was too shocked to cry. My intestines broke loose and choked my throat!

The newsman explains 'oh, it's not a war on terror now. These men are fighting for their buddies.' True enough, a heroic example of warriors and human love. True brave hearts all. I was so sad, but why get in this situation anyway? Because the bobbing heads were told some guy I'd never heard of had blown up the twin towers?

Revenge?

Reminds me of a gang of bank robbers caught out in the parking lot killed one by one by an army of cops and civilians alike… fighting for their buddies? Maybe it wasn't such a good idea afterall. They were at the bank to make some real money not get killed!

Fighting terror with terror. That will never work. Those troopers, as brave as they were, were still terrorized (well, I was), as were the children and civilians and farmers, pilots and the fighters in the hills. It sounds horrible to say it, but where the 101st goes, dead children will follow. Must be some kind of commie traitor to say that…right? Buck up man, it's true. You know a real man or woman will admit if they are wrong, or if something was a mistake or maybe that was not the way to go. Admit the truth at least. I saw kids killed for nothing in Vietnam and you see it now on the news. Suicide bomber, yes, you'd do the same thing if Russia was stupid enough to invade the U.S. In Vietnam, I saw our bullets hit children!

You know in Vietnam we had very little comradery. The Puking Buzzards we proudly called ourselves or even the 'one oh worst'. This medic had few friends. Most of us were forced into being in the 101st and most were legs, but when the bullets were screaming by, things changed. Most of the time, however, we didn't give a damn about the 'no slack' battalion. Many of the officers were not respected at all. The staff officers tried to get up on stage and drive us on with the 'Airborne' spirit. No one responded and the officers were laughed off. It was shocking. Welcome to the real world.

After seeing the film, I watched the movie *Taps*. You know the film where young Tom Cruise blasts away with a M-60 against American Army soldiers and cops! George C. Scott, famous for portraying Patton, this time plays a 101st airborne general who is totally about 'honor'. The symbols here are scary. A person's honor IS all they have, but the message in the film is honor doesn't mean a damn thing next to a dead boy. It means nothing next to hurt civilians either. It turns into shame if you ask me.

What is with our Army now? The book *Not a Good Day to Die* by Sean Naylor is about total chaos in Afghanistan on Operation Anaconda. It paints an ugly picture.

It seems after Colonel Beckwith's disaster at Desert One in the failed attempt to rescue the American hostages held by Iran everybody works together now. In Naylor's book, every special operations group that can speak English and some that can't are all mixed together driving around in Toyotas, in the snow, getting lost, and when not pinned down by the locals, they get murdered by our gunships. Navy Seals in the same trucks with Delta Force and Rangers and Green Berets while foreign jet zoomies drop a bomb here or there.

Of course, the 101st Airborne are in the act, too, setting up blocking forces that never seemed to work. Imagine, Mexico trying to take back Los Angeles then Monterey then crossing the Sierra Nevada to attack Edwards Air Force Base. Sorry to be so negative, but if the King has no clothes why be a fool and play along?

Another special worth watching is "Vietnam Requiem". Although I am not in the film, its all about me and the Hawk Recon. Again, you will see the 101st Airborne shot to shit and several of the main characters in this book in combat with the camera in their face. Now, with the 101st in Europe; God help us!

Make peace not war! You'll get your chance to really defend America soon enough.

THE END

Epilogue

Who Lost the War?

Well by now we know we were tricked and fooled. Made fools of...well yes, and no? Some of us just wanted to blow stuff up, travel to exotic lands and test our bravery against others. But that's the young male ego, the root of all evil they say. Foolish, yes, but these people myself included were not tricked or fooled. We just didn't give a damn. Actually, while the male ego accounts for all wars, most broken families and most bank robberies, it also produces great physicians, writers, artists and chefs in large proportions in case you haven't noticed.

But what got me and a lot of others was the relentless and extreme propaganda from the 6 o'clock news and Walter Cronkite. Over and over, it was reported that the V.C. and NVA had murdered the entire family of a certain village chief for helping the South or U.S. In fact, over 2,000 teachers and artists and politicians were reported murdered during the Tet uprising in Hue. What compassionate red-blooded American wouldn't want to stop children's heads from ending up on pikes? That's one reason I went. I still can't say if that was true and would like to look into it now. But if it was true those responsible didn't deserve the right to run a country. The 'communists' and their troops should have been buried in shallow unmarked graves as many were. We know, we dug them up to see who they were from time to time!

However, I can relate the story of the Hawk Recon setting up an ambush outside a peaceful village one night in July '69. An enemy V.C. tax collection team was supposed to shake down the ville for money and rice. Well, they did, and murdered the mayor, a woman who stood up to them and said, "No". On departing the village, the stupid V.C. walked back the way they had come and right into the Hawks! Lt. Bill

Drypolcher and his recon boys noticed something amiss when strangers started walking by and even stepping over the ambushers. Bill just shot one, point blank, about 6 times just to make sure, as other Hawks also fired some up! Later Bill and Dewy, a squad leader, were awarded Vietnamese Crosses for Gallantry.

But mostly, the war was a lie and murderous theft of America's wealth. L.B.J. and his 'lovely' wife owned some part of Bell Helicopter from Fort Worth, Texas during the war or while he was president. What's wrong with that picture? I don't feel we 'lost' the war at all; we gave it back to the South Vietnamese where it belonged. Chicken shit for sure; but the thing to do at that late date.

The 'legal' excuse for the war was: the 'dirty reds' attacked 2 of our destroyers in a storm at night... long 'admitted' as a lie. It was lucky one or both 'tin cans' weren't somehow blown up and sunk, the usual way war opens for business. Remember the Maine? 9/11? Oklahoma court house? 101st Airborne crash in Newfoundland? Something always gets blown up!

However, according to one author, we were attacking North Vietnam with 'Nasty Boats' (like PT boats) captained by Norwegian skippers... so to be fair why wouldn't the North hit American Navy ships? Maybe it did happen. Just too many lies!

Long ago, but after the war, Mike Wallace of CBS figured out that General William 'Wastemoreland' was underplaying the enemy strength to keep the war going and perhaps finally win (he hoped) to his own envisioned everlasting glory. It's said still today that the Tet uprising was a moral victory for our enemy, but a total defeat for them. Not at all. We should have known our enemy had the man and woman power to rise up again and again, which they did!

People mention all the explosives left behind and the toxins deforming the children. I know the feeling, believe me, I saw our young men blown apart by our own bombs... and mines... while I walked through. I must add that, my handsome little boy died at age 4 from unknown causes.

So, Vietnam veterans I ask you: did you ever learn the Vietnamese word for hello? I didn't, even though I had a dictionary. I ask our young soldiers of today: you tough Seals, Rangers, snipers etc., are you ready to hurt and kill little boys and girls and women? That's what will happen, the bottom line. You okay with that? How about kicking in the doors of nice hard-working families? "War is Hell" they say. I spit on that! Speaking of Navy Seals…what happened with that 4-man team that got wiped out plus the 30 or 40 or more killed trying to rescue them? Was that arrogance or plain male egos with a lot of brain washing? My heroes are the Army Special Op team leaders that, once getting off the chopper, looked around and saw flat desert, houses and a highway nearby, said," Abort! Get back on this fucking bird!"

What gives our leaders the right to terrorize innocents? Remember the My Lai Massacre? The signal from that disgrace is, because everyone got off, it's cool … no one will say a thing. In my opinion, that entire company or so should all be tried for murder! To get away with that slaughter is simply a disgrace for every American, every civilian and every soldier…forever! It will never be forgotten. I get called on the subject today, in Vietnam. I have to explain what happened: I can't! I have to mention it was those other 'people'… the 101st never went south of Lang Co bridge when I was around. I usually mention one of our chopper pilots stopped some of the murders and saved a little boy by ordering his door gunner to fire on the Americans if they didn't cease! Remember why it all happened: so L.B.J. could sell aircraft and 'Wastemoreland' could become a rich Cesar! The pilot who saved the boy was finally awarded the 'soldier's medal' for doing the right thing!

The book "Tiger Force" was written by 2 clowns and about our close sister element of the 101st. The accounts of some of the murders are probably accurate as I can verify. But the descriptions of a recon platoon in action was simply stupid and inaccurate! The cover photo didn't even portray Americans like it tried to. It was ARVNs dressed like an American recon platoon! So, the truth of the accusations are cast in doubt due to the crappy book! But, of course, the authors got their award.

It's a reflection of our people: what our government does. We get the government we deserve. Like L.B.J. an accused murderer several times over! Do you believe one power hungry male egotist like that is running things?

Can you believe the number of countries we have sacked, over thrown, invaded, terrorized and abused since Vietnam? Like a bully who gets his ass kicked by some little Asian kid and then gets even meaner in his shame! One fool is not running that show...it's a greedy group...it's also our disgrace. Ralph Nader told me our real leaders are the C.E.O.s.

So what about all the shootings now? Who's doing that and why? I hear nothing about it. What about the gamers obsessed with killing? What's with the fascination for the sniper...does everyone want to be a murderer or assassin? I don't...now.

I talked to Pappy Boyington once and he said:

"Show me a hero...and I'll show you a bum!"

Glossary

91B2P	paratrooper medic
AG	assistant gunner – a belt feeder usually
Airborne	101st had many names but always airborne: paratrooper
Air Cavalry	Helicopter borne infantry division. Slang – 'Horse they never rode and road they never crossed' due to their divisional patch of a horse's head and diagonal stripe.
Air assault	for non-paratrooper chopper riders
Air Mobile	from Vietnam
AIT	advanced individual training
Almost Airborne	slang for 82 Airborne Division
ARVN	S. Vietnamese Army
ASAP	as soon as possible…almost never fast or soon.
Band aid	medic
Big Band aid	head medic
Big Dead One	slang for 1st Infantry Division
Big Pill	head medic
Bloody Bayonet, the Herd	slang for 173 Airborne Brigade
Boonie Rat	soldier who lives in the jungle, outside any wire or base
Buy the farm	Die, also zapped, hit, blown away, all fucked up,

CA	combat assault choppers usually, if 'hot' good for 1 air medal
Cherry	fucking new guy
CID	criminal investigation division
Co	Vietnamese for girl
CO	conscientious objector – didn't kill or carry weapon…usually
CO	commanding officer
Chieu Hoi	enemy traitor to other side…us.
Click	1 kilometer, never miles
Cobra	skinny attack chopper, 2 crew with rockets and mini-guns, only chopper without American Indian name.
Chopper	name for birds…never copter like TV news police
Claymore mine	command detonated bomb
C&C	command and control…like a C&C bird full of officers.
CIB	combat infantryman badge
CMB	combat medics badge…both for combat only!
CP	command point…where leaders hung out.
C Ration	C rats: canned food or dried
Crispy critters	bodies burned well done
DEROS	tour over, leave Vietnam or other country
Di Di Mau	run, hurry
DXed	exchange an item
DZ	drop zone usually parachutes
Electric Butterknife	slang for Green Berets in the 60s: the only Special Forces at the time
Electric Strawberry	slang for 25th infantry Division

FAC	any spotter a/c usually single engine L-19 'bird dog'
FNG	a cherry, fucking new guy
Frag	fragmentation hand grenade
Freak	normal dope smoker
Funny 4th	slang for 4th infantry Division
Grunt	soldier
Gook	slang for Asian, respectfully: Sir Charles in Nam
H&E	high explosive of any kind
Hooch	any shelter, poncho to a brick house
Humping	busting trail, hiking
Jar Heads	slang for Marines
Juicers vs. Freaks	drinkers vs. smokers usually the same
Laager	camped, set up
LAW	light anti-tank weapon
LBJ	short for Long Binh jail…in country prison, named for president
Leg	most of the Army…those not paratroopers
Lifer	career soldier, 20 years or more
Line doggie	infantry
Loach	scout chopper…1 pilot and 1 gunner…hot!
Log Bird	a helicopter supply ship
LURP	long ranger recon patrol, also LRRP 5-man teams usually
LZ	landing zone usually choppers
NCO	noncommissioned officer…Sgt. and up to just before Lt.
NCOIC	noncommissioned officer in charge: a Sgt. of some sort
NDP	night defensive position or perimeter
No Slack	2/327th battalion pass word and motto

NVA	north Vietnamese regulars
OJT	on the job training
PLF	parachute landing fall
Phu gas	mixture of gasoline like napalm
Pill	medic
Point man	leader sometimes cutting through jungle
Puff	puff the magic dragon, a gunship
Puking Buzzards or 1-0-worst	slang for 101st Airborne Division
Red Legs	artillery personnel
REMP	rear echelon mother fucker, also spelled with a 'F'
RIF	Reconnaissance in force, large group usually
RPD	fast firing machine gun with 200 round drum and bipod, NVA/VC
RPG	rocket propelled grenade, also a SAM
RTO	our famous radio men usually with a officer or NCOIC
Ruck	rucksack or pack
Ruck up	leave, get your ass out to the boonies, down the trail etc.
Seiko	watch made in Japan pronounced SEEKO in the 60s
Sir Charles	name of our enemy soldiers with great respect!
SITREP	situation report on radio
Slack man	second behind point man, back up
Slick	cargo chopper sans rockets and large guns
SOP	standard operating procedure
Spooky	gunship, C-119, C-130 or DC-3 possibly O-2-A
Swabbies	slang for Navy
Tabs	heat tabs, blue tablets for heating food

Tango	trail or blue feature on map
Thump gun	M-79 grenade launcher/shot gun rounds
TOC	tactical operations center, headquarters or fire control center
TOP	slang for company sergeant, often well liked, last stop before becoming an officer
VC	Viet Cong, Communist forces against own government
Willie Peter	white phosphorous shells
World, The	home, USA usually
Zoomies	slang for Airforce also: Air Farse